Supporting Lifelong Learning
Volume 1

This book brings together a number of texts from Europe, North America and Australia to illustrate, explore and challenge some of the ideas and assumptions which underpin notions of lifelong learning. The chapters trace the transition from notions of learning as a psychological or cognitive phenomenon occurring in the minds of individual learners, towards more social and situated accounts which emphasize the role of culture and social participation. These different accounts of learning have far reaching implications for all those involved.

Supporting Lifelong Learning, Volume 1: Perspectives on learning argues that the 'learning' aspect of 'lifelong learning' has received surprisingly little attention in discussions of how to promote more effective and inclusive approaches. In examining this issue more closely it will appeal to those who are involved in supporting learners in the workplace, the classroom or the community. It will also appeal to postgraduate and doctorate level students with an interest in post-school education and training.

This book is one of three Readers prepared for the Open University MA Course: E845 *Supporting Lifelong Learning*. The three separate volumes provide an in-depth examination of lifelong learning from the perspectives of teaching and learning, organizing learning and policy making. They bring together for the first time theories from a diverse range of disciplines that are now central to our understanding of lifelong learning and provide a new and distinctive contribution to the field.

Roger Harrison is a Lecturer in Education at The Open University.

Fiona Reeve is a Lecturer in Lifelong Learning at The Open University.

Ann Hanson is Staff Tutor in Education at The Open University in the North West.

Julia Clarke is a Research Fellow at The Open University.

Supporting Lifelong Learning, Volume 1: Perspectives on learning

The companion volumes in this series are:

Supporting Lifelong Learning, Volume 2: Organizing learning
Edited by Fiona Reeve, Marion Cartwright and Richard Edwards

Supporting Lifelong Learning, Volume 3: Making policy work
Edited by Richard Edwards, Nod Miller, Nick Small and Alan Tait

All of these Readers are part of a course: *Supporting Lifelong Learning* (E845), that is itself part of the Open University Masters Programme in Education.

The Open University Masters Programme in Education
The Open University Masters Programme in Education is now firmly established as the most popular postgraduate degree for education professionals in Europe, with over 3,000 students registering each year. The Masters Programme in Education is designed particularly for those with experience of teaching, the advisory service, educational administration or allied fields.

Structure of the Masters Programme in Education
The Masters Programme is a modular degree, and students are, therefore, free to select from the programme which best fits in with their interests and professional goals. Specialist lines in management, applied linguistics and lifelong learning are also available. Study within the Open University's Advanced Diploma can also be counted towards a Masters Degree, and successful study within the Masters Programme entitles students to apply for entry into the Open University Doctorate in Education programme.

OU-Supported Open Learning
The Masters Programme in Education provides great flexibility. Students study at their own pace, in their own time, anywhere in the European Union. They receive specially prepared study materials, supported by tutorials, thus offering the chance to work with other students.

The Doctorate in Education
The Doctorate in Education is a part-time doctoral degree, combining taught courses, research methods and a dissertation designed to meet the needs of professionals in education and related areas who are seeking to extend and deepen their knowledge and understanding of contemporary educational issues. The Doctorate in Education builds upon successful study within the Open University Masters Programme in Education.

How to apply
If you would like to register for this programme, or simply find out more information about available courses, please write for the *Professional Development in Education* prospectus to the Call Centre, PO Box 724, The Open University, Walton Hall, Milton Keynes, MK7 6ZW, UK (Telephone 0 (0 44) 1908 653231). Details can also be viewed on our web page http://www.open.ac.uk

Supporting Lifelong Learning
Volume I

Perspectives on learning

Edited by
Roger Harrison, Fiona Reeve,
Ann Hanson and Julia Clarke

ROUTLEDGE / FALMER
Taylor & Francis Group

The Open
University

London and New York

First published 2002 by RoutledgeFalmer
11 New Fetter Lane, London EC4P 4EE

Simultaneously published in the USA and Canada
by RoutledgeFalmer
29 West 35th Street, New York, NY 10001

RoutledgeFalmer is an imprint of the Taylor & Francis Group

Typeset in Goudy by
Florence Production Ltd, Stoodleigh, Devon
Printed and bound in Great Britain by
St Edmundsbury Press, Bury St Edmunds, Suffolk

British Library Cataloguing in Publication Data
A catalogue record for this book is available from the
British Library

Library of Congress Cataloging in Publication Data
A catalog record for this book has been requested

ISBN 0–415–25926–6 (hbk)
ISBN 0–415–25927–4 (pbk)

Contents

Illustrations

Figures

Table

Acknowledgements

We are indebted to the following for allowing us to make use of copyright material:

Chapter 1: Rogers, A. (1996) 'Learning and adult education', in A. Rogers *Teaching Adults*. Buckingham and Philadelphia: Open University Press. Reproduced by permission of Open University Press.

Chapter 2: Rogers, C. (1967) 'The interpersonal relationships in the facilitation of learning', in R. Leeper (ed.) *Humanizing Education*. Alexandria, VA: Association for Supervision and Curriculum Development. Copyright © ASCD. Reprinted by permission. All rights reserved.

Chapter 3: Schön, D. (1983) 'From technical rationality to reflection-in-action', in *The Reflective Practitioner: How Professionals Think in Action*. New York: Basic Books. Copyright © 1983 by Basic Books, Inc. Reprinted by permission of Basic Books, a member of Perseus Books, L.L.C. Territory granted: World excluding the UK and Commonwealth. UK and British Commonwealth rights granted by Ashgate Publishing Ltd © Schon, D. (1991) *The Reflective Practitioner: How Professionals Think in Action*. Avebury: Ashgate Publishing Ltd.

Chapter 4: Clarke, J. 'Deconstructing domestication: women's experience and the goals of critical pedagogy'. Newly commissioned work.

Chapter 5: Usher, R., Bryant, I. and Johnston, R. (1997) 'Reconfiguring the "other": self and experience in adult learning', in R. Usher, I. Bryant and R. Johnston, *Learning Beyond the Limits: Adult Education and the Postmodern Challenge*. London and New York: Routledge. Reproduced by permission of Taylor & Francis Ltd.

Chapter 6: Boud, D. and Walker, D. (1998) 'Promoting reflection in professional courses: the challenge of context', *Studies in Higher Education*, 23(2): 191–206. Reproduced by permission of Taylor & Francis Ltd.

Chapter 7: Lave, J. and Wenger, E. (1991) 'Legitimate peripheral participation in communities of practice', in J. Lave and E. Wenger, *Situated Learning*. Cambridge: Cambridge University Press. Reproduced by permission of Cambridge University Press.

Chapter 8: Eraut, M., Alderton, J., Cole, G. and Senker, P. (1998) 'Learning from other people at work', in F. Coffield (ed.) *Learning at Work*. Bristol: The Policy Press. Reproduced by permission of The Policy Press.

Chapter 9: Guile, D. and Young, M. (1999) 'Beyond the institution of apprenticeship: towards a social theory of learning as the production of knowledge', in P. Ainley and H. Rainbird (eds) *Apprenticeship: Towards a New Paradigm of Learning*. London: Kogan Page. Reproduced by permission of Kogan Page.

Chapter 10: Mayes, T. 'The technology of learning in a social world'. Newly commissioned work.

Chapter 11: Hamilton, M. (2000) 'Sustainable literacies and the ecology of lifelong learning', originally prepared as a working paper for the Global Colloquium on Supporting Lifelong Learning (online). Milton Keynes: The Open University. Available at http://www.open.ac.uk/lifelong-learning Reproduced by permission of The Open University.

Chapter 12: Baynham, M. (2000) 'Academic writing in new and emergent discipline areas', in M. R. Lea and B. Stierer (eds) *Student Writing in Higher Education*. Buckingham and Philadelphia: SRHE and Open University Press. Reproduced by permission of Open University Press.

Chapter 13: Zukas, M. and Malcolm, J. (2000) 'Pedagogies for lifelong learning: building bridges or building walls?', originally prepared as a working paper for the Global Colloquium on Supporting Lifelong Learning (online). Milton Keynes: The Open University. Available at http://www.open.ac.uk/lifelong-learning. Reproduced by permission of The Open University.

While the publishers have made every effort to contact copyright holders of the material used in this volume, they would be grateful to hear from any they were unable to contact.

Introduction

Perspectives on learning

Roger Harrison, Fiona Reeve, Ann Hanson and Julia Clarke

In recent times we have seen a loosening of the boundaries around concepts of adult learning, symbolized by contemporary discourses of 'lifelong learning'. Learning is now seen as a key feature of participation in social and economic life. Learning as a preparation for life has been displaced by learning as an essential strategy for successful negotiation of the life course, as the conditions in which we live and work are subject to ever more rapid change. Traditional distinctions between formal and informal learning, or between different institutional contexts, become less significant since learning might occur in the workplace, the home, the car, the internet cafe, as well as the college. We learn not only for the purposes of gaining formal qualifications but also to obtain and keep employment, develop expertise in a leisure activity, deal with changes in relationships, or manage personal finances. We learn from colleagues, friends, parents and children. We learn through mentoring, television and books, as well as various forms of 'web-ucation' and 'e-learning'. There seems to be no aspect of human experience that does not lend itself to appropriation as a pedagogical project; a situation that has raised questions for some about the nature and intent of the lifelong learning project as a whole (Alheit, 1998). In contemporary conditions learning becomes not only 'lifelong', suggesting learning as relevant throughout the life course, but also 'life-wide', suggesting learning as an essential aspect of our whole life experience, not just that which we think of as 'education'. Whilst this adds to the difficulty of making generalizations about learning, it also serves to stimulate interest in wider understandings of the processes of learning. These wider understandings extend the reach of 'learning' beyond the institutional settings and formats of 'education' and constitute a serious challenge to many established ideas of how, why, where and with whom learning might occur.

It is perhaps surprising then that whilst notions of lifelong learning have achieved a high profile within discourses of adult education and training,

The Introduction was written especially for this volume.

the learning aspect of lifelong learning has received rather less attention. When we hear or read about lifelong learning it is usually as part of an injunction to learn more, and more efficiently, in the cause of realizing our personal potential and securing national economic competitiveness. Attention is thus directed towards the alleged outcomes of learning, rather than the processes through which it might be achieved. Attention is also directed towards the 'lifelong' aspects of lifelong learning, with the implication that there is no escape and no hiding place from the requirement to learn. Such descriptive and prescriptive discourses have been effective in rallying a wide constituency behind the idea that lifelong learning is not only imperative but also a 'good thing', whilst eliding the possibility of more critical and analytical engagement with what it actually means. In particular these discourses are remarkable in the extent to which they pass over questions about the nature, processes or purposes of learning.

This book brings together a number of texts from Europe, North America and Australia to illustrate, explore and challenge some of the ideas and assumptions that underpin notions of learning within current discourses of lifelong learning. Some of them will be familiar to those involved in supporting learners, in fact they might well constitute the theoretical touchstone of their practices. The work of Carl Rogers, for example, is foundational to the learner-centred rhetoric, if not always the practice, of many formal and informal initiatives in lifelong learning currently being developed in the UK and elsewhere. Similarly Donald Schön has become a key reference point for those who see their professional identity in terms of the 'reflective practitioner' and who understand professional knowledge as constituted through 'reflective practice'. These seminal texts still provide powerful and persuasive accounts of learning, accounts that have had far-reaching effects on pedagogic practices and assumptions about learner identity and the construction of knowledge. Indeed, a central theme running through this book is that ideas about learning are closely implicated in shaping ideas about pedagogy, identity and knowledge construction. For example, a perspective that views the learning process as a transmission from teacher to learner would tend to emphasize the efficient organization of knowledge into manageable chunks and the skills of the teacher in communicating these to learners. Here the role of the learner is simply to annex the knowledge of others, rather than to critique this knowledge or adapt it to their own situation. In contrast a view of learning as occurring through reflection on experience would emphasize the central role of the learner in constructing new knowledge through processing the raw material of experience, and the skills of the teacher in facilitating this process. Here the role of the learner is pivotal both to the learning process and to the definition of what counts as knowledge. Research by Jean Lave and Etienne Wenger indicates a very different view of learning as primarily a social rather than an individual activity; as something that occurs with or without the existence of teachers and curricula; with knowledge being generated through co-participation in 'communities of practice'. Here the focus of interest shifts from the minds of individual learners to the social and cultural context in which they are operating. Learner identity can no longer be understood in terms of the freewheeling, autonomous and self-directed individual, but as relational, context dependent and embedded in social practices. Further possibilities are introduced within a New Literacy Studies perspective, discussed in this volume by Mary Hamilton, where the focus of interest is not on pedagogy, but on the workings of power in culture and politics. Here the questions that come into focus are about which forms of learning, and which learners, are privileged and which are marginalized in contemporary discourses of lifelong learning. Each of these perspectives is examined within the chapters in this book.

The above might suggest the possibility of clear delineation between theories of learning; of defining and positioning each in relation to the others so that their similarities and differences can be clearly seen. In fact, as Alan Rogers (Chapter 1) indicates, such clear-cut boundaries are hard to draw. Lifelong learning is a large and complex field, traversed by many disciplinary traditions, ranging from psychology to anthropology, social theory, linguistics, feminism and post-structuralism. It is a field characterized by shifting discourses of what we mean by learners and learning, and pedagogical practices characterized by hybridity and fluidity rather than purity or constancy. There is a similar danger inherent in presenting learning theories within a linear or developmental framework. The sequence of chapters in this book might suggest a clear progression, with each new theory positioned as a corrective to previous misconceptions. But to present such a progressive narrative would be misleading. It would, for example, imply some degree of consensus about the direction in which we might locate 'progress'. We would adopt a different stance, viewing theory as a series of understandings that are located in, and emerge from, particular historical, social and cultural settings. From this perspective theories of learning can be viewed as discourses about learning that bring into focus certain aspects and characteristics of the learning process whilst excluding others from the picture. Each approach might present itself as progressive, but with different values and purposes.

At risk of falling into the 'reductionist, binary, and reificatory logic' (Fenwick, 2000) of such classificatory systems, we propose the following three frames of understanding within which the chapters in this collection might be grouped.

First, learning might be understood as making sense of experience through a process of reflection. This is a 'constructivist' account of learning in which learners take on the central role as meaning makers as they process, interpret and generalize from their own lived experience. In doing so they create mental structures or frames of understanding that can then be used in other situations. Learning is presented as a dynamic process in which the individual learner is the central actor, and knowledge is seen as temporary, contingent and constructed by the learner. It is a view of learning and the learner that the writings of Carl Rogers and Donald Schön have been enormously influential in promoting and has been enthusiastically taken up by many practitioners who have sought to privilege the lived experience of the learner as a counter to more traditional, discipline-based pedagogic practices. In recent times it has been used as part of a legitimating rationale for those curriculum innovations such as work-based learning, recording achievement, the assessment of prior learning, and the use of ICT, which seek to devolve control of the pace, place and subject of learning to the learner. In doing so they raise important questions about the role and status of those who support learning, suggesting activities such as 'facilitating', 'mentoring' and 'coaching' as more appropriate than 'teaching'.

Critiques of experiential theories of learning have emerged from feminist and postmodern perspectives, among others. It is this latter that is explored here by Robin Usher, Ian Bryant and Rennie Johnston. Their analysis draws attention to the absence of any consideration of the effects of culture and power within these accounts of learning and representations of the learner. Viewing learners as individualized, rational processors of experience, detached from history, sociality and human practices, is revealed as neither natural or neutral, but part of a culturally and politically located understanding of what it means to be a person and a learner. Their postmodern analysis introduces a sceptical and questioning attitude towards taken-for-granted notions of identity, culture and knowledge, suggesting that they are not as stable, universal or foundational as they might appear. In a similar spirit of deconstruction, Julia Clarke takes a feminist perspective towards the critical pedagogy of Paulo Freire, illuminating the way in which the liberation/domestication binary legitimates a gendered interpretation of emancipation that has the effect of marginalizing the desires and interests of many women. Using this critical lens, what is presented as a universal vision of emancipation can be seen as a partial and ideological agenda that represents the interests of some groups in society while imposing its own form of oppression on others. These chapters help to illustrate how such critical perspectives can offer analytical tools for tracing the effects of power in discourses of learning that claim universality and neutrality.

As long-standing advocates of the use of reflection in supporting learning and professional development, David Boud and David Walker in their chapter expose and critique a range of practices that in their view are in danger of subverting the more radical and provocative aspects of reflection. In particular they are wary of the use of reflection in contexts where its potential is constrained and the messy and challenging processes of critical reflection are replaced by simplified and technical formulae. Their contribution is a timely response to critiques of reflective practice that point out that for many practitioners, contemporary conditions of employment have led to an erosion of opportunities for exercising professional judgement. The introduction of market forces, performance targets and quality audits into many areas of work can be seen as decreasing the scope for professional autonomy, and increasing the tendency towards 'instrumental' and 'recipe following' forms of reflection. They also take on board the postmodern critique of reflection as individualized and universalized processes that pass over the influence of the broader social, cultural and political context in which they are embedded. For Boud and Walker an awareness that experience is open to multiple readings, and an understanding that context shapes notions of learning, are essential components of critical reflection on practice.

The chapter by Jean Lave and Etienne Wenger introduces our second frame of understanding. Here the concern with context is taken a stage further in suggesting that it is the social situation and its attendant social practices that create the possibilities for learning. Rather than occupying the centre of the frame, heroically creating meaning from personal experience, the individual learner is relegated to the role of participant in a collective process of negotiating meaning within a particular context and community of practice. By suggesting that learning can *only* be understood as a social process this perspective displaces the more traditional preoccupations of learning theory with what goes on in the mind of the individual learner. Here it is not the learner but the social and cultural context that occupies the centre of the theoretical frame. Knowledge, skills and understanding are entirely contingent on the specific context in which they occur and the interactions through which they are generated. The idea of knowledge as a stable commodity that belongs to an individual and that can be transmitted, assessed and accredited is undermined by this account of learning, with significant implications for current practices of supporting and accrediting learners. The research reported by Michael Eraut, Jane Alderton, Gerald Cole and Peter Senker on informal learning in the workplace can be read as supportive to many aspects of the above account, showing learning as highly situated and dependent on social relations within the workplace. The evidence they present constitutes a powerful argument for the significance of the informal learning gained through social relations with those who might be colleagues, mentors, line managers or other carriers of specialist knowledge. An important dimension introduced by their analysis is that they show how individuals are simultaneously engaged on a number of learning careers spanning a range of social contexts. Participation is multiple and complex, with learners carrying knowledge from one setting, resituating and integrating it in others. A feature of Lave and Wenger's chapter is that whilst providing a detailed account of how learning occurs through participation in communities of practice they do not move on to suggest strategies for improving pedagogy. The chapters by David Guile and Michael Young, and by Terry Mayes, begin to explore some of the pedagogic implications of taking this view of learning, and in particular they focus on the potential role of Information and Communication Technologies (ICT) in facilitating this move. Viewing learning as a social rather than an individual process opens up significant and exciting new possibilities for 'thinking practices differently', turning on their heads many traditional notions of learning and supporting learners.

Our third frame of understanding is not so much a theory about how learning occurs as a critical account of the work language does in establishing understandings and expectations about what is learned, how it is learned and what aspects are valued through assessment. Viewing learning as 'literacy practices' helps to extend the discussion about its nature and effects, bringing into view wider sociocultural and political questions that are largely absent from behaviourist, reflective and situated accounts of learning. Mary Hamilton develops this critique, pointing to the role of social institutions and power relations in constituting and sustaining certain privileged and elite forms of literacy practice. Hamilton argues that a move towards valuing vernacular literacies opens up possibilities for a wider and more inclusive vision of lifelong learning. In doing so she brings into focus those forms of learning that people engage in outside the domain of formal education – the 'life-wide' dimension of lifelong learning – and allows us to reflect on those distinctions that position some forms of learning as fundable and worthy of accreditation and others as not. Mike Baynham's chapter is based on empirical research into the forms of literacy practices required by students in higher education. His study indicates that these are far from being the settled and closely defined packages of study skills that one might expect, but rather a set of shifting and constantly renegotiated meanings as to what constitutes academic knowledge and what it means to be a student in higher education. As well as illustrating the diversity of literacy practices required by different disciplinary areas, and the lack of clarity in communicating these to students, his study provides an insight into the dynamic process of meaning making. He shows students and tutors engaged in the construction their own understandings of the literacy practices required, drawing on resources from their personal and practical experience of the world as well as the codes and practices of the academic institution. Even within the relatively bounded and regulated context of higher education we begin to see how meanings are not fixed, but always in flux and therefore open to negotiation and change.

The final chapter by Miriam Zukas and Janice Malcolm provides a different map of the territory we have traversed in this book. Their project is to look across the highly segmented terrain of lifelong learning in the UK, focusing on those who they term 'educators'; on the identity positions available to them and the effects of these on the nature and content of learning. Here they draw on the notion of 'communities of practice' to suggest that the different contexts of adult, further and higher education have developed their own distinctive pedagogic practices. For them, lifelong learning is a 'virtual concept' that has mobilized surprisingly little discussion about the possibility, or even desirability, of continuity or connectivity between the pedagogic practices it includes. Although the focus of their study is on teaching rather than learning, their chapter nevertheless provides an appropriate conclusion to this volume. By drawing attention to the different assumptions and value judgements embedded in conceptual models of teaching and learning they emphasize the importance of taking a critical stance towards technical and formulaic attempts to capture 'best practice'. What such formulations fail to acknowledge is the diversity of perspectives on learning that are available and the practical and ethical implications of these for learners and those who support learning.

References

Alheit, P. (1998) On a Contradictory Way to the 'Learning Society': A critical approach, *Studies in the Education of Adults*, 66–82.

Fenwick, T. (2000) Expanding Conceptions of Experiential Learning: A review of the five contemporary perspectives on cognition, *Adult Education Quarterly*, Vol. 50, 243–272.

Chapter 1

Learning and adult education

Alan Rogers

Learning theories

It is important to stress the fact that there are many strategies for learning, because some recent writers have suggested that there is only one way in which all learning is done (we shall talk about one or two of these strategies later in this section). We need to be wary of adopting any all-embracing theory of learning that implies exclusivity.

It will be useful to summarise the many different learning theories briefly. They may be divided for simplicity's sake into three main groups. There are the *behaviourist* theories, mostly of the stimulus–response variety of differing degrees of complexity. There are the *cognitive* theories, based on a different view of the nature of knowledge. And there are those theories that have been called *humanist*; these rely on various analyses of personality and of society.

Before looking at these in more detail, one or two comments need to be made. First, it is tempting to identify the stimulus–response learning theories with the 'conformist' view of education and the humanist with the 'liberation' view. There is some truth is this in that the humanists often talk in terms of liberation. But his is too simplistic: the divide between these two approaches runs right through all three sets of theories. The behavioural theories range from a simple reinforcement of the desired responses through to an exploration of the many different possible responses; the cognitive theories can talk at one extreme of the discipline of the subject and at the other end of the continuum of open discovery learning; and the humanist theories can describe the importance of role imitation in attitudinal development on the one hand and the freedom of the learning group on the other.

Second, however, there does seem to be a correlation between each of these groups of learning theories and the three main elements in the teaching–learning encounter. Education consists of a dynamic interaction involving three parties – the teacher-planner, the student participant(s), and the subject-matter. Each of the three groups of learning theories tends to

This is an edited version of a chapter previously published in *Teaching Adults*, 1996, Buckingham and Philadelphia: Open University Press.

Learning theories	Conformist-oriented	(continuum)	Liberation-oriented
Behavioural; teacher-centred	Reinforcement of desired responses	-----------------------	Exploration of different responses
Cognitive; subject-centred	Discipline of subject	------------------------------	Discovery learning
Humanist; learner-centred	Imitation of norms	----------------------	Group learning

Figure 1.1 Learning theories.

exalt the primacy of one of these three elements. Behavioural theories stress the role of the teacher-agent in providing the stimulus and selecting and reinforcing the approved responses; cognitive theories emphasise the content of the material; while the humanist theories (the most complex group) direct attention to the active involvement of the student participant.

Behaviourist theories

This group of theories suggests that we learn by receiving stimuli from our environment that provoke a response. The teacher can direct this process by selecting the stimuli and by reinforcing the approved responses while discouraging the 'wrong' responses. Learning is thus brought about by an association between the desired responses and the reinforcement (rewards and punishments through a complicated system of success and failure indicators).

These theories stress the active role of the teacher-agent. The student-learner is often seen as more passive. Although the learner offers a variety of responses, it is only the teacher who can determine the 'right' response and who can reward it appropriately, discouraging the other responses. Feedback, the return from the learner to the teacher, thus stands on its own, separate from and following after the learning process.

The behaviourist theories are based on a view of knowledge that distinguishes sharply between right and wrong. They assume that knowledge is truth and can be known; it is independent of both teacher and learner; it is the same for all learners.

Stimulus–response theories are not seen by their proponents as just applicable to low-level learning. They also apply at more advanced levels. Nor are they confined to skill learning; they form the basis for cognitive and attitudinal learning as well – to the understanding of historical processes and the appreciation of music. Indeed, the general validity of the theory is that it is often seen to underlie most of the other theories of learning. Cognitive theories stress the inherent demands of the subject-matter but they still rely on an assumption that responses are called out by different stimuli. And humanist theories urge that the stimuli arise from our social and life context, that the variety of our responses is dependent on our individual experiences and personalities, and that at an early stage of life we all learn by a system of approvals and disapprovals that indicate whether our social patterns of behaviour are acceptable or not. Stimulus and response form part of almost all theories of learning in some form or other.

Cognitive theories

Since the 1960s, a number of theories have emerged that direct attention to the activity of the learner in processing the response and to the nature of knowledge itself. These form a distinct group.

These theories point to the active engagement of the mind in learning. They stress the processes involved in creating responses, the organisation of perceptions, the development of insights. In order to learn, understanding is necessary. The material must be marshalled step by step and then mastered. The setting of goals is related to each part of the material encountered. Feedback is an essential part of the process of learning, not separate from it.

Although the learner is seen to be active rather than passive, the activity itself is controlled by the inherent structure of knowledge itself. The material that the teacher-agent orders and that the learner seeks to master dominates the process. The words 'must' and 'necessary' and 'discipline', which occur frequently in connection with this view of learning, reveal that teacher and learner are faced by something that is bigger than both of them, something to which they must adapt themselves. The world of knowledge lies outside of themselves.

This group of views is not confined to the acquisition of new knowledge or the development of new understandings. It applies to learning new skills and new attitudes as well.

Both kinds of learning theories, behavioural and cognitive, posit hierarchies of learning: that there are strategies for low-level learning and strategies for higher-level learning. Learning advances as more and more learning takes place; there are higher levels of learning that not all learners attain to.

Bloom, who drew a distinction between learning in the cognitive domain and learning in the affective domain, may be taken as an example of this. He suggests (1965) that the steps to learning in each domain parallel each other. Thus the process of cognitive learning consists of the recall and recognition of *knowledge*; *comprehension*, understanding the material, exploring it more actively; the *application* of the comprehended knowledge, using it in concrete situations; then exploring each new situation by breaking it down into its constituted parts (*analysis*) and building it up into new concepts (*synthesis*); and finally *evaluation* in which the learners come to assess the new knowledge, to judge its value in relation to the realisation of their goals. On the affective side, there is a similar progression: *receiving* stimuli, paying attention, developing awareness, being willing to receive and eventually using selective attention; then *responding* willingly, the emergence of a sense of satisfaction with the response; third, *valuing* the concepts and the process they are engaged in, making an assessment that the activity is worth doing, so that the learners come to express their preferences and eventually their commitment; then *conceptualising*, making judgements, attaching concepts to each of the values they have identified; and finally *organising* these values into a system that in the end comes to characterise each individual. He suggests that the steps to learning are the same in all learners. Gagné (1972) too drew up a progression of learning from the simple 'signal' learning through stimulus–response to the very complex 'problem-solving' learning.

Humanist theories

Such hierarchies however do not seem to characterise many forms of humanist learning theories. These are more recent in origin and are not so coherent as those in the other two groups.

Humanist learning theories spring from an understanding of the major contemporary changes in culture – away from the certainties of empirical science, the relatively simple and universally valid conclusions of objective research, the stability and general applicability of scientific laws, the generally accepted values, the positivism of August Comte and others – into the modern world of living complexity, uncertainty, instability, the uniqueness of individual response and the conflicts of values (Schein, 1972). Humanist

Bloom		Gagné
Cognitive	*Affective*	Signal
		Stimulus–response
Knowledge	Receiving	Chaining
Comprehension	Responding	Verbal association
Application	Valuing	Multiple discrimination
Analysis–synthesis	Conceptualising	Concept learning
Evaluation	Organising	Principle learning
		Problem solving

Figure 1.2 Bloom and Gagné: hierarchies of learning.

learning theories stress once more the active nature of the learner. Indeed, the learner's actions largely create the learning situation. They emphasise the urges and drives of the personality, movements towards (for example) increased autonomy and competence, the compulsion towards growth and development, the active search for meaning, the fulfilment of goals that individuals set for themselves. They stress the particular social settings within which learning operates. Learning and setting goals for oneself are seen to be natural processes, calling into play the personal learning abilities that the learners have already developed and which they seek to enhance. Learning comes largely from drawing upon all the experience that goes to make up the self and upon the resources of the wider community. Motivation for learning comes from within; and the material on which the learning drive fastens is the whole of life, the cultural and interpersonal relationships that form the social context.

These views also stress the autonomy of the learners and emphasise that all the other theories talk about 'controls', about the learner being controlled by the stimuli, by the teacher, by the subject-matter. The humanist views on the other hand see learning as part of a process of conflict in which the learners are seeking to take control of their own life processes. It is the engagement of the learners with the world around them and with themselves that creates the learning milieu. The material on which they exercise their learning skills is less important than the goals they have set themselves. The role of the teacher is to increase the range of experiences so that the student participants can use these in any way they please to achieve their own desired learning changes.

It will be necessary for us to spend a little more time looking at these newer views, for they will influence the way in which adult education will develop over the coming years, before we can draw some general conclusions from them. It will be convenient to divide them into two main groups: those that focus on the *personality* factors and those that focus on the social or *environmental* context with which the learner is in dialogue.

Personality theories

Most personality learning theories depend on prior concepts relating to the distribution of personality types along a spectrum of one kind or another – between the extrovert and the introvert, for instance, or between those who see the 'locus of control' as within themselves and those who see it as outside of themselves ('I was ill because I ate bad meat' as against 'the food in that restaurant made me ill'), or between the fatalist and the self-confident (Rotter, 1982).

Those who locate people on such external–internal scales tend to suggest that people placed at the external end of the continuum have a general expectancy that positive reinforcements are not under their control; that they may tend to lack self-confidence, to possess feelings of inferiority, even to expect failure and to rely more on luck, fate, chance or God. They suggest that in terms of learning, these people often feel that what they don't know is so vast and what they do know is so small that they may be discouraged from attempting to master new fields. At the opposite extreme, it is suggested, are those who believe that reinforcement is contingent on their own behaviour. These people are usually thought to be more independent, resisting manipulation; they will act, pay attention and (if they feel it necessary to the achievement of some goal they have set for themselves) remember. They are seen to draw upon the information and other resources provided by their environment, to select activities in which they have already been successful, and to feel confident that what they already know will help them to master further skills and knowledge. Most people however are thought to occupy mid-points between these two extremes or to display characteristics of both of these types at different times and in different circumstances.

Various learning theories have been built on these analyses of personality types, for instance, in the work of Carl Rogers (1974), Abraham Maslow (1968) and Cy Houle (1961). The importance of attitudes in the learning process and the relationship of attitudes to knowledge is the great contribution of these theories to our understanding of learning. Learning does not just affect the head (as so much in cognitive learning theories suggests). Berne (1970), for instance, built his view of learning to a large extent on the difference within each person of the 'parent' (P), the 'adult' (A) and the 'child' (C). He argued that communication between people may go seriously wrong if these attitudes become confused, if the lines get crossed, if for example one person speaking as 'adult' is responded to as 'child'.

Environmental learning theories

These writers emphasise that 'no man is an island'. The learning process, especially when self-impelled in the way the personality theorists suggest, calls upon the resources of the environment in which the learner is situated. But these writers go further than this: they suggest that learning is created by the active encounter between the person and the outside world more than by the inner drives and urges. Four main sets of social and environmental learning theories may be identified.

In brief, *human communications theory* indicates that communications link people together into an organisation to achieve a common purpose. Communication is not just a one-way tool; it is a system or network of events. Communication is a transaction, a series of two-way processes that involve a source (initiator), a transmission, a message and a receiver. There is inevitably interference and distortion in the transmission, and feedback is a necessary, though independent, part of the process in order to check whether that has been received is perceived as being equivalent to what has been sent. Interpretation is an essential element of the transaction, and in this the receiver is active, not passive. Learning is thus a process of change that comes about through reactions to the continuous reception of messages that is the inevitable consequence of each person being part of a human communications network or society.

Human communications theory tends towards the 'external' end of the scale; *social learning theory* on the other hand stresses the 'internal' factors. It is based on the study of the interaction of the individual and the social environment. The interaction starts with the members of the family and widens out from there, and much of the learning consists of imitation and the internalisation of value systems acquired from others. Recent studies, for instance, have stressed the need for direct human contact in attitudinal development; and the importance of peer group pressure has also become clear. Like the human communications theory, this is not just a stimulus–response theory. It emphasises the active engagement of the person with the environment, a dialectic with all the potential for conflict and the need for conflict resolution.

Some modern learning theories have seen the engagement of the individual with the environment in a holistic sense – the *total environment*, not just the social environment. The physical world in which we live, the built environment that we have made for ourselves, the mental world that we have created (what the French call *mentalités*) as well as the social environment are all elements with which we are bound in a perpetual engagement.

Some writers have seen this engagement in terms of a struggle, a desperate search for freedom. Habermas (1978), like Carl Rogers, views human life as a quest for self-emancipation, a search for autonomy through self-formative processes. Like others, he has drawn on the seminal work of Paulo Freire (1972) who identified three stages of learning: activities that are task-related; second, activities concerned with personal relationships; and third, what he calls 'conscientization', a concept that implies the transformation of the awareness of surrounding reality, the development of a concern for change, and a realistic assessment of the resources of and hindrances to such a process and the conflicts it is bound to provoke. Learning is only learning when it leads to action for change.

Habermas similarly identifies three kinds of learning, which form something of a hierarchy:

- *instrumental learning* – how to manipulate the environment; the acquisition of skills and understanding needed to control the world we live in (it is interesting that Habermas places scientific learning on the lowest rung of his scale);
- *communicative learning* – learning changes in the realm of interpersonal relations and concerned with increasing interpersonal understanding;

- *emancipatory learning* – self-understanding, awareness and transformation of cultural and personal presuppositions that are always with us and affect the way we act.

Habermas suggests that these different kinds of learning have different methods of investigation, of teaching and of evaluation. Any teaching–learning situation will call upon all three kinds of learning in different proportions. Because the teaching–learning encounter is part of the wider struggle of the individual and his/her total environment, it will involve a complete transformation of the relationship between learner, teacher (mediator of knowledge) and knowledge (sometimes seen as 'competencies').

A further group of humanist learning theories relate to what is called *paradigm transformation*. This view argues that the environment we live in is the result of our own creative processes; that we build, name and manipulate the environment for ourselves; and that learning is a process of rebuilding, renaming and remanipulating that environment. It calls for the modification and adaptation of those paradigms (i.e. accepted and usually unchallenged world-pictures on which we build our lives) that underlie our personality and all our actions.

One way of looking at this is to use the metaphor of 'learning maps' (Rogers, 1993). People draw maps in their head: they place every experience, concept and activity on this map at some distance from themselves at the centre of these maps. Those who like cooking and feel themselves to be good at it, for example, will locate 'cooking' close to the self-centre, whereas they may well locate 'computers' closer to the periphery because they feel less at ease with this feature of modern society or because it seems to be distant from their main preoccupations. Learning, it has been suggested, is easiest among those subjects that are close to the centre; and this implies that learning includes a process of redrawing these maps so as to bring the desired learning subjects closer to the self-centre. So long as adults feel that any subject is 'not for me', they will experience great difficulties in learning.

Perhaps the most influential expressions of this group of theories is George Kelly's 'personal construct theory'. Kelly (1955) argues that learning is not something determined by external influences but that we create our own learning. By observing and reflecting on experience, we form our own personal constructs (units of meaning) from our ideas, feelings, memories and evaluations about events, places and people in our lives. In this way, we make sense of the world and manipulate it rather than respond to stimuli. The act of learning is then largely initiated by the learner, exploring and extending his or her own understanding, holding what has been called a 'learning conversation with him-/herself'.

This school of thought rejects the notion of knowledge existing outside of ourselves, an objective reality to be discovered by research. Rather all knowledge is contingent; it is 'contested and provisional'. What exist are the various 'acts of knowing' that we all engage in. Knowledge creation does not mean so much the uncovering of hidden truth as the construction of new perceptions. Those who search after truth are faced with choosing between all the various 'acts of knowing'. The focus thus switches from trying to establish the validity of the knowledge itself to the criteria by which we can judge the validity of the questions asked and the answers arrived at in each individual case; how can we determine which 'act of knowing' carries with it some experiential validity for ourselves?

Some have gone further. They have denied the existence of the mind as a finite, fixed entity in favour of 'a dynamic, ever-changing flux with unknown potential'. They claim that those psychologists who speak in terms of fixed measures like intelligence, aptitude and personality traits for what are seen by others to be 'temporary stabilised states' are to be regarded as perpetuating myths and creating blocks to a 'true' perception of the personality as fluid and active in its own quest.

We are thus back with the views that see learning as dependent on the innate drives of men and women towards autonomy and understanding in an attempt to control rather than be controlled, in a search for liberation. But it is a different form of theory. Learning is not seen by these writers as merely the satisfaction of a sense of urges, seeking a state of rest and harmony, the diminishing of a sense of anxiety, the relief of tension. Rather, learning through life is to be viewed as an active engagement with our environment and with ourselves, a struggle that may actually increase tension, a dialectic in which we seek to alter both our environment and ourselves in the constant search for something better, some ideal, a struggle that will never end. Learning is seen as the process by which our sense of discontent with the now and here and the search for transcendence expresses itself in a quest for perfectibility.

Experiential learning and the learning cycle

There is growing consensus that experience forms the basis of all learning. Many modern writers suggest that at the heart of all learning is the search for meaning in experience. Mezirow (1981) has stressed this above all else. Learning is creating meanings, finding the keys, making sense of experience – a process that is as natural to all adults as breathing.

The process by which this search for meaning is conducted is, according to many contemporary writers, *critical reflection on experience*. Freire and others have suggested that learning is accomplished by critically analysing experience. They have spoken of a learning cycle starting with experience, proceeding through reflection on experience, and leading to action, which in its turn becomes the concrete experience for further reflection and thus the next stage of the cycle (Figure 1.3a). They argue that action is an

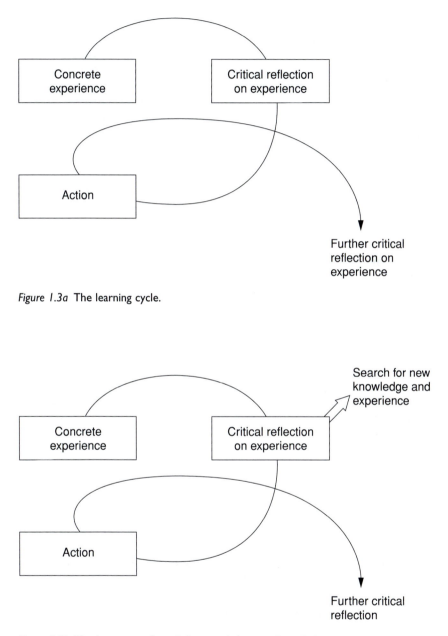

Figure 1.3a The learning cycle.

Figure 1.3b The learning cycle and the search for new knowledge.

essential part of the learning process, not a result of learning, not an add-on at the end. Without action, learning has not effectively taken place.

We need to modify this learning cycle in three ways if we are to understand it fully. First, the process of reflection is complex. It involves making a judgement on experience, assessing it in the light of some other standard that is drawn from other experience, either one's own or other people's experience. It means trying to determine how to explain the experience, to assess in what ways the experience could have been different. Farmers, faced with a new pest or disease, will ask their neighbours, 'What is it? We have never seen it before'; they thus reveal that they have first searched their own experience and are now actively seeking to access the experience of others.

In learning through critical reflection on experience there is the active search for new material against which experience can be judged. The learning cycle needs then to be adapted as shown in Figure 1.3b.

Second, as David Kolb (1984) has pointed out, critical reflection will lead in some cases to the drawing of conclusions, to developing generalisations, general principles ('abstract conceptualisation' as he puts it). Critical reflection can be seen as asking questions about experience in the light of other experience; abstract conceptualisation may be seen as identifying possible answers. Hypotheses are formed from the process of critical reflection on experience, which can be tested in new situations (Figure 1.3c).

Third, however, learning includes goals, purposes, intentions, choice and decision making, and it is not at all clear where these elements fit into the learning cycle. Decisions are needed to determine which other forms of experience are used for critical reflection; decisions are certainly needed before translating abstract conceptualisation into active experimentation; and decisions and goals occur at other points in the cycle. These have tended to be omitted from discussions of the learning cycle (Figure 1.3d).

There is then a widespread acceptance that critical reflection on experience leading to action forms a large part of the process of learning. But it is probably unacceptable to suggest (as some writers do) that this is *the* way in which we learn. As we have seen above, there are many different strategies of learning, and we clearly use them all at some time or other. Critical reflection on experience would seem to be the key strategy in the process of creating meaning out of experience; it is certainly the main way in which critical learning is developed. But there is more to learning than the search for meanings.

The importance of new knowledge cannot be exaggerated. It is against new knowledge, against our earlier experience or against the experience of others, however that is mediated to us (through teaching or speech or the written word or observation, etc.), that we measure the experience that forms the basis of learning, that we pass judgement on it, that we seek to make meaning; it is through such other knowledge that we reflect critically on experience. Without new knowledge there can be no critical reflection.

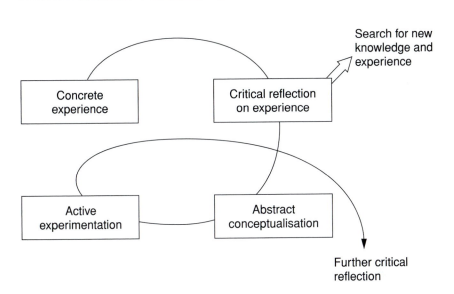

Figure 1.3c The learning cycle and conceptualisation.

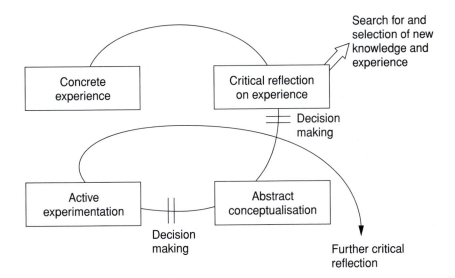

Figure 1.3d The learning cycle and decision making.

Learning styles

One common element in modern discussions of adult learning relates to what are called 'learning styles'. We have all engaged for the whole of our lives in natural learning and from time to time in the more purposeful and structured 'learning episodes'. In the course of this, we have developed our own learning styles.

The subject of learning styles is too extensive to explore fully in these pages, but an outline of recent current thinking is necessary. The most relevant material is that based on the learning cycle that David Kolb elaborated and which is discussed above. The argument goes like this. Each of the stages of the learning cycle calls for different learning approaches and appeals to different kinds of persons.

Every individual develops through experience one or more *preferred* learning styles. It is important to stress that we all tend to use all of these styles, we do not confine our learning efforts to one only. But we prefer to use one or perhaps two modes of learning above the others; we feel stronger at learning through one approach rather than through any of the others. What is clear is that we all learn actively and that we do it in different ways (see Figure 1.4).

Two conclusions for the teacher of adults come from this view of learning styles. The first is that in any adult learning group there will always be people with a range of different learning styles. We can never assume that all our student participants will prefer to learn only through one form of activity. This means that it is necessary for any teacher to adopt a wide range of teaching–learning activities in order to help those who prefer to learn through active engagement with experience, those who prefer to reflect critically, those who prefer to develop more generalised views, and those who prefer to experiment and test out other people's theories.

The second conclusion is that the development of understandings about learning styles was never intended to enable the teacher of adults to put people into a particular learning style category. It was developed to help explain what is going on. Some student participants will wish to strengthen those learning styles with which they feel less comfortable, which they feel are weaker. Some activists may thus wish to develop their skills of critical reflection or abstract conceptualisation, for example. But others will seek to use their strongest style to maximise their learning. It is never safe to rely upon any one conclusion in adult education.

There is still much that is not known about learning styles. We do not know for instance whether we use exactly the same learning styles for all learning situations. For example, if Habermas is right and there are three quite different kinds of learning, it is not clear if our learning styles will vary according to the kind of learning being engaged in. Emancipatory learning may call for more reflective styles than for activist styles. Again we do not

Active learners
Some people prefer to learn by doing something immediately. They don't bother to wait to listen to all the instructions, to read the manual first but get on with the job. These people get impatient when someone tells them all about the task first. When they have finished one activity, they want to pass quickly to the next one. They want to see as many new things as possible; they like to meet lots of new people. They will often volunteer to take the lead in any activity. They like short-term goals and are usually bored by the slower work of implementing and consolidating a programme. They tend to believe what they are told. These people want to find out things for themselves.

Reflective learners
Some people prefer to 'wait and see', to sit back and watch others doing the task first, to listen to the talk of others. These people don't give the first answer that comes into their heads; when they are asked a question, they take time to think, they hesitate and are often uncertain. These people tend to like sharing their learning with others because this helps them to collect different opinions before they make up their minds.

Theorising learners
Some people like to build systems, to get down to first principles. They speak in general rather than in concrete terms. They question the basic assumptions. They try to make coherent pictures out of complex material (they often represent ideas in diagrams showing relationships). They try to be objective, detached; they are less sympathetic to human feelings, to other people's subjective judgements. These people want the world to be logical; they do not like too many different opinions.

Experimental learners
Some people like to experiment, to apply our new insights. They try to find new and more effective ways of doing things. They take short cuts or devise new modes of working. They tend to be confident, energetic, impatient of what they see as too much talk. They like solving problems and see new situations as a challenge from which they can learn a good deal. They like being shown how to do something but become frustrated if they are not allowed to do it for themselves very quickly.

Figure 1.4 Preferred learning styles.

Source: Adapted from the works of Kolb, 1976, 1984; Honey and Mumford, 1986.

know if these learning styles are common to all societies and all cultures or whether they are culture-bound (most of the research has been undertaken in Western rich societies). Equally we do not know if learning styles remain the same with ageing: do older learners continue to learn through the style they preferred when they were younger? While learning styles theories have been tested empirically with certain learning groups in a limited range of cultures (Honey and Mumford, 1986), these aspects have not yet been properly studied.

Concerns of the teacher of adults

Some practical conclusions may be drawn from all of this for the teacher of adults.

The existence of natural 'learning episodes' suggests a series of principles for those whose function is to create purposeful, systematic and structured learning opportunities for adults. The task of the teacher is twofold – to build upon these processes but at the same time to seek to go beyond them in a number of ways:

- not just to use but also to build up and enhance the participants' existing learning techniques, to help to make them more efficient;
- to start with the specific issue but then to help the learner to move from the concrete to the more general, to draw out the principles underlying the particular instances;
- to help the learner make the learning more permanent, more available for later use, rather than being simply a one-off incident of learning;
- to urge that the process should not stop once the immediate task is completed but lead on to further purposeful learning.

These form part of the goals of the teacher, using as our base the natural learning processes of our adult student participants.

Some of the more important considerations to be drawn from the adult learning episodes and borne in mind during the planning and teaching process are summarised in Figure 1.5.

Conclusion

There are many different theories about learning. Most of them rely upon some form of stimulus–response, but recent work suggests that the individual is engaged in learning through a process of active interrelating with either new knowledge or with his/her social or total environment. Learning takes place in a number of different domains, and different strategies are called into play to cope with different types of learning. All these theories have something to teach us about what we are doing, they each contribute to the list of factors that will make for the effective teaching of adults.

Characteristics	Implications
1 Episodic, not continuous	• Rely on short bursts of learning activity. • Break material into manageable units; but hook each one on to other items of learning.
2 Problem-centred, not curriculum-oriented; immediate goals based on needs and intentions; concrete situation; immediate, not future application; short term	• Make relevant to students' needs for motivation. • Be aware of students' intentions. • Students to set goals. • Start where they are, not necessarily at the beginning. • Do activity now, not prepare for it in the future.
3 Learning styles	• Be aware of different learning styles; build up learning skills.
• analogical thinking; use of existing knowledge and experience	• Relate new material to existing experience and knowledge. • Be sensitive to range and use of experience.
• trial and error	• Discovery learning; students to be active, not passive recipients. • Need for reinforcement; build in feedback. • Need for practice.
• meaningful wholes	• Move from simplified wholes to more complex wholes. • Help students to build up units to create whole; select out essential units from non-essential.
• less memory; but imitation	• Rely on understanding for retention, not memory. • Use of demonstration.
4 Lack of interest in general principles	• Move from concrete to general, not from general to concrete; encourage questioning of general principles; build up relationships.
• stops when need is met	• Remotivate to further learning.

Figure 1.5 The learning episode and the implications for the teacher of adults.

Rather than suggest that any one of these groups of learning theories is 'right' and the others are 'wrong', I have directed attention to the 'natural learning episode', those incidents in which adults throughout their lives engage in purposeful and structured learning using their own preferred learning style in order to achieve a particular goal or solve a specific problem. These episodes remind us that our student participants are already experienced learners; and they will help us to understand more clearly how to structure our own learning opportunities for adults. Our purpose as teachers of adults is to go beyond this natural learning process – to help the learners to make its results more permanent; to help them to draw out general principles; to use the process to lead on to further purposeful learning; to encourage them, in short, to become free in their own learning. We can use the characteristics of these learning episodes as a basis for creating adult learning episodes for our student participants.

References

Berne, E. (1970) *Games People Play*. Harmondsworth: Penguin.

Bloom, B.S. (1965) *Taxonomy of Educational Objectives*. London: Longman.

Freire, P. (1972) *Pedagogy of the Oppressed*. Harmondsworth: Penguin.

Gagné, R.M. (1972) Domains of Learning, *Interchange*, 3(1): 1–8.

Habermas, J. (1978) *Knowledge and Human Interest*. London: Heinemann.

Honey, P. and Mumford, A. (1986) *Manual of Learning Styles*. London: Peter Honey.

Houle, C.O. (1961) *The Inquiring Mind: a Study of the Adult who Continues to Learn*. Madison, WI: University of Wisconsin Press.

Kelly, G.A. (1955) *Psychology of Personal Constructs*, 2 vols. New York: McGraw-Hill.

Kolb, D.A. (1976) *Learning Style Inventory Technical Manual*. Boston, MA: McBer.

Kolb, D.A. (1984) *Experiential Learning: Experience as the Source of Learning and Development*. Englewood Cliffs, NJ: Prentice-Hall.

Maslow, A.H. (1968) *Towards a Psychology of Being*. New York: Van Nostrand.

Mezirow, J. (1981) A critical theory of adult learning and education, *Adult Education*, 3: 3–24.

Rogers, A. (1993) Adult learning maps and the teaching process, *Studies in the Education of Adults*, 22(2): 199–220.

Rogers, C. (1974) *On Becoming a Person*. London: Constable.

Rotter, J.B. (1982) *The Development and Applications of Social Learning Theory*. New York: Praeger.

Schein, E.H. and Kommers, D.W. (1972) *Professional Education*. New York: McGraw-Hill.

Chapter 2

The interpersonal relationship in the facilitation of learning

Carl R. Rogers

I wish to begin this chapter with a statement that may seem surprising to some and perhaps offensive to others. It is simply this: Teaching, in my estimation, is a vastly overrated function.

Having made such a statement, I scurry to the dictionary to see if I really mean what I say. *Teaching* means 'to instruct'. Personally, I am not much interested in instructing another in what she should know or think, though others seem to love to do this. 'To impart knowledge or skill'. My reaction is, why not be more efficient, using a book or programmed learning? 'To make to know'. Here my hackles rise. I have no wish to *make* anyone know something. 'To show, guide, direct'. As I see it, too many people have been shown, guided, directed. So I come to the conclusion that I *do* mean what I said. Teaching is, for me, a relatively unimportant and vastly overvalued activity.

But there is more in my attitude than this. I have a negative reaction to teaching. Why? I think it is because it raises all the wrong questions. As soon as we focus on teaching, the question arises, what shall we teach? What, from our superior vantage point, does the other person need to know? I wonder if, in this modern world, we are justified in the presumption that we are wise about the future and the young are foolish. Are we *really* sure as to what they should know? Then there is the ridiculous question of coverage. What shall the course cover? This notion of coverage is based on the assumption that what is taught is what is learned; what is presented is what is assimilated. I know of no assumption so obviously untrue. One does not need research to provide evidence that this is false. One needs only to talk with a few students.

But I ask myself, 'Am I so prejudiced against teaching that I find no situation in which it is worthwhile?' I immediately think of my experiences in Australia long ago. I became much interested in the Australian Aborigines.

This is an edited version of an article previously published in *Humanizing Education*, 1967, Alexandria, VA: Association for Supervision and Curriculum Development.

Here is a group that for more than 20,000 years has managed to live and exist in a desolate environment in which modern man would perish within a few days. The secret of the Aboriginal's survival has been teaching. He has passed on to the young every shred of knowledge about how to find water, about how to track game, about how to kill the kangaroo, about how to find his way through the trackless desert. Such knowledge is conveyed to the young as being *the* way to behave, and any innovation is frowned upon. It is clear that teaching has provided him the way to survive in a hostile and relatively unchanging environment.

Now I am closer to the nub of the question that excites me. Teaching and the imparting of knowledge makes sense in an unchanging environment. This is why it has been an unquestioned function for centuries. But if there is one truth about modern man, it is that he lives in an environment that is *continually changing*. The one thing I can be sure of is that the physics that is taught to the present-day student will be outdated in a decade. The teaching in psychology will certainly be out of date in twenty years. The so-called 'facts of history' depend very largely upon the current mood and temper of the culture. Chemistry, biology, genetics, and sociology are in such flux that a firm statement made today will almost certainly be modified by the time the student gets around to using the knowledge.

We are, in my view, faced with an entirely new situation in education where the goal of education, if we are to survive, is the *facilitation of change and learning*. The only man who is educated is the man who has learned how to learn; the man who has learned how to adapt and change; the man who has realized that no knowledge is secure, that only the process of *seeking* knowledge gives a basis for security. Changingness, a reliance on *process* rather than upon static knowledge, is the only thing that makes any sense as a goal for education in the modern world.

So now with some relief I turn to an activity, a purpose, that really warms me – the facilitation of learning. When I have been able to transform a group – and here I mean all the members of a group, myself included – into a community of *learners*, then the excitement has been almost beyond belief. To free curiosity; to permit individuals to go charging off in new directions dictated by their own interests; to unleash the sense of inquiry; to open everything to questioning and exploration; to recognize that everything is in process of change – here is an experience I can never forget. I cannot always achieve it in groups with which I am associated, but when it is partially or largely achieved, then it becomes a never-to-be-forgotten group experience. Out of such a context arise true students, real learners, creative scientists and scholars, and practitioners, the kind of individuals who can live in a delicate but ever-changing balance between what is presently known and the flowing, moving, altering problems and facts of the future.

But do we know how to achieve this new goal in education or is it a will-o'-the-wisp that sometimes occurs, sometimes fails to occur, and thus offers little real hope? My answer is that we possess a very considerable knowledge of the conditions that encourage self-initiated, significant, experiential, 'gut-level' learning by the whole person. We do not frequently see these conditions put into effect because they mean a real revolution in our approach to education and revolutions are not for the timid. But we do find examples of this revolution in action.

We know – and I will briefly mention some of the evidence – that the initiation of such learning rests not upon the teaching skills of the leader, not upon scholarly knowledge of the field, not upon curricular planning, not upon use of audio-visual aids, not upon the programmed learning used, not upon lectures and presentations, not upon an abundance of books, though each of these might at one time or another be utilized as an important resource. No, the facilitation of significant learning rests upon certain attitudinal qualities that exist in the personal *relationship* between the facilitator and the learner.

We came upon such findings first in the field of psychotherapy, but now there is evidence that shows these findings apply in the classroom as well. We find it easier to think that the intensive relationship between therapist and client might possess these qualities, but we are also finding that they *may* exist in the countless interpersonal interactions between the teacher and pupils.

Qualities that facilitate learning

What are these qualities, these attitudes, that facilitate learning? Let me describe them very briefly, drawing illustrations from the teaching field.

Realness in the facilitator of learning

Perhaps the most basic of these essential attitudes is realness or genuineness. When the facilitator is a real person, being what she is, entering into a relationship with the learner without presenting a front or a façade, she is much more likely to be effective. This means that the feelings that she is experiencing are available to her, available to her awareness, that she is able to live these feelings, be them, and able to communicate them if appropriate. It means that she comes into a direct personal encounter with the learner, meeting her on a person-to-person basis. It means that she is *being* herself, not denying herself.

Seen from this point of view it is suggested that the teacher can be a real person in her relationship with her students. She can be enthusiastic, can be bored, can be interested in students, can be angry, can be sensitive and sympathetic. Because she accepts these feelings as her own, she has no need to impose them on her students. She can like or dislike a student product without implying that it is objectively good or bad or that the student is good or bad. She is simply expressing a feeling for the product, a feeling that exists within herself. Thus, she is a person to her students, not a faceless embodiment of a curricular requirement nor a sterile tube through which knowledge is passed from one generation to the next.

It is obvious that this attitudinal set, found to be effective in psychotherapy, is sharply in contrast with the tendency of most teachers to show themselves to their pupils simply as roles. It is quite customary for teachers rather consciously to put on the mask, the role, the façade of being a teacher and to wear this façade all day, removing it only when they have left the school at night.

But not all teachers are like this. Take Barbara Shiel. She gave her pupils a great deal of responsible freedom, and I will mention some of the reactions of her students later. But here is an example of the way she shared herself with her pupils – not just sharing feelings of sweetness and light, but anger and frustration. She had made art materials freely available, and students often used these in creative ways, but the room frequently looked like a picture of chaos. Here is her report of her feelings and what she did with them.

> I find it maddening to live with the mess – with a capital M! No one seems to care except me. Finally, one day I told the children . . . that I am a neat, orderly person by nature and that the mess was driving me to distraction. Did they have a solution? It was suggested there were some volunteers who could clean up . . . I said it didn't seem fair to me to have the same people clean up all the time for others – but it would solve it for me. 'Well, some people like to clean,' they replied. So that's the way it is.
>
> (Shiel, 1966)

I hope this example puts some lively meaning into the phrases I used earlier, that the facilitator 'is able to live these feelings, be them, and able to communicate them if appropriate'. I have chosen an example of negative feelings because I think it is more difficult for most of us to visualize what this would mean. In this instance, Miss Shiel is taking the risk of being transparent in her angry frustrations about the mess. And what happens? The same thing that, in my experience, nearly always happens. These young people accept and respect her feelings, take them into account, and work out a novel solution that none of us, I believe, would have suggested. Miss Shiel wisely comments, 'I used to get upset and feel guilty when I became angry. I finally realized the children could accept *my* feelings too. And it is important for them to know when they've "pushed me". I have my limits, too' (Shiel, 1966).

Just to show that positive feelings, when they are real, are equally effective, let me quote briefly a college student's reaction, in a different course:

> Your sense of humour in the class was cheering; we all felt relaxed because you showed us your human self, not a mechanical teacher image. I feel as if I have more understanding and faith in my teachers now. I feel closer to the students too.

Another says:

> You conducted the class on a personal level and therefore in my mind
> I was able to formulate a picture of you as a person and not as merely
> a walking textbook.

Another student in the same course:

> It wasn't as if there was a teacher in the class, but rather someone whom
> we could trust and identify as a 'sharer.' You were so perceptive and
> sensitive to our thoughts, and this made it all the more 'authentic' for
> me. It was an 'authentic' *experience*, not just a class.
>
> (Bull, 1966)

I trust I am making it clear that to be real is not always easy, nor is it achieved
all at once, but it is basic to the person who wants to become that revolutionary individual, a facilitator of learning.

Prizing, acceptance, trust

There is another attitude that stands out in those who are successful in facilitating learning. I have observed this attitude. I have experienced it. Yet, it
is hard to know what term to put to it so I shall use several. I think of it as
prizing the learner, prizing her feelings, her opinions, her person. It is a caring
for the learner, but a non-possessive caring. It is an acceptance of this other
individual as a separate person, having worth in her own right. It is a basic
trust – a believe that this other person is somehow fundamentally trust-
worthy. Whether we call it prizing, acceptance, trust, or by some other term,
it shows up in a variety of observable ways. The facilitator who has a considerable degree of this attitude can be fully acceptant of the fear and hesitation
of the student as she approaches a new problem as well as acceptant of the
pupil's satisfaction in achievement. Such a teacher can accept the student's
occasional apathy, her erratic desires to explore byroads of knowledge, as
well as her disciplined efforts to achieve major goals. She can accept personal
feelings that both disturb and promote learning – rivalry with a sibling,
hatred of authority, concern about personal adequacy. What we are describing is a prizing of the learner as an imperfect human being with many
feelings, many potentialities. The facilitator's prizing or acceptance of the
learner is an operational expression of her essential confidence and trust in
the capacity of the human organism.

I would like to give some examples of this attitude from the classroom
situation. Here any teacher statements would be properly suspect since many
of us would like to feel we hold such attitudes and might have a biased
perception of our qualities. But let me indicate how this attitude of prizing,

of accepting, of trusting appears to the student who is fortunate enough to experience it.

Here is a statement from a college student in a class with Dr Morey Appell:

> Your way of being with us is a revelation to me. In your class I feel important, mature, and capable of doings things on my own. I want to think for myself and this need cannot be accomplished through text-books and lectures alone, but through living. I think you see me as a person with real feelings and needs, an individual. What I say and do are significant expressions from me, and you recognize this.
>
> (Appell, 1959)

The facilitator who cares, who prizes, who trusts the learner creates a climate for learning so different from the ordinary classroom that any resemblance is purely coincidental.

Empathic understanding

A further element that establishes a climate for self-initiated, experiential learning is empathic understanding. When the teacher has the ability to understand the student's reactions from the inside, has a sensitive awareness of the way the process of education and learning seems *to the student*, then again the likelihood of significant learning is increased.

This kind of understanding is sharply different from the usual evaluative understanding, which follows the pattern of 'I understand what is wrong with you.' When there is a sensitive empathy, however, the reaction in the learner follows something of this pattern, 'At last someone understands how it feels and seems to be *me* without wanting to analyse me or judge me. Now I can blossom and grow and learn.'

This attitude of standing in the other's shoes, of viewing the world through the student's eyes, is almost unheard of in the classroom. One could listen to thousands of ordinary classroom interactions without coming across one instance of clearly communicated, sensitively accurate, empathic under-standing. But it has a tremendously releasing effect when it occurs.

Let me take an illustration from Virginia Axline, dealing with a second grade boy. Jay, age 7, has been aggressive, a troublemaker, slow of speech and learning. Because of his 'cussing', he was taken to the principal, who paddled him, unknown to Miss Axline. During a free work period, Jay fashioned very carefully a man of clay down to a hat and a handkerchief in his pocket. 'Who is that?' asked Miss Axline. 'Dunno,' replied Jay. 'Maybe it is the principal. He has a handkerchief in his pocket like that.' Jay glared at the clay figure. 'Yes,' he said. Then he began to tear the head off and looked up and smiled. Miss Axline said, 'You sometimes feel like twisting his head off, don't you? You get so mad at him.' Jay tore off one arm, another, then beat the figure to a pulp with his fists. Another boy, with the perception of the young, explained, 'Jay is mad at Mr X because he licked him this noon.' 'Then you must feel lots better now,' Miss Axline commented. Jay grinned and began to rebuild Mr X (Axline, 1944).

The other examples I have cited also indicate how deeply appreciative students feel when they are simply *understood* – not evaluated, not judged, simply understood from their *own* point of view, not the teacher's. If any teacher set herself the task of endeavouring to make one non-evaluative, acceptant, empathic response per day to a student's demonstrated or verbalized feeling, I believe she would discover the potency of this currently almost non-existent kind of understanding.

What are the bases of facilitative attitudes?

A 'puzzlement'

It is natural that we do not always have the attitudes I have been describing. Some teachers raise the question, 'But what if I am *not* feeling empathic, do *not*, at this moment, prize or accept or like my students. What then?' My response is that realness is the most important of the attitudes mentioned, and it is not accidental that this attitude was described first. So if one has little understanding of the student's inner world and a dislike for the students or their behaviour, it is almost certainly more constructive to be *real* than to be pseudo-empathic or to put on a façade of caring.

But this is not nearly as simple as it sounds. To be genuine, or honest, or congruent, or real means to be this way about *oneself*. I cannot be real about another because I do not *know* what is real for him. I can only tell, if I wish to be truly honest, what is going on in me.

Let me take an example. Early in this chapter I reported Miss Shiel's feelings about the 'mess' created by the art work. Essentially she said, 'I find it maddening to live with the mess! I'm neat and orderly and it is driving me to distraction.' But suppose her feelings had come out somewhat differently in the disguised way that is much more common in classrooms at all levels. She might have said, 'You are the messiest children I've ever seen! You don't care about tidiness or cleanliness. You are just terrible!' This is most definitely *not* an example of genuineness or realness, in the sense in which I am using these terms. There is a profound distinction between the two statements, which I should like to spell out.

In the second statement she is telling nothing of herself, sharing none of her feelings. Doubtless the children will *sense* that she is angry, but because children are perceptively shrewd, they may be uncertain as to whether she is angry at them or has just come from an argument with the principal. It has none of the honesty of the first statement in which she tells of her *own* upsetness, of her *own* feeling of being driven to distraction.

Another aspect of the second statement is that it is all made up of judgements or evaluations, and like most judgements, they are all arguable. Are these children messy, or are they simply excited and involved in what they are doing? Are they *all* messy, or are some as disturbed by the chaos as she? Do they care nothing about tidiness, or is it simply that they don't care about it every day? If a group of visitors were coming, would their attitude be different? Are they terrible, or simply children? I trust it is evident that when we make judgements, they are almost never fully accurate and hence cause resentment and anger as well as guilt and apprehension. Had she used the second statement, the response of the class would have been entirely different.

I am going to some lengths to clarify this point because I have found from experience that to stress the value of being real, of *being* one's feelings, is taken by some as a licence to pass judgements on others, to project on others all the feelings that one should be 'owning'. Nothing could be further from my meaning.

Actually the achievement of realness is most difficult, and even when one wishes to be truly genuine, it occurs but rarely. Certainly it is not simply a matter of the *words* used, and if one is feeling judgemental, the use of a verbal formula that sounds like the sharing of feelings will not help. It is just another instance of a façade, of a lack of genuineness. Only slowly can we learn to be truly real. For first of all, one must be close to one's feelings, capable of being aware of them. Then one must be willing to take the risk of sharing them as they are, inside, not disguising them as judgements, or attributing them to other people. This is why I so admire Miss Shiel's sharing or her anger and frustration, without in any way disguising it.

A trust in the human organism

It would be most unlikely that one could hold the three attitudes I have described, or could commit herself to being a facilitator of learning unless she has come to have a profound trust in the human organism and its potentialities. If I distrust the human being, then I *must* cram her with information of my own choosing lest she go her own mistaken way. But if I trust the capacity of the human individual for developing her own potentiality, then I can provide her with many opportunities and permit her to choose her own way and her own direction in her learning.

It is clear, I believe, that the teachers rely basically upon the tendency towards fulfilment, towards actualization, in their students. They are basing their work on the hypothesis that students who are in real contact with problems that are relevant to them wish to learn, want to grow, seek to discover, endeavour to master, desire to create, move towards self-discipline. The teacher is attempting to develop a quality of climate in the classroom and a quality of personal relationship with students that will permit these natural tendencies to come to their fruition.

Living the uncertainty of discovery

I believe it should be said that this basically confident view of the human being and the attitudes toward students that I have described do not appear suddenly, in some miraculous manner, in the facilitator of learning. Instead, they come about through taking risks, through *acting* on tentative hypotheses. I can only state that I started my career with the firm view that individuals must be manipulated for their own good; I only came to the attitudes I have described and the trust in the individual that is implicit in them because I found that these attitudes were so much more potent in producing learning and constructive change. Hence, I believe that it is only by risking herself in these new ways that the teacher can *discover*, for herself, whether or not they are effective, whether or not they are for her.

I will then draw a conclusion, based on the experiences of the several facilitators and their students that have been included up to this point. When a facilitator creates, even to a modest degree, a classroom climate characterized by all that she can achieve of realness, prizing, and empathy; when she trusts the constructive tendency of the individual and the group; then she discovers that she has inaugurated an educational revolution. Learning of a different quality, proceeding at a different pace, with a greater degree of pervasiveness, occurs. Feelings – positive, negative, confused – become a part of the classroom experience. Learning becomes life and a very vital life at that. The student is on the way, sometimes excitedly, sometimes reluctantly, to becoming a learning, changing being.

Evidence from students

Certainly before the research evidence was in, students were making it clear by their reactions to student-centred or person-centred classrooms that an educational revolution was underway. This kind of evidence persists to the present day.

The most striking learnings of students exposed to such a climate are by no means restricted to greater achievement in the three Rs. The significant learnings are the more personal ones – independence, self-initiated and responsible learning, release of creativity, a tendency to become more of a person. I can only illustrate this by picking, almost at random, statements from students whose teachers have endeavoured to create a climate of trust, of prizing, of realness, of understanding, and above all, of freedom. Here is one of a number of statements made by students in a course on poetry led (not taught) by Dr Samuel Moon.

In retrospect, I find that I have actually enjoyed this course, both as a class and as an experiment, although it had me quite unsettled at times. This, in itself, made the course worthwhile since the majority of my courses this semester merely had me bored with them and the whole process of 'higher education.' Quite aside from anything else, due mostly to this course, I found myself devoting more time to writing poetry than to writing short stories, which temporarily interfered with my writing class.

... I should like to point out one very definite thing which I have gained from the course; this is an increased readiness on my part to listen to and to seriously consider the opinions of my fellow students. In view of my past attitude, this alone makes the course valuable. I suppose the real result of any course can be expressed in answer to the question, 'Would you take it over again?' My answer would be an unqualified 'Yes.'

(Moon, 1966: 227)

I should like to add to this several comments from Dr Bull's sophomore students in a class in adolescent psychology. The first two are midsemester comments.

This course is proving to be a vital and profound experience for me ... This unique learning situation is giving me a whole new conception of just what learning is ... I am experiencing a real growth in this atmosphere of constructive freedom ... the whole experience is challenging.

I feel that the course had been of great value to me ... I'm glad to have had this experience because it has made me think ... I've never been so personally involved with a course before, especially *outside* the classroom. It has been frustrating, rewarding, enjoyable, and tiring!

The other comments are from the end of the course:

This course is not ending with the close of the semester for me, but continuing ... I don't know of any greater benefit which can be gained from a course than this desire for further knowledge.

I feel as though this type of class situation has stimulated me more in making me realize where my responsibilities lie, especially as far as doing required work on my own. I no longer feel as though a test date is the criterion for reading a book. I feel as though my future work will be done for what *I* will get out of it, not just for a test mark.

I think that now I am acutely aware of the breakdown in communications that does exist in our society from seeing what happened in our class . . . I've grown immensely. I know that I am a different person than I was when I came into that class . . . It has done a great deal in helping me understand myself better . . . thank you for contributing to my growth.

My idea of education has been to gain information from the teacher by attending lectures. The emphasis and focus were on the teacher . . . One of the biggest changes that I experienced in this class was my outlook on education. Learning is something more than a grade on a report card. No one can measure what you have learned because it's a personal thing. I was very confused between learning and memorization. I could memorize very well, but I doubt if I ever learned as much as I could have. I believe my attitude toward learning has changed from a grade-centred outlook to a more personal one.

(Bull, 1966)

If you wish to know what this type of course seems like to a sixth grader, let me give you a sampling of the reactions of Miss Shiel's youngsters, misspellings and all.

I feel that I am learning self ability [sic]. I am learning not only school work but I am learning that you can learn on your own as well as someone can teach you.

I like this plan because there is a lot of freedom. I also learn more this way than the other way you don't have to wate [sic] for others you can go at your own speed rate and it also takes a lot of responsibility.

(Shiel, 1966)

Or let me take two more, from Dr Appell's graduate class:

I have been thinking about what happened through this experience. The only conclusion I come to is that if I try to measure what is going on, or what I was at the beginning, I have got to know what I was when I started – and I don't . . . so many things I did and feel are just lost . . . scrambled up inside . . . They don't seem to come out in a nice little pattern or organization I can say and write . . . There are so many things left unsaid. I know I have only scratched the surface, I guess. I can feel so many things almost ready to come out . . . maybe that's enough. *It seems all kinds of things have so much more meaning now than ever before* . . . This experience has had meaning, has done things to me and I am not sure how much or how far just yet. I think I am going to be a better me in the fall. *That's one thing I am sure of.*

(Appell, 1963)

You allow no play, yet I'm learning. Since the term began I seem to feel more alive, more real to myself. I enjoy being alone as well as with other people. My relationships with children and other adults are becoming more emotional and involved. Eating an orange last week, I peeled the skin off each separate orange section and liked it better with the transparent shell off. It was juicier and fresher tasting that way. I began to think, that's how I feel sometimes, without a transparent wall around me, really communicating my feelings. I feel that I'm growing, how much, I don't know. I'm thinking, considering, pondering and learning.

(Appell, 1959)

I can't read these student statements – sixth grade, college, graduate level – without being deeply moved. Here are teachers, risking themselves, *being* themselves, *trusting* their students, adventuring into the existential unknown, taking the subjective leap. And what happens? Exciting, incredible *human* events. You can sense persons being created, learnings being initiated, future citizens rising to meet the challenge of unknown worlds. If only one teacher out of a hundred dared to risk, dared to be, dared to trust, dared to understand, we would have an infusion of a living spirit into education that would, in my estimation, be priceless.

The effect upon the instructor

Let me turn to another dimension that excites me. I have spoken of the effect upon the *student* of a climate that encourages significant, self-reliant, personal learning. But I have said nothing about the reciprocal effect upon the instructor. When she has been the agent for the release of such self-initiated learning, the faculty member finds herself changed as well as her student. One such says:

To say that I am overwhelmed by what happened only faintly reflects my feelings. I have taught for many years but I have never experienced anything remotely resembling what occurred. I, for my part, never found in a classroom so much of the whole person coming forth, so deeply involved, so deeply stirred. Further, I question if in the traditional setup, with its emphasis on subject matter, examinations, grades, there is, or there can be a place for the 'becoming' person with his deep and manifold needs as he struggles to fulfill himself. But this is going far afield. I can only report to you what happened and to say that I am grateful and that I am also humbled by the experience. I would like you to know this for it has enriched my life and being.

(Rogers, 1961: 313)

Another faculty member reports as follows:

Rogers has said that relationships conducted on these assumptions mean 'turning present day education upside down.' I have found this to be true as I have tried to implement this way of living with students. The experiences I have had have plunged me into relationships which have been significant and challenging and beyond compare for me. They have inspired me and stimulated me and left me at times shaken and awed with their consequences for both me and the students. They have led me to the fact of what I can only call . . . the tragedy of education in our time – student after student who reports this to be his first experience with total trust, with freedom to be and to move in ways most consistent for the enhancement and maintenance of the core of dignity which somehow has survived humiliation, distortion, and corrosive cynicism.

(Appell, 1959)

Too idealistic?

Some readers may feel that the whole approach of this chapter – the belief that teachers can relate as persons to their students – is hopelessly unrealistic and idealistic. They may see that in essence it is encouraging both teachers and students to be creative in their relationship to each other and in their relationship to subject matter, and feel that such a goal is quite impossible. They are not alone in this. I have heard scientists at leading schools of science and scholars in leading universities arguing that it is absurd to try to encourage all students to be creative – we need hosts of mediocre technicians and workers, and if a few creative scientists and artists and leaders emerge, that will be enough. That may be enough for them. It may be enough to suit you. I want to go on record as saying it is *not* enough to suit me. When I realize the incredible potential in the ordinary student, I want to try to realise it. We are working hard to release the incredible energy in the atom and the nucleus of the atom. If we do not devote equal energy – yes, and equal money – to the release of the potential of the individual person then the enormous discrepancy between our level of physical energy resources and human energy resources will doom us to a deserved and universal destruction.

I am sorry I can't be coolly scientific about this. The issue is too urgent. I can only be passionate in my statement that people count, that interpersonal relationships *are* important, that we know something about releasing human potential, that we could learn much more, and that unless we give strong positive attention to the human interpersonal side of our educational dilemma, our civilization is on its way down the drain. Better courses, better curricula, better coverage, better teaching machines will never resolve our dilemma in a basic way. Only persons acting like persons in their relationships with their students can even begin to make a dent on this most urgent problem of modern education.

Summary

Let me try to state, somewhat more calmly and soberly, what I have said with such feeling and passion.

I have said that it is most unfortunate that educators and the public think about, and focus on, *teaching*. It leads them into a host of questions that are either irrelevant or absurd so far as real education is concerned.

I have said that if we focused on the facilitation of *learning* – how, why, and when the student learns, and how learning seems and feels from the inside – we might be on a much more profitable track.

I have said that we have some knowledge, and could gain more, about the conditions that facilitate learning, and that one of the most important of these conditions is the attitudinal quality of the interpersonal relationship between facilitator and learner.

Those attitudes that appear effective in promoting learning can be described. First of all is a transparent realness in the facilitator, a willingness to be a person, to be and live the feelings and thoughts of the moment. When this realness includes a prizing, caring, a trust and respect for the learner, the climate for learning is enhanced. When it includes a sensitive and accurate emphatic listening, then indeed a freeing climate, stimulative of self-initiated learning and growth, exists. The student is *trusted* to develop.

I have tried to make plain that individuals who hold such attitudes, and are bold enough to act on them, do not simply modify classroom methods – they revolutionize them. They perform almost none of the functions of teachers. It is no longer accurate to call them *teachers*. They are catalysers, facilitators, giving freedom and life and the opportunity to learn, to students.

I have brought in the cumulating research evidence that suggests that individuals who hold such attitudes are regarded as effective in the classroom; that the problems that concern them have to do with the release of potential, not the deficiencies of their students; that they seem to create classroom situations in which there are not admired children and disliked children, but in which affection and liking are part of the life of every child; that in classrooms approaching such a psychological climate, children learn more of the conventional subjects.

But I have intentionally gone beyond the empirical findings to try to take you into the inner life of the student – elementary, college, and graduate – who is fortunate enough to live and learn in such an interpersonal relationship with a facilitator, in order to let you see what learning feels like when it is free, self-initiated and spontaneous. I have tried to indicate how it even changes the student–student relationship – making it more aware, more caring, more sensitive, as well as increasing the self-related learning of significant material. I have spoken of the change it brings about in the faculty member.

Throughout, I have tried to indicate that if we are to have citizens who can live constructively in this kaleidoscopically changing world, we can *only* have them if we are willing for them to become self-starting, self-initiating learners. Finally, it has been my purpose to show that this kind of learner develops best, so far as we now know, in a growth-promoting, facilitative relationship with a *person*.

References

Appell, Morey L. (1959) 'Selected student reactions to student-centered courses', unpublished manuscript, Indiana State University.

Appell, Morey L. (1963) 'Self-understanding for the guidance counselor', *Personnel Guidance Journal*, October, pp. 143–148.

Axline, Virginia M. (1944) 'Morale on the school front', *Journal of Educational Research*, pp. 521–533.

Bull, Patricia (1966) 'Student reactions, Fall, 1965', unpublished manuscript, New York State University College.

Moon, Samuel F. (1966) 'Teaching the self,' *Improving College and University Teaching, 14* Autumn, pp. 213–229.

Rogers, Carl R. (1961) *On Becoming a Person*, Boston: Houghton Mifflin.

Shiel, Barbara J. (1966) 'Evaluation: a self-directed curriculum, 1965', unpublished manuscript, n.p.

Chapter 3

From Technical Rationality to reflection-in-action

Donald Schön

The dominant epistemology of practice

According to the model of Technical Rationality – the view of professional knowledge that has most powerfully shaped both our thinking about the professions and the institutional relations of research, education, and practice – professional activity consists of instrumental problem solving made rigorous by the application of scientific theory and technique. Although all occupations are concerned, in this view, with the instrumental adjustment of means to ends, only the professions practice rigorously technical problem solving based on specialized scientific knowledge.

The prototypes of professional expertise are the 'learned professions' of medicine and law and, close behind these, business and engineering. These are, in Nathan Glazer's terms, the 'major' or 'near-major' professions (Glazer, 1974: 345). They are distinct from 'minor' professions such as social work, librarianship, education, divinity and town planning. In the essay from which these terms are drawn, Glazer (1974) argues that the schools of the minor professions are hopelessly non-rigorous, dependent on representatives of academic disciplines, such as economics or political science, who are superior in status to the professions themselves. But what is of greatest interest from our point of view is that Glazer's distinction between major and minor professions rests on a particularly well-articulated version of the model of Technical Rationality. The major professions are 'disciplined by an unambiguous end – health, success in litigation, profit – which settles men's minds' (ibid.: 363) and they operate in stable institutional contexts. Hence they are grounded in systematic, fundamental knowledge, of which scientific knowledge is the prototype, or else they have 'a high component of strictly technological knowledge based on science in the education which they provide' (ibid.: 349). In contrast, the minor professions suffer from shifting,

This is an edited version of an article previously published in *The Reflective Practitioner*, 1983, New York: Basic Books; 1991, Avebury: Ashgate Publishing Ltd.

ambiguous ends and from unstable institutional contexts of practice, and are *therefore* unable to develop a base of systematic, scientific professional knowledge. For Glazer, the development of a scientific knowledge base depends on fixed, unambiguous ends because professional practice is an instrumental activity. If applied science consists of cumulative, empirical knowledge about the means best suited to chosen ends, how can a profession ground itself in science when its ends are confused or unstable?

The systematic knowledge base of a profession is thought to have four essential properties. It is specialized, firmly bounded, scientific and standardized. This last point is particularly important, because it bears on the paradigmatic relationship that holds, according to Technical Rationality, between a profession's knowledge base and its practice. In Wilbert Moore's words:

> If every professional problem were in all respects unique, solutions would be at best accidental, and therefore have nothing to do with expert knowledge. What we are suggesting, on the contrary, is that there are sufficient uniformities in problems and in devices for solving them to qualify the solvers as professionals . . . professionals apply very general principles, *standardized* knowledge, to concrete problems . . .
>
> (Moore, 1970: 56)

This concept of 'application' leads to a view of professional knowledge as a hierarchy in which 'general principles' occupy the highest level and 'concrete problem solving' the lowest. As Edgar Schein has put it, there are three components to professional knowledge:

1 An *underlying discipline* or *basic science* component upon which the practice rests or from which it is developed.
2 An *applied science* or *'engineering'* component from which many of the day-to-day diagnostic procedures and problem-solutions are derived.
3 A *skills and attitudinal* component that concerns the actual performance of services to the client, using the underlying basic and applied knowledge.

(Schein, 1973: 39)

The application of basic science yields applied science. Applied science yields diagnostic and problem solving techniques, which are applied in turn to the actual delivery of services. Applied science is said to 'rest on' the foundation of basic science. And the more basic and general the knowledge, the higher the status of its producer.

When the representatives of aspiring professions consider the problem of rising to full professional status, they often ask whether their knowledge base has the requisite properties and whether it is regularly applied to the everyday problems of practice. Thus, in an article entitled 'The librarian: from occupation to profession' the author states that:

> the central gap is of course the failure to develop a general body of scientific knowledge bearing precisely on this problem, in the way that the medical profession with its auxiliary scientific fields has developed an immense body of knowledge with which to cure human diseases.
>
> (Goode, 1966: 39)

The sciences in which he proposes to ground his profession are 'communications theory, the sociology or psychology of mass communications, or the psychology of learning as it applies to reading' (Goode, 1966: 39). Unfortunately, however, he finds that:

> most day-to-day professional work utilizes rather concrete rule-of-thumb local regulations and rules and major catalog systems . . . The problems of selection and organization are dealt with on a highly empiricist basis, concretely, with little reference to general scientific principles.
>
> (Goode, 1966: 39)

And a social worker, considering the same sort of question, concludes that 'social work is already a profession' because it has a basis in:

> theory construction via systematic research. To generate valid theory that will provide a solid base for professional techniques requires the application of the scientific method to the service-related problems of the profession. Continued employment of the scientific method is nurtured by and in turn reinforces the element of *rationality*.
>
> (Greenwood, 1966: 11)

It is by progressing along this route that social work seeks to 'rise within the professional hierarchy so that it, too, might enjoy maximum prestige, authority, and monopoly which presently belong to a few top professions' (Greenwood, 1966: 19).

If the model of Technical Rationality appeared only in such statements of intent, or in programmatic descriptions of professional knowledge, we might have some doubts about its dominance. But the model is also embedded in the institutional context of professional life. It is implicit in the institutionalized relations of research and practice, and in the normative curricula of professional education. Even when practitioners, educators, and researchers question the model of Technical Rationality, they are party to institutions that perpetuate it.

From the point of view of the model of Technical Rationality institutionalized in the professional curriculum, real knowledge lies in the theories and techniques of basic and applied science. Hence, these disciplines should come first. 'Skills' in the use of theory and technique to solve concrete problems should come later on, when the student has learned the relevant science – first, because he cannot learn skills of application until he has learned applicable knowledge; and second, because skills are an ambiguous, secondary kind of knowledge. There is something disturbing about calling them 'knowledge' at all.

Again, medicine is the prototypical example. Ever since the Flexner Report, which revolutionized medical education in the early decades of the twentieth century, medical schools have devoted the first two years of study to the basic sciences – chemistry, physiology, pathology – as 'the appropriate foundation for later clinical training' (Thorne, 1973: 30). Even the physical arrangement of the curriculum reflects the basic division among the elements of professional knowledge:

> The separation of the medical school curriculum into two disjunctive stages, the preclinical and the clinical, reflects the division between theory and practice. The division also appears in the location of training and in medical school facilities. The sciences of biochemistry, physiology, pathology and pharmacology are learned from classrooms and laboratories, that is, in formal academic settings. More practical training, in clinical arts such as internal medicine, obstetrics and pediatrics, takes place in hospital clinics, within actual institutions of delivery.
>
> (Thorne, 1973: 31)

The origins of Technical Rationality

It is striking that the dominant model of professional knowledge seems to its proponents to require very little justification. How comes it that in the second half of the twentieth century we found in our universities a dominant view of professional knowledge as the application of scientific theory and technique to the instrumental problems of practice?

The answer to this question lies in the last three hundred years of the history of Western ideas and institutions. Technical Rationality is the heritage of Positivism, the powerful philosophical doctrine that grew up in the nineteenth century as an account of the rise of science and technology and as a social movement aimed at applying the achievements of science and technology to the well-being of mankind. It became institutionalized in the modern university, founded in the late nineteenth century when Positivism was at its height, and in the professional schools that secured their place in the university in the early decades of the twentieth century.

Since the Reformation, the history of the West has been shaped by the rise of science and technology and by the industrial movement that was both cause and consequence of the increasingly powerful scientific world-view. As the scientific world-view gained dominance, so did the idea that human progress would be achieved by harnessing science to create technology for the achievement of human ends. This Technological Programme[1] became a major theme for the philosophers of the Enlightenment in the eighteenth century, and by the late nineteenth century had been firmly established as a pillar of conventional wisdom. By this time, too, the professions had come to be seen as vehicles for the application of the new sciences to the achievement of human progress. The engineers, closely tied to the development of industrial technology, became a model of technical practice for the other professions. Medicine, a learned profession with origins in the medieval universities, was refashioned in the new image of a science-based technique for the preservation of health. And statecraft came to be seen as a kind of social engineering. As the professions evolved and proliferated, they became, increasingly, the principal agents of the Technological Programme.

As the scientific movement, industrialism, and the Technological Programme became dominant in Western society, a philosophy emerged that sought both to give an account of the triumphs of science and technology and to purge mankind of the residues of religion, mysticism and metaphysics that still prevented scientific thought and technological practice from wholly ruling over the affairs of men. It was in this spirit that, in the first half of the nineteenth century, Auguste Comte first expressed the three principal doctrines of Positivism. First, there was the conviction that empirical science was not just a form of knowledge but the only source of positive knowledge of the world. Second, there was the intention to cleanse men's minds of mysticism, superstition, and other forms of pseudoknowledge. And finally, there was the programme of extending scientific knowledge and technical control to human society.

As Positivists became increasingly sophisticated in their efforts to explain and justify the exclusivity of scientific knowledge, they recognized to what extent observational statements were theory-laden, and found it necessary to ground empirical knowledge in irreducible elements of sensory experience. They began to see laws of nature not as facts inherent in nature but as constructs created to explain observed phenomena, and science became for them a hypothetico-deductive system. In order to account for his observations, the scientist constructed hypotheses, abstract models of an unseen world that could be tested only indirectly through deductions susceptible to confirmation or disconfirmation by experiment. The heart of scientific inquiry consisted of the use of crucial experiments to choose among competing theories of explanation.

In the light of Positivist doctrines such as these, practice appeared as a puzzling anomaly. Practical knowledge exists, but it does not fit neatly into Positivist categories. We cannot readily treat it as a form of descriptive knowledge of the world, nor can we reduce it to the analytic schemas of logic and mathematics. Positivism solved the puzzle of practical knowledge in a way that had been foreshadowed by the Technological Programme and by Comte's programme for applying science to morality and politics. Practical knowledge was to be construed as knowledge of the relationship of means to ends. Given agreement about ends,[2] the question, 'How ought I to act?' could be reduced to a merely instrumental question about the means best suited to achieve one's ends. Disagreement about means could be resolved by reference to facts concerning the possible means, their relevant consequences, and the methods for comparing them with respect to the chosen ends of action. Ultimately, the instrumental question could be resolved by recourse to experiment. And as men built up scientific understandings of cause and effect, causal relationships could be mapped on to instrumental ones. It would be possible to select the means appropriate to one's ends by applying the relevant scientific theory. The question, 'How ought I to act?' could become a scientific one, and the best means could be selected by the use of the science-based technique.

In the late nineteenth and early twentieth centuries, the professions of engineering and medicine achieved dramatic successes in reliably adjusting means to ends and became models of instrumental practice. The engineer's design and analysis of materials and artefacts, the physician's diagnosis and treatment of disease, became prototypes of the science-based, technical practice that was destined to supplant craft and artistry. For according to the Positivist epistemology of practice, craft and artistry had no lasting place in rigorous practical knowledge.

Universities came of age in the United States, assumed their now familiar structure and styles of operation, in the late nineteenth and early twentieth centuries when science and technology were on the rise and the intellectual hegemony of Positivism was beginning to be established. Although other traditions of thought were never wholly extinguished in American universities – indeed, in some places managed to preserve a kind of local dominance – nevertheless in the United States more than in any other nation except Germany the very heart of the university was given over to the scientific enterprise, to the ethos of the Technological Programme, and to Positivism.

But for this, the professionalizing occupations paid a price. They had to accept the Positivist epistemology of practice that was now built into the very tissue of the universities. And they had also to accept the fundamental division of labour on which Veblen (1962) had placed so great an emphasis. It was to be the business of university-based scientists and scholars to create the fundamental theory that professionals and technicians would apply to practice. The function of the professional school would be:

> the transmission to its students of the generalized and systematic knowledge that is the basis of professional performance.
>
> (Hughes, 1973: 660)

But this division of labour reflected a hierarchy of kinds of knowledge that was also a ladder of status. Those who create new theory were thought to be higher in status than those who apply it, and the schools of 'higher learning' were thought to be superior to the 'lower'.

Emerging awareness of the limits of Technical Rationality

Following World War II, the United States Government began an unparalleled increase in the rate of spending for research. As government spending for research increased, research institutions proliferated. Some were associated with the universities, others stood outside them. All were organized around the production of new scientific knowledge and were largely promoted on the basis of the proposition that the production of new scientific knowledge could be used to create wealth, achieve national goals, improve human life, and solve social problems. Nowhere was the rate of increase in research spending more dramatic, and nowhere were the results of that spending more visible, than in the field of medicine. The great centres of medical research and teaching were expanded, and new ones were created. The medical research centre, with its medical school and its teaching hospital, became the institutional model to which other professions aspired. Other professions, hoping to achieve some of medicine's effectiveness and prestige, sought to emulate its linkage of research and teaching institutions, its hierarchy of research and clinical roles, and its system for connecting basic and applied research to practice.

The prestige and apparent success of the medical and engineering models exerted a great attraction for the social sciences. In fields such as education, social work, planning, and policy making, social scientists attempted to do research, to apply it, and to educate practitioners, all according to their perceptions of the models of medicine and engineering. Indeed, the very language of social scientists, rich in reference to measurement, controlled experiment, applied science, laboratories and clinics, was striking in its reverence for these models.

However, both the general public and the professionals have become increasingly aware of the flaws and limitations of the professions. The professions have suffered a crisis of legitimacy rooted both in their perceived failure to live up to their own norms and in their perceived incapacity to help society achieve its objectives and solve its problems. Increasingly, we have become aware of the importance to actual practice of phenomena – complexity, uncertainty, instability, uniqueness and value-conflict – that do not fit the model of Technical Rationality. Now, in the light of the Positivist origins of Technical Rationality, we can more readily see why these phenomena are so troublesome.

From the perspective of Technical Rationality, professional practice is a process of problem *solving*. Problems of choice or decision are solved through the selection, from available means, of the one best suited to established ends.

But with this emphasis on problem solving, we ignore problem *setting*, the process by which we define the decision to be made, the ends to be achieved, the means that may be chosen. In real-world practice, problems do not present themselves to the practitioner as givens. They must be constructed from the materials of problematic situations that are puzzling, troubling and uncertain. In order to convert a problematic situation to a problem, a practitioner must do a certain kind of work. He must make sense of an uncertain situation that initially makes no sense. When professionals consider what road to build, for example, they deal usually with a complex and ill-defined situation in which geographic, topological, financial, economic and political issues are mixed up together. Once they have somehow decided what road to build and go on to consider how best to build it, they may have a problem they can solve by the application of available techniques; but when the road they have built leads unexpectedly to the destruction of a neighbourhood, they may find themselves again in a situation of uncertainty.

It is this sort of situation that professionals are coming increasingly to see as central to their practice. They are coming to recognize that although problem setting is a necessary condition for technical problem solving, it is not itself a technical problem. When we set the problem, we select what we will treat as the 'things' of the situation, we set the boundaries of our attention to it, and we impose upon it a coherence that allows us to say what is wrong and in what directions the situation needs to be changed. Problem setting is a process in which, interactively, we *name* the things to which we will attend and *frame* the context in which we will attend to them.

Even when a problem has been constructed, it may escape the categories of applied science because it presents itself as unique or unstable. In order to solve a problem by the application of existing theory or technique, a practitioner must be able to map those categories on to features of the practice situation. When a nutritionist finds a diet deficient in lysine, for example, dietary supplements known to contain lysine can be recommended. But a unique case falls outside the categories of applied theory; an unstable situation slips out from under them. A nutritionist attempting a planned nutritional intervention in a rural Central American community may discover that the intervention fails because the situation has become something other than the one planned for.

Technical Rationality depends on agreement about ends. When ends are fixed and clear, then the decision to act can present itself as an instrumental problem. But when ends are confused and conflicting, there is as yet no 'problem' to solve. A conflict of ends cannot be resolved by the use of techniques derived from applied research. It is rather through the non-technical process of framing the problematic situation that we may organize and clarify both the ends to be achieved and the possible means of achieving them.

Similarly, when there are conflicting paradigms of professional practice, such as we find in the pluralism of psychiatry, social work or town planning, there is no clearly established context for the use of technique. There is contention over multiple ways of framing the practice role, each of which entrains a distinctive approach to problem setting and solving. And when practitioners do resolve conflicting role frames, it is through a kind of inquiry that falls outside the model of Technical Rationality. Again, it is the work of naming and framing that creates the conditions necessary to the exercise of technical expertise.

We can readily understand, therefore, not only why uncertainty, uniqueness, instability and value conflict are so troublesome to the Positivist epistemology of practice but also why practitioners bound by this epistemology find themselves caught in a dilemma. Their definition of rigorous professional knowledge excludes phenomena they have learned to see as central to their practice. And artistic ways of coping with these phenomena do not qualify, for them, as rigorous professional knowledge.

This dilemma of 'rigour or relevance' arises more acutely in some areas of practice than in others. In the varied topography of professional practice, there is a high, hard ground where practitioners can make effective use of research-based theory and technique, and there is a swampy lowland where situations are confusing 'messes' incapable of technical solution. The difficulty is that the problems of the high ground, however great their technical interest, are often relatively unimportant to clients or to the larger society, whereas in the swamp are the problems of greatest human concern. Shall the practitioner stay on the high, hard ground where he can practise rigorously, as he understands rigour, but where he is constrained to deal with problems of relatively little social importance? Or shall he descend to the swamp where he can engage the most important and challenging problems if he is willing to forsake technical rigour?

In 'major' professions such as medicine, engineering or agronomy there are zones where practitioners can function as technical experts. But there are also zones where the major professions resemble the minor ones. Medical technologies, such as kidney dialysis, generate demands in excess of the willingness of the nation to invest in medical care. Engineering that seems powerful and elegant when judged from a narrowly technical perspective may also carry unacceptable risks to environmental quality or human safety. Large-scale, industrialized agriculture destroys the peasant economies of the developing worlds. How should professionals take account of such issues as these?

There are those who choose the swampy lowlands. They deliberately involve themselves in messy but crucially important problems and, when asked to describe their methods of inquiry, they speak of experience, trial and error, intuition, and muddling through.

Other professionals opt for the high ground. Hungry for technical rigour, devoted to an image of solid professional competence, or fearful of entering a world in which they feel they do not know what they are doing, they choose to confine themselves to a narrowly technical practice.

Many practitioners have responded to the dilemma of rigour or relevance by cutting the practice situation to fit professional knowledge. This they do in several ways. They may become selectively inattentive to data that fall outside their categories. Designers of management information systems may simply avoid noticing, for example, how their systems trigger games of control and evasion. They may use 'junk categories' to explain away discrepant data,[3] as technical analysts sometimes attribute the failure of their recommendations to 'personality' or to 'politics'. Or they may try to force the situation into a mould that lends itself to the use of available techniques. Thus, an industrial engineer may simplify the actual arrangement of a manufacturing system in order to make it easier to analyse; or, more ominously, members of the helping professions may get rid of clients who resist professional help, relegating the categories such as 'problem tenant' or 'rebellious child'. All such strategies carry a danger of misreading situations, or manipulating them, to serve the practitioner's interest in maintaining his confidence in his standard models and techniques. When people are involved in the situation, the practitioner may preserve his sense of expertise at his clients' expense.

Schein (1973), Glazer (1974) and Simon (1972) propose three different approaches to the limitations of Technical Rationality and the related dilemma of rigour or relevance. All three employ a common strategy, however. They try to fill the gap between the scientific basis of professional knowledge and the demands of real-world practice in such a way as to preserve the model of Technical Rationality. Schein does it by segregating convergent science from divergent practice, relegating divergence to a residual category called 'divergent skill'. Glazer does it by attributing convergence to the major professions, which he applauds, and divergence to the minor professions, which he dismisses. Simon does it by proposing a science of design that depends on having well-formed instrumental problems to begin with.

Yet the Positivist epistemology of practice, the model of professional knowledge to which these writers cling, has fallen into disrepute in its original home, the philosophy of science. Among philosophers of science no one wants any longer to be called a Positivist, and there is a rebirth of interest in the ancient topics of craft, artistry and myth – topics whose fate Positivism once claimed to have sealed. It seems clear, however, that the dilemma that afflicts the professions hinges not on science *per se* but on the Positivist view of science. From this perspective, we tend to see science, after the fact, as a body of established propositions derived from research. When we recognize their limited utility in practice, we experience the dilemma of rigour or relevance. But we may also consider science before the fact as a process in which scientists grapple with uncertainties and display arts of inquiry akin to the uncertainties and arts of practice.

Let us then reconsider the question of professional knowledge; let us stand the question on its head. If the model of Technical Rationality is incomplete, in that it fails to account for the practical competence in 'divergent' situations, so much the worse for the model. Let us search, instead, for an epistemology of practice implicit in the artistic, intuitive processes that some practitioners do bring to situations of uncertainty, instability, uniqueness and value conflict.

Reflection-in-action

When we go about the spontaneous, intuitive performance of the actions of everyday life, we show ourselves to be knowledgeable in a special way. Often we cannot say what it is that we know. When we try to describe it we find ourselves at a loss, or we produce descriptions that are obviously inappropriate. Our knowing is ordinarily tacit, implicit in our patterns of action and in our feel for the stuff with which we are dealing. It seems right to say that our knowing is *in* our action.

Similarly, the workaday life of the professional depends on tacit knowing-in-action. Every competent practitioner can recognize phenomena – families of symptoms associated with a particular disease, peculiarities of a certain kind of building site, irregularities of materials or structures – for which he cannot give a reasonably accurate or complete description. In his day-to-day practice he makes innumerable judgements of quality for which he cannot state adequate criteria, and he displays skills for which he cannot state the rules and procedures. Even when he makes conscious use of research-based theories and techniques, he is dependent on tacit recognitions, judgements and skilful performances.

On the other hand, both ordinary people and professional practitioners often think about what they are doing, sometimes even while doing it. Stimulated by surprise, they turn thought back on action and on the knowing that is implicit in action. They may ask themselves, for example, 'What features do I notice when I recognize this thing? What are the criteria by which I make this judgement? What procedures am I enacting when I perform this skill? How am I framing the problem that I am trying to solve?' Usually, reflection on knowing-in-action goes together with reflection on the stuff at hand. There is some puzzling, or troubling, or interesting phenomenon with which the individual is trying to deal. As he tries to make sense of it, he also reflects on the understandings that have been implicit in his action, understandings that he surfaces, criticizes, restructures and embodies in further action.

It is this entire process of reflection-in-action that is central to the 'art' by which practitioners sometimes deal well with situations of uncertainty, instability, uniqueness and value conflict.

Knowing-in-action. Once we put aside the model of Technical Rationality, which leads us to think of intelligent practice as an *application* of knowledge to instrumental decisions, there is nothing strange about the idea that a kind of knowing is inherent in intelligent action. Common sense admits the category of know-how, and it does not stretch common sense very much to say that the know-how is *in* the action – that a tightrope walker's know-how, for example, lies in, and is revealed by, the way he takes his trip across the wire, or that a big-league pitcher's know-how is in his way of pitching to a batter's weakness, changing his pace, or distributing his energies over the course of a game. There is nothing in common sense to make us say that know-how consists of rules or plans that we entertain in the mind prior to action. Although we sometimes think before acting, it is also true that in much of the spontaneous behaviour of skilful practice we reveal a kind of knowing that does not stem from a prior intellectual operation.

As Gilbert Ryle has put it:

> What distinguishes sensible from silly operations is not their parentage but their procedure, and this holds no less for intellectual than for practical performances. 'Intelligent' cannot be defined in terms of 'intellectual' or 'knowing *how*' in terms of 'knowing *that*'; 'thinking what I am doing' does not connote 'both thinking what to do and doing it.' When I do something intelligently . . . I am doing one thing and not two. My performance has a special procedure or manner, not special antecedents.
> (Ryle, 1949: 32)

Over the years, several writers on the epistemology of practice have been struck by the fact that skilful action often reveals a 'knowing more than we can say'.

Psycholinguists have noted that we speak in conformity with rules of phonology and syntax that most of us cannot describe.[4] Alfred Schutz (1962) and his intellectual descendants have analysed the tacit, everyday know-how that we bring to social interactions such as the rituals of greeting, ending a meeting, or standing in a crowded elevator. Birdwhistell (1970) has made comparable contributions to a description of the tacit knowledge embodied in our use and recognition of movement and gesture. In these domains, too, we behave according to rules and procedures that we cannot usually describe and of which we are often unaware.

In examples like these, knowing has the following properties:

- There are actions, recognitions and judgements that we know how to carry out spontaneously; we do not have to think about them prior to or during their performance.
- We are often unaware of having learned to do these things; we simply find ourselves doing them.
- In some cases, we were once aware of the understandings that were subsequently internalized in our feeling for the stuff of action. In other cases, we may never have been aware of them. In both cases, however, we are usually unable to describe the knowing that our action reveals.

It is in this sense that I speak of knowing-*in*-action, the characteristic mode of ordinary practical knowledge.

Reflecting-in-action. If common sense recognizes knowing-in-action, it also recognizes that we sometimes think about what we are doing. Phrases such as 'thinking on your feet', 'keeping your wits about you', and 'learning by doing' suggest not only that we can think about doing but that we can think about doing something while doing it. Some of the most interesting examples of this process occur in the midst of a performance.

Big-league baseball pitchers speak, for example, of the experience of 'finding the groove':

> Only a few pitchers can control the whole game with pure physical ability. The rest have to learn to adjust once they're out there. If they can't, they're dead ducks.

> [You get] a special feel for the ball, a kind of command that lets you repeat the exact same thing you did before that proved successful.

> Finding your groove has to do with studying those winning habits and trying to repeat them every time you perform.
>
> (Maslow, 1981: 34)

I do not wholly understand what it means to 'find the groove'. It is clear, however, that the pitchers are talking about a particular kind of reflection. What is 'learning to adjust once you're out there'? Presumably it involves noticing how you have been pitching to the batters and how well it has been working, and on the basis of these thoughts and observations, changing the way you have been doing it. When you get a 'feel for the ball' that lets you 'repeat the exact same thing you did before that proved successful', you are noticing, at the very least, that you have been doing something right, and your 'feeling' allows you to do that something again. When you 'study those winning habits', you are thinking about the know-how that has enabled you to win. The pitchers seem to be talking about a kind of reflection on their patterns of action, on the situations in which they are performing, and on the know-how implicit in their performance. They are reflecting *on* action and, in some cases, reflecting *in* action.

When good jazz musicians improvise together, they also manifest a 'feel for' their material and they make on-the-spot adjustments to the sounds they hear. Listening to one another and to themselves, they feel where the music is going and adjust their playing accordingly. They can do this, first of all, because their collective effort at musical invention makes use of a schema – a metric, melodic and harmonic schema familiar to all the participants – that gives a predictable order to the piece. In addition, each of the musicians has at the ready a repertoire of musical figures that he can deliver at appropriate moments. Improvisation consists of varying, combining and recombining a set of figures within the schema that bounds and gives coherence to the performance. As the musicians feel the direction of the music that is developing out of their interwoven contributions, they make new sense of it and adjust their performance to the new sense they have made. They are reflecting-in-action on the music they are collectively making and on their individual contributions to it, thinking what they are doing and, in the process, evolving their way of doing it. Of course, we need not suppose that they reflect-in-action in the medium of words. More likely, they reflect through a 'feel for the music' that is not unlike the pitcher's 'feel for the ball'.

Much reflection-in-action hinges on the experience of surprise. When intuitive, spontaneous performance yields nothing more than the results expected for it, then we tend not to think about it. But when intuitive performance leads to surprises, pleasing and promising or unwanted, we may respond by reflecting-in-action. Like the baseball pitcher, we may reflect on our 'winning habits'; or like the jazz musician, on our sense of the music we have been making; or like the designer, on the misfit we have unintentionally created. In such processes, reflection tends to focus interactively on the outcomes of action, the action itself, and the intuitive knowing implicit in the action.

Let us consider an example that reveals these processes in some detail.

In an article entitled 'If you want to get ahead, get a theory', Inhelder and Karmiloff-Smith describe a rather unusual experiment concerning 'children's processes of discovery in action' (Inhelder and Karmiloff-Smith, 1975: 195). They asked their subjects to balance wooden blocks on a metal bar. Some of the blocks were plain wooden blocks, but others were conspicuously or inconspicuously weighted at one end. The authors attended to the spontaneous processes by which the children tried to learn about the properties of the blocks, balance them on the bar, and regulate their actions after success or failure.

They found that virtually all children aged 6 to 7 began the task in the same way:

> *all* blocks were systematically first tried at their geometric centre.
> (Inhelder and Karmiloff-Smith, 1975: 202)

And they found that slightly older children would not only place all blocks at their geometric centre but that:

> when asked to add small blocks of varying shapes and sizes to blocks already in balance, they added up to ten blocks precariously one on top of the other at the geometric centre rather than distributing them at the extremities.
> (ibid.: 203)

They explain this persistent and virtually universal behaviour by attributing to the children what they call a 'theory-in-action': a 'geometric centre theory' of balancing, or, as one child put it, a theory that 'things always balance in the middle'.

Of course, when the children tried to balance the counterweighted blocks at their geometric centres, they failed. How did they respond to failure? Some children made what the authors called an 'action-response':

> They now placed the very same blocks more and more systematically at the geometric centre, with only very slight corrections around this point. They showed considerable surprise at not being able to balance the blocks a second time ('Heh, what's wrong with this one, it worked before') ... Action sequences then became reduced to: Place carefully at geometric centre, correct very slightly around this centre, abandon all attempts, declaring the object 'impossible' to balance.
>
> (Inhelder and Karmiloff-Smith, 1975: 203)

Other children, generally between the ages of 7 and 8, responded in a very different ways. When the counterweighted blocks failed to balance at their geometric centres, these children began to decentre them. They did this first with conspicuously counterweighted blocks. Then:

> gradually, and often almost reluctantly, the 7 to 8 year olds began to make corrections also on the inconspicuous weight blocks ... At this point, we observed many pauses during action sequences on the inconspicuous weight items.
>
> (ibid.: 205)

Later still:

> As the children were now really beginning to question the generality of their geometric centre theory, a negative response at the geometric centre sufficed to have the child rapidly make corrections toward the point of balance.
>
> (ibid.)

And finally:

> children paused *before* each item, roughly assessed the weight distribution of the block by lifting it ('you have to be careful, sometimes it's just as heavy on each side, sometimes it's heavier on one side'), inferred the probable point of balance and then placed the object immediately very close to it, without making any attempts at first balancing at the geometric centre.
>
> (ibid.)

The children now behaved as though they had come to hold a theory-in-action that blocks balance, not at their geometric centres, but at their centres of gravity.

This second pattern of response to error, the authors call 'theory-response'. Children work their way toward it through a series of stages. When they are first confronted with a number of events that refute their geometric centre theories-in-action, they stop and think. Then, starting with the conspicuous-weight blocks, they begin to make corrections away from the geometric centre. Finally, when they have really abandoned their earlier theories-in-action, they weigh all the blocks in their hands so as to infer the probable point of balance. As they shift their theories of balancing from geometric centre to centre of gravity, they also shift from a 'success orientation' to a 'theory orientation'. Positive and negative results come to be taken not as signs of success or failure in action but as information relevant to a theory of balancing.

It is interesting to note that as the authors observe and describe this process, they are compelled to invent a language. They describe theories-in-action that the children themselves cannot describe:

> Indeed, although the (younger) child's action sequences bear eloquent witness to a theory-in-action implicit in his behavior, this should not be taken as a capacity to conceptualize explicitly on what he is doing and why.
>
> (Inhelder and Karmiloff-Smith, 1975: 203)

Knowing-in-action, which the child may represent to himself in terms of a 'feel for the blocks', the observers redescribe in terms of 'theories'. I shall say that they convert the child's know*ing*-in-action to know*ledge*-in-action.

A conversion of this kind seems to be inevitable in any attempt to talk about reflection-in-action. One must use words to describe a kind of knowing, and a change of knowing, which are probably not originally represented in words at all. Thus, from their observations of the children's behaviour, the authors make verbal descriptions of the children's intuitive understandings. These are the authors' theories about the children's knowing-in-action. Like all such theories, they are deliberate, idiosyncratic constructions, and they can be put to experimental test:

> just as the child was constructing a theory-in-action in his endeavour to balance the blocks, so we, too, were making on-the-spot hypotheses about the child's theories and providing opportunities for negative and positive responses in order to verify our own theories!
>
> (ibid.: 199)

Reflecting-in-practice. The block-balancing experiment is a beautiful example of reflection-in-action, but it is very far removed from our usual images of professional practice. If we are to relate the idea of reflection-in-action to professional practice, we must consider what a practice is and how it is like and unlike the kinds of action we have been discussing.

The word 'practice' is ambiguous. When we speak of a lawyer's practice, we mean the kinds of things he does, the kinds of clients he has, the range of cases he is called upon to handle. When we speak of someone practising the piano, however, we mean the repetitive or experimental activity by which he tries to increase his proficiency on the instrument. In the first sense, 'practice' refers to performance in a range of professional situations. In the second, it refers to preparation for performance. But professional practice also includes an element of repetition. A professional practitioner is a specialist who encounters certain types of situations again and again. This is suggested by the way in which professionals use the word 'case' – or project, account, commission, or deal, depending on the profession. All such terms denote the units that make up a practice, and they denote types of family-resembling examples. Thus, a physician may encounter many different 'cases of measles'; a lawyer, many different 'cases of libel'. As a practitioner experiences many variations of a small number of types of cases, he is able to 'practise' his practice. He develops a repertoire of expectations, images and techniques. He learns what to look for and how to respond to what he finds. As long as his practice is stable, in the sense that it brings him the same types of cases, he becomes less and less subject to surprise. His knowing-in-practice tends to become increasingly tacit, spontaneous and automatic, thereby conferring upon him and his clients the benefits of specialization.

On the other hand, professional specialization can have negative effects. In the individual, a high degree of specialization can lead to a parochial narrowness of vision. When a profession divides into subspecialities, it can break apart an earlier wholeness of experience and understanding. Thus people sometimes yearn for the general practitioner of earlier days, who is thought to have concerned himself with the 'whole patient', and they sometimes accuse contemporary specialists of treating particular illnesses in isolation from the rest of the patient's life experience. Further, as a practice becomes more repetitive and routine, and as knowing-in-practice becomes increasingly tacit and spontaneous, the practitioner may miss important opportunities to think about what he is doing. He may find that, like the younger children in the block-balancing experiment, he is drawn into patterns of error that he cannot correct. And if he learns, as often happens, to be selectively inattentive to phenomena that do not fit the categories of his knowing-in-action, then he may suffer from boredom or 'burn-out' and afflict his clients with the consequences of his narrowness and rigidity. When this happens, the practitioner has 'over-learned' what he knows.

A practitioner's reflection can serve as a corrective to over-learning. Through reflection, he can surface and criticize the tacit understandings that have grown up around the repetitive experiences of a specialized practice, and can make new sense of the situations of uncertainty or uniqueness that he may allow himself to experience.

Practitioners do reflect *on* their knowing-in-practice. Sometimes, in the relative tranquillity of a post-mortem, they think back on a project they have undertaken, a situation they have lived through, and they explore the understandings they have brought to their handling of the case. They may do this in a mood of idle speculation, or in a deliberate effort to prepare themselves for future cases.

But they may also reflect on practice while they are in the midst of it. Here they reflect-in-action, but the meaning of this term needs now to be considered in terms of the complexity of knowing-in-practice.

A practitioner's reflection-in-action may not be very rapid. It is bounded by the 'action-present', the zone of time in which action can still make a difference to the situation. The action-present may stretch over minutes, hours, days, or even weeks or months, depending on the pace of activity and the situational boundaries that are characteristic of the practice. Within the give-and-take of courtroom behaviour, for example, a lawyer's reflection-in-action may take place in seconds; but when the context is that of an antitrust case that drags on over years, reflection-in-action may proceed in leisurely fashion over the course of several months. An orchestra conductor may think of a single performance as a unit of practice, but in another sense a whole season is his unit. The pace and duration of episodes of reflection-in-action vary with the pace and duration of the situations of practice.

When a practitioner reflects in and on his practice, the possible objects of his reflection are as varied as the kinds of phenomena before him and the systems of knowing-in-practice that he brings to them. He may reflect on the tacit norms and appreciations that underlie a judgement, or on the strategies and theories implicit in a pattern of behaviour. He may reflect on the feeling for a situation that has led him to adopt a particular course of action, on the way in which he has framed the problem he is trying to solve, or on the role he has constructed for himself within a larger institutional context.

Reflection-in-action, in these several modes, is central to the art through which practitioners sometimes cope with the troublesome 'divergent' situations of practice.

When the phenomenon at hand eludes the ordinary categories of knowledge-in-practice, presenting itself as unique or unstable, the practitioner may surface and criticize his initial understanding of the phenomenon, construct a new description of it, and test the new description by an on-the-spot experiment. Sometimes he arrives at a new theory of the phenomenon by articulating a feeling he has about it.

When he finds himself stuck in a problematic situation that he cannot readily convert to a manageable problem, he may construct a new way of setting the problem – a new frame that, in what I shall call a 'frame experiment', he tries to impose on the situation.

When he is confronted with demands that seem incompatible or inconsistent, he may respond by reflecting on the appreciations that he and others have brought to the situation. Conscious of a dilemma, he may attribute it to the way in which he has set his problem, or even to the way in which he has framed his role. He may then find a way of integrating, or choosing among, the values at stake in the situation.

In his mid-thirties, sometime between the composition of his early work *The Cossacks* and his later *War and Peace*, Leo Nikolayevich Tolstoy became interested in education. He started a school for peasant children on his estate at Yasnaya Polyana, he visited Europe to learn the latest educational methods, and he published an educational journal, also called *Yasnaya Polyana*. Before he was done (his new novel eventually replaced his interest in education), he had built some seventy schools, had created an informal teacher-training programme, and had written an exemplary piece of educational evaluation.

For the most part, the methods of the European schools filled him with disgust, yet he was entranced by Rousseau's writings on education. His own school anticipated John Dewey's later approach to learning by doing, and bore the stamp of his conviction that good teaching required 'not a method but an art'.

An artful teacher sees a child's difficulty in learning to read not as a defect in the child but as a defect 'of his own instruction'. So he must find a way of explaining what is bothering the pupil. He must do a piece of experimental research, then and there, in the classroom. And because the child's difficulties may be unique, the teacher cannot assume that his repertoire of explanations will suffice, even though they are 'at the tongue's end'. He must be ready to invent new methods and must 'endeavour to develop in himself the ability of discovering them'.

Researchers at the Massachusetts Institute of Technology (MIT) have undertaken a programme of in-service education for teachers, a programme organized around the idea of on-the-spot reflection and experiment, very much as in Tolstoy's art of teaching. In this Teacher Project,[5] the researchers have encouraged a small group of teachers to explore their own intuitive thinking about apparently simple tasks in domains such as mathematics, physics, music, and the perceived behaviour of the moon. The teachers have made some important discoveries. They have allowed themselves to become confused about subjects they are supposed to 'know'; and as they have tried to work their way out of their confusions, they have also begun to think differently about learning and teaching.

Early in the project, a critical event occurred. The teachers were asked to observe and react to a videotape of two boys engaged in playing a simple game. The boys sat at a table, separated from one another by an opaque screen. In front of one boy, blocks of various colours, shapes and sizes were arranged in a pattern. In front of the other, similar blocks were lying on the table in no particular order. The first boy was to tell the second one how to reproduce the pattern. After the first few instructions, however, it became clear that the second boy had gone astray. In fact, the two boys had lost touch with one another, though neither of them knew it.

In their initial reactions to the videotape, the teachers spoke of a 'communications problem'. they said that the instruction giver had 'well-developed verbal skills' and that the receiver was 'unable to follow directions'. Then one of the researchers pointed out that, although the blocks contained no green squares – all squares were orange and only triangles were green – she had heard the first boy tell the second to 'take a green square'. When the teachers watched the videotape again, they were astonished. That small mistake had set off a chain of false moves. The second boy had put a green thing, a triangle, where the first boy's pattern had an orange square, and from then on all the instructions became problematic. Under the circumstances, the second boy seemed to have displayed considerable ingenuity in his attempts to reconcile the instructions with the pattern before him.

At this point, the teachers reversed their picture of the situation. They could see why the second boy behaved as he did. He no longer seemed stupid; he had, indeed, 'followed instructions'. As one teacher put it, they were now 'giving him reason'. They saw reasons for his behaviour; and his errors, which they had previously seen as an inability to follow directions, they now found reasonable.

Later on in the project, as the teachers increasingly challenged themselves to discover the meanings of a child's puzzling behaviour, they often spoke of 'giving him reason'.

In examples such as these, something falls outside the range of ordinary expectations. The banker has a feeling that something is wrong, though he cannot at first say what it is. The physician sees an odd combination of diseases never before described in a medical text. Tolstoy thinks of each of his pupils as an individual with ways of learning and imperfections peculiar to himself. The teachers are astonished by the sense behind a student's mistake. In each instance, the practitioner allows himself to experience surprise, puzzlement, or confusion in a situation that he finds uncertain or unique. He reflects on the phenomena before him, and on the prior understandings that have been implicit in his behaviour. He carries out an experiment that serves to generate both a new understanding of the phenomena and a change in the situation.

When someone reflects-in-action, he becomes a researcher in the practice context. He is not dependent on the categories of established theory and technique, but constructs a new theory of the unique case. His inquiry is not limited to a deliberation about means that depends on a prior agreement about ends. He does not keep means and ends separate, but defines them interactively as he frames a problematic situation. He does not separate thinking from doing, ratiocinating his way to a decision that he must later convert to action. Because his experimenting is a kind of action, implementation is built into his inquiry. Thus reflection-in-action can proceed, even in situations of uncertainty or uniqueness, because it is not bound by the dichotomies of Technical Rationality.

Although reflection-in-action is an extraordinary process, it is not a rare event. Indeed, for some reflective practitioners it is the core of practice. Nevertheless, because professionalism is still mainly identified with technical expertise, reflection-in-action is not generally accepted – even by those who do it – as a legitimate form of professional knowing.

Many practitioners, locked into a view of themselves as technical experts, find nothing in the world of practice to occasion reflection. They have become too skilful at techniques of selective inattention, junk categories and situational control, techniques that they use to preserve the constancy of their knowledge-in-practice. For them, uncertainty is a threat; its admission is a sign of weakness. Others, more inclined toward and adept at reflection-in-action, nevertheless feel profoundly uneasy because they cannot say what they know how to do, cannot justify its quality or rigour.

For these reasons, the study of reflection-in-action is critically important. The dilemma of rigour or relevance may be dissolved if we can develop an epistemology of practice that places technical problem solving within a broader context of reflective inquiry, shows how reflection-in-action may be rigorous in its own right, and links the art of practice in uncertainty and uniqueness to the scientist's art of research. We may thereby increase the legitimacy of reflection-in-action and encourage its broader, deeper, and more rigorous use.

Notes

1   I first used this term in *Technology and Change* (New York: Delacorte Press, 1966).
2   Of course, the problem of the lack of agreement about ends has engaged the attention of many of the protagonists of the positivist epistemology of practice. Approaches to this problem have ranged from the search for an ultimate end, to which all others could be subordinated; to a 'universal solvent' for ends, as in the utility functions of the welfare economists; to the 'piecemeal social engineering' proposed by Karl Popper. For a discussion of these, their defects and merits, see Frankel, C. 'The relation of theory to practice: some standard views', in C. Frankel *et al.* (eds) (1968) *Social Theory and Social Intervention*, Cleveland: Case Western Reserve University Press.
3   The term is taken from Geertz, C. 'Thick description: toward an interpretive theory of culture', in Geertz, C. (1973) *The Interpretation of Cultures*, New York: Basic Books.
4   The whole of contemporary linguistics and psycholinguistics is relevant here – for example, the work of Chomsky, Halle, and Sinclair.
5   The staff of the Teacher Project consisted of Jeanne Bamberger, Eleanor Duckworth and Margaret Lampert. My description of the incident of 'giving the child reason' is adapted from a project memorandum by Lampert.

References

Birdwhistell, R.L. (1970) *Kinesics and Context*, Philadelphia: University of Pennsylvania Press.

Glazer, N. (1974) 'Schools of the minor professions', *Minerva*.

Goode, W. (1966) 'The librarian: from occupation to profession', in H. Vollmer and D. Mills (eds) *Professionalization*, Englewood Cliffs, NJ: Prentice-Hall.

Greenwood, E. (1966) 'Attributes of a profession', in H. Vollmer and D. Mills (eds) *Professionalization*, Englewood Cliffs, NJ: Prentice-Hall.

Hughes, E. (1973) 'Higher education and the professions', in C. Kaysen (ed.) *Content and Context: Essays on College Education*, New York: McGraw-Hill.

Inhelder, B. and Karmiloff-Smith, A. (1975) 'If you want to get ahead, get a theory', *Cognition*, vol. 3, no. 3: 195–212.

Maslow, J.E. (1981) 'Grooving on a baseball afternoon', *Mainliner*, May: 34.

Moore, W.E. (1970) *The Professions*, New York: Russell Sage Foundation.

Ryle, G. (1949) 'On knowing how and knowing that', in G. Ryle *The Concept of Mind*, London: Hutchinson.

Schein, E. (1973) *Professional Education*, New York: McGraw-Hill.

Schutz, A. (1962) *Collected Papers*, The Hague: Nijhoff.

Simon, H. (1972) *The Sciences of the Artificial*, Cambridge, MA: MIT Press.

Thorne, B. (1973) 'Professional education in medicine', in E. Hughes, B. Thorne, A. DeBaggis, A. Gurin and D. Williams *Education for the Professions of Medicine, Law, Theology and Social Welfare*, New York: McGraw-Hill.

Veblen, T. (1962) *The Higher Learning in America*, New York: Hill and Wang (reprint of 1918 edition).

Chapter 4

Deconstructing domestication
Women's experience and the goals of critical pedagogy

Julia Clarke

Introduction

Critical pedagogy refers to a particular strand of educational practice, associated most commonly with the name of the Brazilian educator, Paulo Freire, whose educational philosophy, politics and *praxis*[1] was directed towards revolutionary social change. This chapter begins with a personal account of my own changing perspective over the past thirty years on the goals of liberation, democracy and social justice, which were often assumed, in the literature of critical pedagogy, to be universal and unproblematic. Among the theoretical understandings that have helped me to make sense of problems arising in my personal and professional experience, I draw upon feminism and deconstruction to explore the ways in which the emancipatory goals of critical pedagogy are embedded in a masculine construction of human subjectivity. This is evident in Freire's account of liberation, which is defined in opposition to domestication. In this account there is thus an implicit denigration of those aspects of human experience – the work of caring for our own and our dependants' physical and emotional needs – that are located in the domestic sphere, and are generally associated with women's lives. After outlining the source of Freire's masculine construction of the liberated subject, I go on to show how this is reflected in accounts of radical education, transformative learning and related strands of adult education practice. Finally, I consider the implications of this critique for adult educators, with reference to themes emerging from my own study of the experiences of work, learning, and domesticity among a particular group of women in Southern England (Clarke, 1998). While there is no intention to generalise from this small-scale study to make universal claims about women's experience, my concluding arguments refer to 'women's experience' as the current state of affairs in which most, but not all, women, and some, but very few, men take on the bulk of domestic and caring work in human societies around the world.

Newly commissioned work.

A problem in my experience

When I began a student work placement as a volunteer tutor for an adult literacy project in 1974, my tutor lent me her copy of Freire's (1972a) *Pedagogy of the Oppressed*, and I embraced critical pedagogy as a form of educational practice grounded in a neo-Marxist analysis of power and oppression. For the next twenty years, I generally articulated the political aims of my adult and community education work in terms of Freire's fundamental thesis that, since education can never be a neutral process, we must choose between engaging in education for liberation, or for domestication. This presented an uncompromising tool for the critical evaluation of my educational practice as I debated with colleagues the ways in which liberation might be achieved through publishing student writing, teaching 'communications skills' to YTS[2] trainees, or running workplace 'basic skills' courses for manual workers. However, the dilemmas and contradictions of critical pedagogy became particularly problematic when I began to reflect on the goals and outcomes of courses called 'Fresh Start for Women', which I was running in the early 1990s.

These Fresh Start courses comprised a negotiated curriculum that included the positive evaluation of skills acquired through unpaid labour in the home, suggesting ways in which these might be represented, developed or transferred to other situations. The curriculum was based on a concern that the years spent doing unpaid work as mothers, carers and providers of domestic services often results in certain ways of being that prevent women from competing in the labour market or pursuing goal-related education or training. Whatever kinds of learning and change we hoped to achieve, it was clear that the material outcomes for participants on these course would depend largely on local opportunities for continuing education, paid work and childcare. In the mainly rural area where I was working, such opportunities are extremely limited. A surprising number of the participants went on to do voluntary work in social welfare organisations – surprising since most of them were living on low incomes and yet still chose to work without pay. The decision of these women to commit themselves to an active role in a community far wider than their immediate family might lead us to claim that our courses engendered a stronger sense of personal agency and a recognition of the value of social participation. I became concerned, however, that our educational practice often seemed to encourage women to take on an additional burden of unpaid labour in the service of others. This posed a question about whether it was in these women's interests to valorise the skills they have developed through caring for others, while these skills are so undervalued in the labour market.

Critical pedagogy is infused with notions of *false consciousness*, which assume there must be a single true or objective way of talking about our experience if we can only clear away the distortions of ideology. This is exemplified in an account of three women's educational projects described by Gilliam Highet (1991: 155), who set out to examine the ways in which these projects were 'still contributing to the socialisation of women into accepting differential social roles'. Highet saw the educator's task as that of 'developing and specifying alternative goals and values in women's education' (ibid.: 164). She suggests, however, that some of the learners she encountered, particularly mothers, would need to change their relationships and attitudes before they could aspire to Highet's 'goals and values'. These women, in Highet's view, are held back in their 'progress towards equality' because 'the sort of relationships which many women have with their children, and the attitudes they hold in relation to their responsibilities towards children . . . often make it difficult to convince women themselves of the importance of creche provision' (ibid.).

Highet's stance illustrates the problem that I have associated with critical pedagogy. The question of what we actually mean by terms like 'progress towards equality', and whether such goals are in women's interests, cannot be separated from the question raised by Highet's assumption that the women in her study do not know what is good for them. These women's relationships and responsibilities are dismissed as the objects of mistaken attitudes, obstacles that prevent women from pursuing our *true interests*.

As a mother, my own experience includes that of making choices about work, education and caring for others that may appear to be against my interests. These interests, however, comprise a constantly shifting and often conflicting jumble of needs, wishes and desires, none of which are more *true* than any others. My questioning of Freire's repression of domestication in his concept of liberation arises from a belief that the desire for involvement in committed relationships, and consequent ambivalence and conflict, does not constitute a case of false consciousness but represent a challenge to the goals and values of critical pedagogy. The appeal of Freire's work to diverse communities of adult educators around the globe can be explained, to a great extent, by his eclectic reworking of ideas from Critical Theory, radical Catholic theology and revolutionary socialism (Mackie, 1980). In the following brief account, my aim is to illustrate some of the ways in which these ideas contribute to notions of human subjectivity and liberation from which women are excluded.

Man's domain: work, history and culture

Critical theorists are united by a concern with the freedom and autonomy of individuals and the transformation of social relations of domination and oppression. The prerequisite for such a transformation is an *ideology critique* that involves examining the historical roots and assumptions of ideologies, analysing the social interests that they serve, and exposing ideological mystifications and distortions of a true reality. Freire's emphasis on education for revolutionary change draws upon the concept of hegemony in the writings of the Italian Marxist, Antonio Gramsci. The aim of hegemony is to univer-salise the values of a dominant or aspiring class so that a consenting popu-lation adopts common understandings of truth, good taste, and the natural order of everyday life. Gramsci's educational aim was to create the possi-bility of a counter-hegemony that would arise from the proletariat through the creation of working-class intellectuals. Counter-hegemony is achieved not through argument against the ideas and practices of the dominant classes, but by developing an alternative set of ideas, beliefs and practices rooted in working-class experience. For Gramsci, a communist revolution represented the end of class divisions. Since he saw the interests of the working classes as generalisable, universal interests, Gramsci believed that, ultimately, a working-class hegemony would prevail over that of a class whose interests were partial and exclusive. A hegemony of universal interests would elimin-ate the need for coercion since hegemony becomes so deeply embedded in society that it becomes the common sense view of reality.

Gramsci argued that the development of a powerful counter-hegemony required working-class intellectuals who were versed in the high status know-ledge of the classics, and the intellectual heritage of the great writers and thinkers of Western civilisation. Freire, on the other hand, while endorsing Gramsci's belief in the importance of education and cultural transformation for the revolutionary process, opposed this kind of learning, in which students are cast as empty vessels into which dominant and oppressive forms of know-ledge could be poured. He described this as *banking education*, which 'inhibits creativity and domesticates (although it cannot completely destroy) the *inten-tionality* of consciousness by isolating consciousness from the world, thereby denying men their ontological and historical vocation of becoming more fully human' (Freire, 1972a: 56).

In Brazil during the 1950s, Paulo Freire developed a strategy for adult education and revolution that would create the social conditions in which man[3] could become more 'fully human'. 'To exist humanly', Freire wrote, 'is to *name* the world, to change it ... Men are not built in silence, but in word, in work, in action-reflection' (Freire, 1972a: 61). A banking educa-tion, Freire argued, was one in which knowledge is regarded as a commodity and learners are assumed to be ignorant, empty vessels, waiting to be filled with a partial knowledge selected for them by representatives of the oppressor class. Freire's educational project starts from topics that are rich in experi-ential meaning for particular groups in particular social contexts but whose 'true' nature may be veiled in oppressive ideologies and myths. In his adult literacy programme, Freirean educators would pose words like WORK, WEALTH, SLUM, or RAIN as problematic, and invite the learners to subject the images that represent these words to a critical examination aimed at action that will transform their meaning in reality. The transformation that takes place is one in which learners cease to identify themselves as objects to whom the experience of work, wealth, slums or rain just happens.

In becoming a subject of that experience, the learner engages in a process of conscientisation.

Freire constructs a hierarchy of 'levels of consciousness', from the lowest level of preoccupation with basic biological problems, through stages of fatalism and naivety to the highest level of 'critically transitive consciousness' that is the goal of conscientisation. The participants in Freire's 'Cultural Action for Freedom' are men whose 'domain of existence is the domain of work, of history, of culture, of values – the domain in which men experience the dialectic between determinism and freedom' (Freire, 1972b: 52). Freire refers to Marx's conception of work as productive labour in order to distinguish men from animals. As well as being the makers of history, 'there is a further fundamental distinction between man's relationships with the world and the animal's contacts with it: only men work'. But, 'for action to be work it must result in significant products, which while distinct from the active agent, at the same time condition him and become the object of his reflection' (ibid.: 56).

Freire (1972b: 79) writes of attempts to thwart the liberation of men so that they might achieve a 'maximum of potential consciousness' as attempts to domesticate the future. Why does Freire choose a term that is generally associated with the taming of nature, with intimate relations and with the home to express a retrogressive desire to maintain the status quo, to 'domesticate the future'? Freire draws his analysis of the social psychology of oppression directly from Erich Fromm, whose humanistic concern for liberation relies on the representation of mother in the timeless images of home, nature, soil and the ocean. These images are constructed in opposition to father's bounded engagement in rational thought and directed movement through time:

> Mother is the home we come from, she is nature, soil, the ocean; father does not represent any such natural home . . . he represents the other pole of human existence; the world of thought, of man-made things, of law and order, of discipline, of travel and adventure. Father is the one who teaches the child, who shows him the road into the world.
>
> (Fromm, 1957: 35)

The imagery of women as part of the natural world matches Freire's description of animals: 'Unlike men, animals are simply *in* the world, incapable of objectifying either themselves or the world. They live a life without time' (Freire, 1972b: 51).

In order to show his child 'the road into the world', the father must detach himself from the world in order to objectify it and to reflect on the nature of his own existence. While some men may choose the 'dehumanizing' road of oppression, 'Nevertheless, because they impregnate the world with their reflective presence, only men can humanize or dehumanize' (Freire, 1972b:

55). Women are biologically incapable of impregnation, and, even meta-phorically, only women and female animals can represent a 'world' that is impregnated by men. Here, Freire's conception of liberation not only excludes women, but depends upon an essentially female world from which men can detach themselves and which, at the same time, humanise by 'impregnating the world with man's curious and inventive presence, imprinting it with the trace of his works' (ibid.). Freire writes of those who 'want to stop time', as those who want to 'domesticate' the future, to 'keep it in line with the present', and claims that 'there is no genuine hope in those who intend to make the future repeat their present, nor in those who see the future as something predetermined. Both have a "domesticated" notion of history' (ibid.: 41).

Liberation thus requires the agency of a rational, unfettered individual travelling the road of progress through time. This concept depends on the idea of domestication as a timeless dimension of animal existence, just as the liberated man depends upon women's domestic activity for his own suste-nance and for the care and nurture of his children. The rationality of man is thus constructed through a separation of his mind from the source of his own physical existence (from 'the world', from mother, from nature, and from his own bodily and emotional needs and desires). This rational subject is then able, whether through ideology critique, counter-hegemony or consci-entisation, to claim individual and collective knowledge of a single, objective 'true reality'. In these discourses, individual emancipation and collective liberation rely on the idea of a community of such rational subjects coming together as equal participants in the public sphere. There is an assumption of common human interests and this assumption underpins much of the educational practice associated with *Critical Pedagogy*.

Critical pedagogy

Teachers engaged in critical pedagogy are united in a view of education as a practice committed to the reduction, or even elimination, of injustice and oppression. Most critical educators would claim that their practice aims to foster both individual transformation and collective action, but there is some disagreement about the relationship between individual and social change. Critical pedagogy encompasses diverse understandings and analyses of the many and varied contexts, forms and relations of oppression. More funda-mental disagreements regarding the utopian goals of critical pedagogy are not always made explicit, but are apparent in the following examples selected from the literature to illustrate some strands of critical pedagogy. I have grouped descriptions of educational practice into loose categories in order to identify distinctive strands. Most practices will contain elements of several strands as I have characterised them here. My aim, in this instance, is not to construct a clearly delineated taxonomy, but to illustrate some of the educational practices that might be included under the broad umbrella of critical pedagogy.

Transformative learning

In his theory of *Transformative Learning*, Jack Mezirow (1991) investigates the perspective transformation involved in achieving emancipatory knowledge. This way of knowing corresponds to Freire's 'critically transitive consciousness' but Mezirow argues that Freire's interest is limited to 'critical reflection on oppressive social norms or practices' through the sociolinguistic praxis of 'naming the world' (1992: 251). Mezirow maintains that transformation can occur through reflection on epistemic and psychological, as well as sociolinguistic, assumptions (ibid.). Transformative learning may be triggered by any event in our personal and social life that challenges the assumptions on which we have based our interpretations of experience. This forces a re-evaluation of those assumptions and the development of new meanings in a process of critical reflection and rational discourse.

This broader agenda relieves educators from the responsibility for generating and sustaining a unitary vision of an alternative or more 'true' reality and allows for the incorporation of New Age notions of spirituality and personal growth into a particularly North American construction of transformative learning. Accounts of practice that refer to this model of transformative learning include descriptions of different kinds of life-changing events that provide opportunities for 'growth and learning' (Morey, 1997: 38). Caring for elderly relatives, contracting a serious illness, the experience of homelessness, or sharing personal life histories all provide opportunities for transformative learning (Merriam *et al.*, 1997; Ettling and Hayes, 1997; Group for Collaborative Inquiry, 1997). It is interesting to note, however, that even in the late 1990s the concerns of transformative educators appeared to be confined within traditionally gendered spheres of interest. Of ten conference papers (Armstrong *et al.*, 1997) linking notions of transformation to theory, learning, pedagogy or community, the seven written by women focus on direct experiences related to physical and emotional issues and relationships in small groups. Meanwhile, the three papers written by men are concerned with global ecology and learning programmes in the big labour unions (O'Sullivan, 1997; Hall and Livingstone, 1997; Livingstone, 1997). Calling upon 'progressive intellectuals' to work with the labour unions so that 'future Gramscis may flourish and enable the working class to withstand future Mussolinis', David Livingstone (1997: 289) argues that the most fertile ground for critical pedagogy is among those communities represented by leaders who are already committed to social change. This echoes a similar assertion by Thomas Heaney and Aimee Horton (1990), who define *Emancipatory Education* as a practice that can only occur when both learners and teachers are already engaged in social movements: 'Emancipatory projects will be defined in collaboration with activist groups and organizations rather than individuals.' In Britain, this approach is most often represented in the literature of *Radical Education*.

Radical education

An example of the radical education strand of critical pedagogy can be found in Tom Lovett's work in Northern Ireland. In his analysis of the social context of Britain in the 1980s, Lovett describes the social fragmentation caused by changes in family life and the relationship between men and women. Lovett suggests that working-class communities have not had the resources to benefit from the 'personal liberation' of the 1970s. Is this a euphemism for women's liberation? Whoever may have been the beneficiaries of this 'personal liberation', the result, in Lovett's view, has been that working-class areas have become 'the victims of a process of mindless violence, the community turning in on itself in the search for thrills, kicks, money' (1988: 142). Lovett recognises a role for women in 'the reconstruction of local working class communities' (ibid.: 160). However, the educational programme for community activists at Ulster People's College is contrasted with other initiatives in community education, offering subjects like 'practical home skills and formal qualifications'. The latter are dismissed as not 'relevant to community action or the problems of social change' (ibid.: 150).

For radical educational projects to 'experience . . . the meaning of a socialist/radical vision', Allman and Wallis advocate a return to the original writings of Marx, Gramsci and Freire. Although lip service is paid to a 'plurality of human interests', these projects are characterised by a continuing 'search for common and, therefore, potentially shared human goals' (Allman and Wallis, 1995: 19). The question of who is included in, or excluded from, these 'shared human goals' warrants a critical feminist enquiry. Nevertheless, a number of women continue to endorse the same 'socialist/radical vision'. For example, in her account of women's involvement in adult education between 1867 and 1919, Julia Swindells presents a particular group of women as the active subjects in radical education. These are not those members of the Mothers' Union who are content to listen to lectures about 'domestic issues' but, rather, the members of the Women's Co-operative Guild, described as 'honest working women' who are literate, articulate, and active in public political life (Swindells, 1995). Patti Lather describes the *ideology critique*, which is central to the radical education strand of critical pedagogy, as one that depends on a 'binary logic with demonizes some "Other" and positions itself as innocent' (1992: 131). What kind of descriptions, I wonder, might be used to describe those 'other' women who do not fit into Swindells' category of 'honest working women'? Jane Thompson pays tribute to the 'vast majority of women' whose 'capacity for survival, and whose potential for resistance, is not in question' (Thompson, 1995: 133). Despite this tribute, however, Thompson regards her task as a teacher of Women's Studies at Ruskin College as one of providing 'ideas and information that rescue women's lives from oblivion' (ibid.: 133). Before they have been rescued, these women are constructed as victims, customers, desistors and those who are impotent in Thompson's argument for a 'really useful knowledge' that 'shifts the emphasis from victims to survivors . . . from customers to activists . . . from impotence to creative anger . . . from those who desist to those who resist' (ibid.: 131, 132).

Border pedagogies

Jane Thompson's construction of learners as alleged 'Others', who need to be rescued from themselves, has been challenged in those critical pedagogies that may be referred to as *Border Pedagogy* (Giroux, 1992); *Pedagogy of Resistance* (McLaren, 1994); or as *pedagogies of desire, of representation* and so on, depending on the particular interest of the protagonist. The 'borders' being traversed in this strand are those between Critical Theory and post-modern developments in Cultural Theory. This encounter leads to a questioning of the oversimplification of categories like race, class, gender or sexuality as if such categories describe objective and essential human attributes and characteristics. The focus, instead, is on the ways in which we represent people, objects and events, and on the social hierarchies and institutional arrangements that make some descriptions more powerful than others.

Debates within the strand of border pedagogies reflect a continuing tension between those who advocate emancipation within the discourse of Critical Theory, and those who, like Elizabeth Ellsworth (1992), have begun to ask, 'Why doesn't this feel empowering?' In her critical and self-reflexive account of teaching an anti-racism course to university students, Ellsworth challenges critical pedagogy's 'conventional notions of dialogue and democracy', which assume that learners can become fully rational and disinterested. Ellsworth argues that, on the contrary, they should be regarded as 'subjects split between the conscious and the unconscious and among multiple social positionings' (1992: 108). In a vitriolic response to Ellsworth's challenge to the simple optimism of critical pedagogy, Giroux accuses her of proposing a 'crippling form of political disengagement' (Giroux, 1988: 171), and Peter McLaren dismisses Ellsworth's stance as one of 'political inertia and moral cowardice' (McLaren, 1988: 68).

Accounts of practice within this disparate body, which I have grouped together under the heading of border pedagogies, are generally located within higher education, and the debates often become abstract and removed from practical engagement with the complexity of concrete situations. Among the 'multiple social positionings' occupied by adults enrolled on courses like 'Fresh Start for Women', are those that might be illuminated through a study of the gendered organisation of domestic labour and paid work. While a goal of liberation is clearly problematic, it is also clear that women continue to be disadvantaged, even oppressed, by these social arrangements. As an adult educator, my work is still directed towards developing critical reflection and introducing new perspectives that serve the interests of learners (and my own) by expanding our awareness of possibilities for personal and social change. It has become clear, however, that this question of interests cannot be resolved with reference to Freire's opposition to liberation or domestication. Of course, education is never a neutral process, but the opposition to liberation/domestication becomes problematic when we consider the extent to which our thinking about *liberation* ignores, denies or suppresses the *domestication* upon which we depend for our physical and emotional sustenance. In Freire's work, the undesirable condition, or process, of domestication denotes a kind of blind acceptance of oppression. This does not allow for a positive association of the domestic sphere with love and with the connectedness of one's own needs and interests to the needs and interests of others. If domestication includes providing shelter, food and clothing for ourselves and our dependants, then whose interests are served by a goal of liberation *from* such domestication? Posing this question led me to feminist theory and deconstruction.

Feminism and deconstruction

Feminism is a political stance, advocating the right of women to participate on equal terms with men in every aspect of human affairs. This definition of feminism allows for very different accounts of what constitutes participation and such accounts must acknowledge that relations of power and oppression operate among and between women as well as between men and women. The categorisation of women as a homogenous group has been effectively challenged by arguments that factors such as race, ethnicity, social class or sexual orientation may constitute more immediate, and sometimes more violent intractable, sites of oppression than those identified in terms of gender alone. And yet definitions of feminism must rest on a concept of gender that allows for all women to somehow be classed as different from all men. This presents a dilemma, which has been polarised within feminist debate as a politics of equality or a politics of difference. A politics of equality is rooted in a view of gender identity as the result of socialisation, in which gender differences are regarded as the cultural differences that are socially constructed around biological differences between the sexes. Early feminists, like Mary Wollstonecraft and Simone de Beauvoir argued for the release of women from the burdens of domesticity to enable us to develop our own rationality and participate alongside men in public life. This view has been described as 'adding women in', and implies a negation of differences between men and women. A politics of difference, on the other hand, is based on a view that there is a dialectical relationship between culture and biology. Although the restriction of gender to just two categories is historically and culturally specific, there are also ways in which notions of masculinity are closely related to the male body and femininity to the female body. Thus gender differences cannot be divorced from biological differences unless we disregard significant aspects of our bodily experience. However, even the notion of experience is problematic, and Judith Butler (1990: 136) argues that gender should be understood as a process of 'doing' rather than 'being'. Through our practical engagement in social relations, institutions and discourses we bring ourselves into line with a gender, which Butler describes as a 'fabrication, a fantasy instituted and inscribed on the surface of our bodies' (ibid.: 136). This echoes the perspective from cultural theory that I have associated with the literature of 'Border pedagogies', a perspective that is illuminated by feminist deconstruction of the gendered dualisms on which Western rationality depends.

Deconstruction has developed from Jaques Derrida's view of language as text based on a 'metaphysics of presence' in which all present states depend, for their meaning, on absent states. This enables us to see how, for example, emotion is subordinated to reason, which both repress and depend upon the concept of emotion for its meaning. Similarly, Freire's concept of liberation depends, for its meaning, on a repression and denial of domestication. A feminist deconstructive perspective exposes the highly gendered nature of Freire's binary thinking, consistent with a pattern of 'phallocentric alignments' that permeate modern Western thought (Grosz, 1993). Feminist writers have shown how modern thinking is founded on a pattern of binary oppositions in which the term associated with masculinity is always privileged. Thus women are continually positioned as inferior through the association of femininity with the subordinate term in these and similar hierarchical dualisms of man/woman, culture/nature, subject/object, mind/body, order/chaos and so on (Hekman, 1990; Plumwood, 1993). A feminist deconstructive approach to this kind of binary thinking involves foregrounding the subordinate terms, not in order to reverse the oppositions and privilege the body or nature, for example above mind or culture, but to displace both terms and open up the way for new meanings.

Deconstructing domestication

In order to look at educational experiences from the standpoint that gives prominence to women's *domestication* I decided to study the biographies of learners who have regarded themselves as primarily responsible for the care of others and yet whose aspirations involve some form of continuing education. I conducted three, hour-long interviews and a series of group meetings with 18 women who had chosen to continue their education despite facing all the barriers most commonly identified as those that prevent participation in continuing education.[4] Each interview followed a similar chronological pattern, beginning with childhood memories of the stories told by, or about, parents and grandparents, moving on through to the present and finishing with hopes and plans for the future. When we tell stories about our lives we construct these within larger narratives or discourses that provide criteria for evaluating the actions of, for example, the good mother, the serious student or the enterprising worker. Critically reviewing the stories that had been transcribed from our interviews enabled these women to consider other possible directions or courses of action that the central characters might have taken. This was not a question of seeing the error of their ways, but one of seeing how their identities are constructed through multiple, changing and often contradictory discourses of work, education and domestic life.

In a single chapter, I cannot begin to represent the complexity of the life histories collected and analysed in the course of this study, nor can I summarise the varied interests and changing desires that motivated each of these 18 women to confound the statistics and participate in continuing education. Themes that emerged from the analysis and discussion of the narratives include questions about public and private life, knowledge, work, autonomy, time, agency and progress. Of particular relevance to the forgoing discussion of the gendered subject in Freire's critical pedagogy are questions of time and definitions of work. Freire (1972b: 41) wrote of 'those who intend to make the future repeat the present' as people with a ' "domesticated" notion of history' for whom there is 'no genuine hope'. This privileges a linear conception of time over the seasonal, biological or cyclical patterns of time that are associated with physical sustenance and growth. It also denies human dependency and the need for us to 'be there' for each other in ways that cannot always be predicted, controlled or accommodated in the forward march of unremitting progress. Karen Davies (1990) cites various explanations for an understanding of linear time as 'male time', which include male power over the development of writing, and over the belief systems of Judaeo-Christian religions that look to the coming of a future Messiah. Instead of a relationship to time in which a task takes 'as long as it takes', linear time is the clock time that paved the way for Fordist mass production and Taylorism, the scientific management of industrial labour. Linear, clock time also dominates educational processes, for example in the measurement of academic and professional competence through performance of written tasks within the strictly controlled time limits of formal examinations. Most of the women in my study spoke of wanting their 'own time', but also accepted that they will always be available for, as one participant said, 'just what falls in your lap'.

Being available for others in this way is not compatible with the kind of labour that Freire dignifies with the status of 'work' as it is currently organised. In his argument that, unlike animals, 'only men work', Freire defined work as action that 'must result in significant products'. Mechtild Hart (1992) posits an alternative view of work that locates the production of *life* rather than *things* as its ultimate purpose, making positive connections between life, work and necessity. This challenges a Marxist view in which the necessity of subsistence labour to meet bodily needs is opposed to freedom, self-realisation and human happiness. Hart calls upon adult educators to challenge the notions of progress and development that are driven by this desire for 'triumph over necessity' that 'always takes the form of mastery: over slaves, over women, over nature' (1992: 121). When they first left school, all of the 18 women in my study worked in shops, offices, catering, hairdressing or factory jobs. At the time of our interviews, when all of them were responsible for the care of dependants, many of the women also worked in part-time care jobs and most of them included among their aspirations for the future a career and professional qualifications in health, social welfare or community work. Financial rewards came very low on their list of interests and desires. For those who chose to work in commercial or manufacturing jobs, all were now suffering from the 'downward mobility' resulting from taking time out of the workplace during periods of rapid technological change.

As a response to such negative consequences for women who choose, or are obliged to take on domestic and caring responsibilities, adult educators put on courses with titles like 'Fresh Start', 'Second Chance' or 'Women Returners'. The notion of a 'fresh start' suggests that those who need such a thing must have taken a wrong turning somewhere. When we invite women to 'return' to the straight and narrow path of organised education, we are denying the value and importance of the productive work and learning that is denigrated when 'domestication' is opposed to 'liberation'. This is not to valorise and celebrate the drudgery, the isolation, the intellectual stagnation and the lack of social standing or financial rewards that are so often features of unpaid work at home. Those features are not the consequences of women's 'domestication', but result from the unequal distribution of domestic labour in the home and the low status and rewards attached to domestic and caring occupations in the public sphere. As a feminist, my agenda for action can include arguing for and supporting policies that seek to redress such inequalities through what Melissa Benn describes as a 'moral ecology', which recognises that for some of us to have more rewarding work and more leisure time, others must have less.[5] This would provide the moral basis for a 'domestic democracy', which involves 'all adults in a household contributing their equitable share to the maintenance of the place where they live' (Benn, 1998: 244). This political agenda cannot be pursued by telling women that we need to be liberated from our own desires, or by denying the value of the domestic and caring work that we do. Instead, we can make a space for the ambivalence and mutability of these desires to be explored in relation to the material conditions of our interconnected lives.

In this chapter I have drawn upon Paulo Freire's early work to highlight the particularly masculine construction of liberation in opposition to domestication that underpins much of the theory and practice of critical pedagogy. In doing so, I owe a debt to Freire's pedagogy for its emphasis on language and the 'problematization' of key words and concepts. Freire acknowledged that the goals of critical pedagogy would change when he wrote,

> Narratives of liberation are always tied to people's stories, and what stories we choose to tell, and the ways in which we decide to tell them, form the provisional basis of what a critical pedagogy of the future might mean.
>
> (Freire, 1993: xii)

Although uncertain about the prospect of a 'critical pedagogy of the future', I now count among my tasks as an adult educator that of deconstructing the narratives and discourses that set up the world of education and work as a privileged 'real world' in opposition to some kind of hinterland of domestication. What are we saying about women's lives when we invite women to 'Return to Learning', and offer them a 'Second Chance' or a 'Fresh Start'? What are we saying about both the desire and the need to care for children or other dependants when we list these activities as 'barriers to learning'? There are clearly many more stories to tell about the domestic experiences of women, and men. The challenge for adult educators is to provide the spaces in which these stories can be told.

Notes

1   *Praxis* – the notion of praxis locates critical reflection in the context of transformative action for material change.
2   YTS = Youth Training Scheme, one of many UK government training schemes for unemployed young people.
3   I make no attempt in this account to add in feminine pronouns or comment on each reference to 'man', 'men' or 'he' since, rather than treating these as the excusable errors of a pre-feminist consciousness, I regard these features as evidence of the masculine world-views and representations of humanity represented in these texts.
4   British and international surveys on motivation and participation in continuing education offer us various typologies of 'non-participants', all of which include people who: have a significant responsibility for the care of dependant/s; are engaged in additional part-time work outside the home; left school with few or no formal qualifications; live in rural areas (McGivney, 1990).
5   Hewitt (1993) reports that in Britain, even when a man and a woman sharing a household are both in full-time work, the average man has 17 hours more leisure time than the average woman.

References

Allman, Paul and Wallis, John (1995) 'Challenging the postmodern condition: Radical adult education for critical intelligence' in M. Mayo and J. Thompson (eds) *Adult Learning, Critical Intelligence and Social Change*, Leicester: National Institute of Adult Continuing Education.

Armstrong, Paul, Miller, Nod and Zukas, Miriam (eds) (1997) *Crossing Borders, Breaking Boundaries: Research in the Education of Adults*, Proceedings of the 27th Annual SCUTREA Conference, London: Birkbeck College.

Benn, Melissa (1998) *Madonna and Child: Towards a New Politics of Motherhood*, London: Jonathan Cape.

Butler, Judith (1990) *Gender Trouble: Feminism and the Subversion of Identity*, London and New York: Routledge.

Clarke, Julia (1998) *Deconstructing domestication: women's experience and the goals of critical pedagogy*, Ph.D. Thesis, University of Southampton.

Davies, Karen (1990) *Women, Time and the Weaving of the Strands of Everyday Life*, Aldershot: Avebury.

Ellsworth, Elizabeth (1992) 'Why doesn't this feel empowering? Working through the repressive myths of critical pedagogy' in Carmen Luke and Jennifer Gore (eds) *Feminisms and Critical Pedagogy*, London and New York: Routledge.

Ettling, Dorothy and Hayes, Naomi (1997) 'Learning to learn: Creating models of transformative education with economically disadvantaged women' in Paul Armstrong, Nod Miller and Miriam Zukas (eds) *Crossing Borders, Breaking Boundaries: Research in the Education of Adults*, Proceedings of the 27th Annual SCUTREA Conference, London: Birkbeck College.

Freire, Paulo (1972a) *Pedagogy of the Oppressed*, Harmondsworth: Penguin.

Freire, Paulo (1972b) *Cultural Action for Freedom*, Harmondsworth: Penguin.

Freire, Paulo (1993) 'Foreword' in Peter McLaren and Peter Leonard (eds) *Paulo Freire: A Critical Encounter*, London and New York: Routledge.

Fromm, Erich (1957) *The Art of Loving*, London: Unwin.

Giroux, Henry (1988) 'Border pedagogy in the Age of Postmodernism', *Journal of Education*, Vol. 170, No. 3, p. 171.

Giroux, Henry (1992) *Border Crossings: Cultural Workers and the Politics of Education*, London and New York: Routledge.

Grosz, Elizabeth (1993) 'Bodies and knowledges: Feminism and the crisis of reason' in L. Alcoff and E. Potter (eds) *Feminist Epistemologies*, London: Routledge.

Group for Collaborative Inquiry (1997) 'Re-writing the boundaries of practice: Storying the work of a transformative pedagogy' in Paul Armstrong, Nod Miller and Miriam Zukas (eds) *Crossing Borders, Breaking Boundaries: Research in the Education of Adults*, Proceedings of the 27th Annual SCUTREA Conference, London: Birkbeck College.

Hall, B., Budd, L. and Livingstone, D. (1997) 'Embracing the world: Transformative learning, human-earth relations, democracy and the quality of life' in Paul Armstrong, Nod Miller and Miriam Zukas (eds) *Crossing Borders, Breaking Boundaries: Research in the Education of Adults*, Proceedings of the 27th Annual SCUTREA Conference, London: Birkbeck College.

Hart, Mechtild (1992) *Working and Educating for Life: Feminist and International Perspectives on Adult Education*, London and New York: Routledge.

Heaney, Thomas and Horton, Aimee (1990) 'Reflective Engagement for Social Change' in Jack Mezirow *Fostering Critical Reflection in Adulthood*, Oxford: Jossey-Bass.

Hekman, Susan J. (1990) *Gender and Knowledge*, Oxford: Blackwell, Polity Press.

Hewitt, P. (1993) *About Time: The Revolution in Work and Family Life*, London: IPPR/Rivers Oram Press.

Highet, Gillian (1991) 'Gender and education: A study of the ideology and practice of community based women's education' in S. Westwood and J.E. Thomas (eds) *Radical Agendas? The Politics of Adult Education*, Leicester: NIACE.

Lather, Patti (1992) 'Post-critical pedagogies: A feminist reading' in Carmen Luke and Jennifer Gore (eds) *Feminisms and Critical Pedagogy*, London and New York: Routledge.

Livingstone, David (1997) 'Working class culture, adult education and informal learning: beyond the "cultural capital" bias to transformative community' in Paul Armstrong, Nod Miller and Miriam Zukas (eds) *Crossing Borders, Breaking Boundaries: Research in the Education of Adults*, Proceedings of the 27th Annual SCUTREA Conference, London: Birkbeck College.

Lovett, Tom (ed.) (1988) *Radical Approaches to Adult Education: A Reader*, London and New York: Routledge.

Mackie, John (ed.) (1980) *Literacy and Revolution: The Pedagogy of Paulo Freire*, London: Pluto Press.

McGivney, Veronica (1990) *Education's for Other People: Access to Education for Non-participant Adults*, Leicester: NIACE.

McLaren, Peter (1994) 'Postmodern and the death of politics' in P. McLaren and P. Lankshear (eds) *Politics of Liberation: Paths from Freire*, London and New York: Routledge.

McLaren, Peter (1988) 'Schooling the post-modern body: Critical pedagogy and the politics of enfleshment', *Journal of Education*, Vol. 170, No. 3, pp. 53–83.

McLaren, Peter and Leonard, Peter (eds) (1993) *Paulo Freire: A Critical Encounter*, London and New York: Routledge.

Merriam, S., Courtenay, B. and Reeves, T.(1997) 'Transformational learning and its link to ego and faith development in HIV-positive adults' in Paul Armstrong, Nod Miller and Miriam Zukas (eds) *Crossing Borders, Breaking Boundaries: Research in the Education of Adults*, Proceedings of the 27th Annual SCUTREA Conference, London: Birkbeck College.

Mezirow, Jack (1991) *Transformative Dimensions of Adult Learning*, San Francisco: Jossey-Bass.

Mezirow, Jack (1992) 'Transformation theory: Critique and confusion', *Adult Education Quarterly*, 42(4): 250–253.

Morey, Oma (1997) 'Breaking the boundaries of eldercare: The nature of transformative learning and the daughters who care' in Paul Armstrong, Nod Miller and Miriam Zukas (eds) *Crossing Borders, Breaking Boundaries: Research in the Education of Adults*, Proceedings of the 27th Annual SCUTREA Conference, London: Birkbeck College.

O'Sullivan, Edmund (1997) 'The dream drives the action: Transformative education for our times' in Paul Armstrong, Nod Miller and Miriam Zukas (eds) *Crossing Borders, Breaking Boundaries: Research in the Education of Adults*, Proceedings of the 27th Annual SCUTREA Conference, London: Birkbeck College.

Plumwood, Valerie (1993) *Feminism and the Mastery of Nature*, London and New York: Routledge.

Swindells, Julia (1995) 'Are we not more than half the nation? Woman and "the radical tradition" of adult education 1867–1919' in M. Mayo and J. Thompson (eds) *Adult Learning, Critical Intelligence and Social Change*, Leicester: National Institute of Adult Continuing Education.

Thompson, Jane (1995) 'Feminism and women's education' in M. Mayo and J. Thompson (eds) *Adult Learning, Critical Intelligence and Social Change*, Leicester: National Institute of Adult Continuing Education.

Chapter 5

Self and experience in adult learning

Robin Usher, Ian Bryant and Rennie Johnston

The self in adult education's traditions of learning

What conception of the self does adult education operate with? Adult education involves processes in which particular kinds of learners (adults) engage
in activities leading to desirable kinds of change. Thus, the very notion of
adult learning as a process where desirable changes are brought about is itself
dependent upon particular yet very often taken-for-granted conceptions of
the self. There are, however, clear if largely implied assumptions about the
nature of the self in the way in which adult learning is typically conceived.
The best way of showing this is by considering the notion of autonomy. As
Boud (1989) points out, 'autonomy' in the context of adult learning refers
both to a goal of self-awareness, of empowerment in the sense of an ability
to exercise choice in relation to needs, and to an approach to learning of
active personal involvement and self-direction.

Autonomy is the government of the self by the self, a freedom from depen-
dence, a situation where one is influenced and controlled only by a source
from within oneself. What prevents autonomy is therefore that which is
outside or 'other' to the self. Amongst the many forms that otherness can
take the most significant in the context of adult education are didactic
teachers and transmitted bodies of formal knowledge. Perhaps the most
significant characteristic of the adult learner has been that of autonomy. As
Candy (1987: 161) points out, the notion of the learner as an autonomous
self is 'so deeply entrenched in the ethos of adult education as to be thought
"obvious" or "self-evident" and to thus be beyond question'. It is this
autonomous self in the form of the adult learner who becomes the centre or
source of experience and knowledge, including self-knowledge.

It is not too difficult to see why this notion of the autonomous self
possessing agency provides a vital rationale and ground for an educational

This is an edited version of a chapter previously pubished in *Learning Beyond the Limits:
Adult Education and the Postmodern Challenge*, 1997, London and New York: Routledge.

practice such as adult learning with its emphasis on personal change. Autonomy defines both a goal for and an approach to the practice of adult education. The rationale is that adult education, by its approach to learning, can bring to the fore and realise the autonomy that is always potentially present in adult selves. This is why the common theme that unites the various and disparate strands or traditions in adult learning is that of empowerment – an empowerment implicated with a particular kind of self who has a natural potential for autonomy and who can be empowered through a particular kind of practice.

Boud (1989: 40–43) refers to four main traditions of learning in adult education: training and efficiency in learning, self-directed learning or andragogy, learner-centred or humanistic, and critical pedagogy and social action. These traditions, although very different, all seek to *remove* something from the process of learning in order that they can attain their goal. Training and efficiency in learning seeks to remove *distractions* that make learning less efficient in the attainment of predefined learning goals. The andragogical tradition seeks to remove the *restrictions* of didactic teachers and formal bodies of knowledge from learning. The humanistic tradition seeks to remove all internal and self-imposed *distortions* on learning whilst the critical tradition seeks to remove the *oppressions* of history and social context from learning.

At this point, it is worth noting the negative imagery. The learning process is characterised as one full of blockages and barriers, things that impede or hold back the self-as-learner from attaining various ends, such as efficacy, autonomy, self-realisation or emancipation, which each tradition posits as the goal of learning. For the self-as-learner the learning process is one beset by distractions, restrictions, barriers and oppressions – all varieties of negative and feared 'otherness', which have to be overcome.

The tradition of training and efficiency in learning depends on a body of predefined knowledge or skills, couched in terms of objectives (often behavioural in nature) and learnt in a planned and efficient way. Pedagogy becomes a technical matter, with the learner receiving pre-planned inputs and producing or enacting predefined outputs; learning becomes a neutral process or system removed from the influence of sociocultural factors. The specificity of learners, differences attributable to biographical factors such as gender, ethnicity and class are either ignored or programmed out. The self that is operative here is the classical scientific self – individualised, undifferentiated, an essentially abstract entity, the 'monological self', the self-contained individual having no transactions with and unaffected by anything 'other' to itself – a kind of pure 'learning machine'.

That is why it is a matter of removing distractions from a learning process whose goal is the acquisition by the learner of new knowledge and skills. This is what autonomy means here. Learners appear to have control of the learning process – the goal is clear, measurable and relevant, the learning process straightforward and flexible; they can work at their own pace and according to their particular circumstances. But, at the same time, this control is largely illusory because the knowledge and skills to be acquired are predefined. The control actually rests with the predefined knowledge and skills, both of which are simply assumed to be neutral 'givens' rather than socioculturally constructed and therefore problematic. Autonomy, therefore, becomes induction into 'givens', predetermined meanings over which the learner has little personal control.

The andragogical tradition has been perhaps the most influential in institutional adult education. As Boud (1989: 41) points out, it is a tradition that emphasises 'the unique goals and interests of individual learners and places these as central in the teaching and learning process'. The focus of the andragogical tradition is the adult learner's experience, considered to be the foundation and most important resource for learning. It is what essentially characterises adults, that which uniquely defines their being as adults (Knowles, 1978, 1985). Thus, in the andragogical tradition, experience is at the centre of knowledge production and acquisition. Using experience becomes not simply a pedagogical device but more significantly an affirmation of the ontological and ethical status of adults, in particular, the mark of their radical difference from children. This tradition is very anti-schooling, seeing as an important part of its mission that of 'liberating' adult learners from its unhappy consequences.

This emphasis assumes that experience provides a different knowledge, a knowledge of the 'real' world drawn from 'life', that is either an alternative or an enriching complement to formal knowledge. Learners are thus not to be seen as empty vessels to be filled with formal knowledge through didactic teaching, but rather as coming to learning situations with valuable resources for learning and with the attributes of self-direction, i.e. knowing their own learning needs, a knowledge not possessed by children.

The emphasis on experience constructs the adult as an active learner who comes to learning situations with personal resources in the form of experience. On the other hand, because of the way in which the self is constructed, this experience is taken as an unproblematic 'given'. Experience is unquestioningly seen as 'present', as an authentic source of knowledge once learners are left free to control their own learning and to realise their inherent self-directing tendencies; once, in other words, they position themselves correctly by freeing themselves from the 'otherness' of knowledge not based on their own experience.

Correspondingly, children's experience is denied a status because it is supposedly less 'authentic' than adults' experience, the assumption being that the child cannot have a self free from otherness. If adult learners are subjected to didactic teaching and a curriculum based on formal knowledge rather than their experience, if, in other words, the conditions of schooling are reproduced, then they revert to being children with a self still dependent on otherness. That the learner's own experience may not come indelibly stamped with the mark of authenticity is not considered.

The rejection of otherness means that andragogy cannot have a conception of experience as culturally constructed, pre-interpreted, complex and multi-stranded. The self is therefore conceived as meaning-*giver*, the originary source of experience and knowledge in relation to experience, with a corresponding failure to recognise that selves, because they are linguistically and socioculturally embedded, are also meaning-*takers*. The meaning of experience comes from 'outside' selves, although at the same time this outside is so much a part of us that we experience it as 'inside'.

The self of andragogy is the transcendental self of the Enlightenment. Persons are seen as individualistic and unitary with a core rationality enabling them to systematically reflect on and know their experience. They are pre-given and decontextualised and, although they are accorded a biography since without it they would have no experience, the assumption is both that they can distance themselves from it and that it is a linear record of the unfolding of the life of an essential self that can be, in principle, always decoded. In general, history, sociality and human practices apart from schooling are considered formative but not essential. It is precisely the quality of remaining 'inside', untouched by an 'outside', of being fully present to oneself, that enables the self-as-learner to exercise its own agency and realise its autonomy. This, then, becomes the justification and potential for the educational interventions by which autonomy can be realised through the removal of restrictions. The emphasis on the 'inside' also makes the andragogical tradition psychologistic (since the 'inside' is always associated with mind and mental activities) and ironically this has opened the door for the colonisation of its practice by psychology. Learners are thrown back on their personal resources that determine the path of their learning – a seeming control by the learner that, in practice, turns out to be illusory.

The humanistic tradition has its theoretical base in humanistic psychology, particularly the work of Carl Rogers (1967, 1983), one of its most significant exponents. Rogers emphasised the importance, first, of 'here and now' experiencing of ourselves and the world, of subjective consciousness and awareness in knowing and acting; second, the process of 'becoming', of choosing ways of living that realise an innate, authentic self, and third, the need to think holistically, in terms of the 'whole' person, the integrated biologically based organism, a unity of thinking, feeling and acting.

Rogers' authentic self, as we have just noted, although it is in many respects different from the rational self, is nonetheless similarly a transcendental non-contingent self, a unitary, self-knowing consciousness, disembodied and disembedded. So long as persons can remain in touch with their authentic core selves, their 'organismic' being, and can be fully themselves, then they will act rationally and responsibly. For Rogers, people become trapped in inauthenticity through oppressive social relations. We have an innate powerful need for external positive regard – for the love and respect of significant others – a need that can only be met by accepting the conditions that they impose for giving us what we desire. This causes us to act inauthentically, against our true selves. As a consequence, we become 'blocked', unhappy and fail to develop our full potential, both generally as persons and particularly as learners.

Social relationships, therefore, exert an oppressive authority – 'anything taken in from others is by definition inimical to authenticity and spontaneity' (Richards, 1989: 109) – and one of the most significant forms this authority can take is the pedagogic relationship. It is the pedagogic relationship that is the main enemy. Unless teachers are 'facilitators', giving up their traditionally didactic role, then this relationship will always be oppressive and will block rather than enable learning. As in the andragogical tradition, schooling and indeed any institutional form of education is seen as doing nothing but harm, and the need, therefore, is to ensure that the learning situation does not replicate this in any way. It must be learner-centred, controlled by the felt needs of learners and geared to optimising their development as whole persons. As Boud (1989: 42) puts it: 'Learners may be constrained by their own early negative experiences of learning and they need the context of a highly supportive and respectful environment to be able to recognise their needs and begin to explore them.'

Here, then, the self is essentially individualistic with an internal organismic rather than a social essence. The social is always 'outside' and oppressively 'other'. There is no recognition that selves might be socially located and no recognition that self and others are mutually constitutive within relationships. All social relationships are seen as inherently manipulative, functioning to distort the autonomy and agency of persons. A person's authentic self is inherently 'good', i.e. it is already socialised and eminently sociable. Social change, therefore, becomes a matter of the individual action of authentic selves; social harmony a product of persons being truly themselves. In learning, the learning of specific subject matter becomes less important than learning about oneself, getting 'in touch' with one's authentic self and acting in accordance with its voice. Learning becomes a means of eliminating self-distortions and inauthenticity in the service of attaining a state of self-knowledge, self-presence and autonomy.

Both the andragogical and humanistic traditions have an individual–society binary opposition at their very heart. The social becomes cast in the role of the oppressive and feared other. As the point of origin, the authentic self is independent of the social realm. Individual autonomy and empowerment lies in liberating oneself from the social and its oppressive effects. In Rogers, for example, the social is something from the outside that gets inside and, like an alien growth, stifles authenticity and potentiality. To be truly autonomous we must therefore expunge the social that is inside us.

These traditions may make much of empowering the individual learner, yet they have shown themselves to be wide open to hijacking by an individualistic and instrumental ethic. The psychologism and individualism of humanistic discourse presented as a concern for the 'person' can lead ultimately and paradoxically to a dehumanisation through the substitution of covert for overt regulation under the guise of 'being human', enabling learners to 'open up', and provide access to their 'inner' world. This is an infiltration of power by subjectivity and a complementary infiltration of subjectivity by power (Rose, 1994).

In the critical pedagogy tradition, the emphasis is on attaining social change rather than personal autonomy, learning in the service of group or collective empowerment rather than individual empowerment. In the critical tradition, there is a rejection of individualism and psychologism, challenging a conception of the self that fails to recognise the effects of social structures and forces. For example, Brah and Hoy (1989) argue that although each of us does have a quality of individual uniqueness, we are socially positioned along power hierarchies constructed through class, race and gender.

Critical pedagogy's self is the exploited self of 'false consciousness' whose experience is rendered inauthentic by distorting ideology and oppressive social structures. Persons are first and foremost socially formed rather than socially isolated individuals. Their experience and knowledge arises from their social formation and positioning, but equally through these is it distorted by false consciousness. Learning in critical pedagogy, therefore, is centred on 'ideology critique', a stripping away of false consciousness. Learners, in dialogue with other learners who are similarly positioned, can understand the nature of their position, develop a 'true' consciousness and take action in conjunction with others to change their situation. Learning becomes, therefore, the acquisition of knowledge of an oppressive world, an awareness and understanding of one's social positioning and, through this knowledge, an ability to change the world and remove oppression.

However, a strong argument can also be made that this tradition is not actually so different from the others. Certainly, there is an emphasis here on the social, but all are as one in seeing the social as negative and distorting. All share a common conception of the relationship of experience to sociality. Critical pedagogy talks, for example, of experience being 'shaped by concrete social conditions' (Brah and Hoy, 1989: 71) but, as in the humanistic tradition, this shaping is conceived as generally negative in its effects. The common feature here is that experiencing in a meaningful and authentic way is seen as the outcome of a freeing from oppressive social relations.

The social is seen in this way by the critical tradition because it is equated with social *forces* that are always portrayed as oppressive and crushing. The dimension of the social is theorised as a solid, reified 'thing', with the inevitable conclusion that the social can do no other than oppress and crush. Of course, this is not to deny that there is oppression or crushing of persons in the lived world, or that this can be explained in social terms. What we want to point to rather is that if sociality is seen purely as social *forces* that crush and oppress, then something very important is being forgotten, namely, that sociality is the *condition* of being a person. This implies, therefore, that it is our social practices that both create us as selves and enable us to be creative, indeed that learning rather than being something located 'inside' is itself a social practice.

Implicit, then, in all the conceptions of the self we have studied so far are two structuring binary opposites; individual/social and voluntarism/determinism. Three of the traditions emphasise or privilege the 'individual' and 'voluntarism' poles whilst critical pedagogy reverses this and privileges the 'social' and 'determinism' poles. The danger with both these positions is that one constructs a totally 'free-wheeling' individualistic self, owing nothing to the social (constructed as oppressive) and where everything important is located 'inside' the person, whilst the other constructs a determined self that owes everything to the social and where conversely everything important (and oppressive) is located 'outside' the person.

There is a tendency in the critical tradition to end up with a conception of the self that is, on the one hand, oversocialised and overdetermined and on the other, patronising in so far as selves have to be seen as normally in a state of false consciousness. In stressing the negative and overwhelming effects of social relations and social structures, persons are made into social 'victims', dupes and puppets, manipulated by ideology and deprived of agency.

The dominant tendency in educational theory and practice has been to privilege the agency of the autonomous self and exclude any notion of determination on the grounds that to admit determination would be to render educational work impossible. However, in rejecting determination a self has to be posited as standing apart from any situatedness, outside of history, sociality and human practices. It is the power of the autonomous self to bestow meanings and shape experience that makes the self the condition and agent of knowledge. There is no situatedness other than the constraints and distortions from which the self can, exercising its agency, free itself by its own willing. In critical pedagogy, the self is shaped by its experiences, meanings are bestowed on them through ideology that becomes the sources of (false) knowledge. The self is socially situated but frees itself and is able to experience truly through collective dialogue and action.

In the end, both these conceptions assume a self that is a unified consciousness with the power of self-presence and the capacity to act rationally. Critical pedagogy, although locating the self in social structures, still assumes a self capable of moving from false to true consciousness – both a unified self, self-knowing and self-present and a rational self capable of knowing its 'true' position and of acting on that knowledge. The critical tradition, in positing a socially embedded self, challenges the dominant conception of the self but the challenge is only partial and ultimately fails because it must also posit a fully rational, self-present self. In effect, then, the self that is operative in all the traditions of adult learning is the monological self of our dominant Western culture.

The place of experience

In all the traditions of adult learning, experience has been accorded a privileged place as the source of learning in a learner-centred pedagogy and at the very centre of knowledge production and knowledge acquisition. One consequent danger is that experience comes to be taken as foundational and authoritative and hence we stop asking questions about it. It has become, in effect, an unquestioned 'given'. The questions that are asked are to do with the knowledge or learning that is the outcome of experience. Adult educators tend to explain learning in terms of foundational experience, since it seems incontrovertible that nothing could be more basic and hence more 'truthful' than someone's experience. Experience seems to be the incontestable evidence, the secure originary point, with the clear implication that explanation must be focused on what is learnt from experience rather than experience itself. Yet, it could be argued, and indeed we shall argue, that experience is not unproblematic that, in fact, rather than the origin of explanation, it is precisely that which is in need of explanation.

This conception of experience – that 'experience is the foundation of, and the stimulus for, learning' (Boud et al., 1993: 8) – is at the heart of pedagogies of experiential learning. The problem is that to see experience as originary in relation to learning fails to recognise that any approach to using experience will generate its own representations of experience and will itself be influenced by the way experience is conceived or represented, by the framework or interpretive grid that will influence how experience is theorised and how it is worked with in practice. In other words, the very *use* of experience presupposes a prior *theory* or epistemology of experience. The discourse and practice of experiential learning presupposes and practises something quite different – a theory of prior experience with experience as the foundational source of knowledge. We would argue that this leads to a failure to consider first, how experience *itself* represents (has meanings) and second, is itself represented (within theories and epistemologies).

Let us explore this second point first, since it links closely with the discussion we have had about the self. We have seen that the dominant conception of the monological self has rationalistic, humanistic and critical variants that, despite the variations, also have important things in common. Similarly, there is a dominant conception of 'monological' experience where the latter is constructed as a 'natural' attribute of selves. This conception is rooted in a rational/empiricist epistemology. Experience is constructed as transparent, giving unmediated access to the world. Language, symbolic systems and discourses are seen simply as neutral vehicles for describing what all rational selves can experience. Knowledge of the world is possible because there is a one-to-one correspondence between the world and the way it is represented through experience. Rational procedures such as reflection can be used by all and enable experience to be sorted, validated and transformed into knowledge. This monological conception of experience, certainly in its rationalistic and humanistic variants, is essentially individualistic and psychologistic. Consciousness is a key attribute with knowledge of the world a function of the autonomous, reflective self – the self as an ideal-knower, independent of contingency and specificity, disembodied and disembedded.

As Michelson (1996) points out, adult education has, throughout its history, tended to construct learning as a process where knowledge is created through the transformation of experience. Experience is *raw material* to be acted upon by the mind through the controlled and self-conscious use of the senses (observation) and the application of reason (reflection). Even the critical tradition in adult education, whilst it seeks to distance itself from the individualism and psychologism by emphasising the constitution of ex-perience within social structures, still retains the notion of 'raw material' and of 'transformation'.

Let us consider these similarities in more detail. First, there is a common emphasis on the potential of selves to experience authentically. Experience provides a privileged access to the truth of reality where reality is itself under-stood as a given. Second, experiencing authentically and knowing truly is a matter of positioning that, whether socially structured or individually orig-inated, is always ultimately a matter of methodical will – in other words, positioning is open to change by eliminating distortion through methodical techniques such as objectivity, reflection, introspection, dialogue and consciousness-raising. Third, there is an elimination of difference. The criti-cal tradition appears to accept difference when it foregrounds the sig-nificance of different social positioning but, because it tends to reify and naturalise categories such as gender, race and class, it actually works to eliminate differences within categories. The very notion of 'positioning' is, therefore, rendered unproblematic to the extent that a potentially liberating practice can become totalising and oppressive. Fourth, all the variants fail to recognise that they are theorising or representing experience. What they think they are doing is simply describing or explaining in a neutral way the essential nature of experience or the nature of the pre-existing self. In effect, however, they are representing or discursively producing experience in a very particular way and with a very particular set of significations. There is nothing neutral about this – on the contrary, it is eminently political and contestable.

We can examine this question of representation more closely by going back to conceptions of the self and looking at their significatory force rather than their content. In other words, the way the self is represented does not merely describe and illuminate a pre-existing self but actually influences people's self-awareness and sense of individuality, the way their subjectivities are constituted.

Representations of the self can be seen as narratives or stories about the self, cultural texts that define subjectivity – Benhabib (1992), for example, refers to the *narrative structure of personal identity*. Our sense of ourselves as self-enclosed, independent, inner-directed, 'sovereign' individuals is produced and maintained by narratives and ways of speaking (Shotter, 1993). These provide meanings through which we define ourselves, meanings that function both as possibilities and constraints in relation to the forming of subjectivity – on the one hand, a set of enabling resources through which selves can be created; on the other, a set of limitations beyond which selves cannot be easily made and remade (Shotter, 1989). Different cultural texts present different sets of possibilities and constraints.

As we have already seen, the dominant narrative projects the self as a natural, existent and universal category. The alternative narrative is one where the self is rather a culturally and historically variable category. Indeed, the very idea that this category of self is definitive of subjectivity is a specifically Western cultural phenomenon. In other cultures and in Western culture at different historical periods, subjectivity, or the sense of self, has been seen as relationally constituted – for example, in relation to family and kinship, to community, to the natural world. Modern subjectivity, however, is rooted in a logic of identity rather than difference and thus bound to a predominantly individualistic or monological conception of human beings as unique selves where subjectivity is inseparably linked to an essentialised and non-relational self.

Feminism, in critiquing this dominant representation of the self, argues that there is no essential pre-existing subjectivity and no universal category of the self. Rather, the self is located in concrete social relations and cultural texts with subjectivity defined by powerful gendered narratives where gender itself is storied into being as a 'natural' or biological attribute of the self (Flax, 1990). Given its central position in the structure of oppressive patriarchy, feminism has sought, therefore, to displace modern Western culture's transcendental, universal and monological self.

The postmodern critique is also directed towards the notion of an essential human nature or true self. Postmodernists would argue that this 'true self' needs to be seen as a character in a narrative, a culturally produced 'fiction' presented in a naturalistic guise so that the narrative is concealed and the self appears as pre-existing and 'natural'. For postmodernists, the self is not a fact, a transcendental being, but an artefact socially, historically and linguistically produced. All social practices, including practices where meaning is attributed to the notion of a 'self', are not just mediated but constituted through language. As Weedon (1987: 33) points out, language is the means by which:

we learn to give voice – meaning – to our experience and to understand it according to particular ways of thinking, particular discourses which pre-date our entry into language. These ways of thinking constitute our consciousness, and the positions with which we identify and structure our sense of ourselves, our subjectivity.

The postmodern story of the self is that of a decentred self, subjectivity without a centre or origin, caught in meanings, positioned in language and the narratives of culture. The self cannot know itself independently of the significations in which it is enmeshed. There is no self-present subjectivity, hence no ultimate transcendental meaning of the self. Meanings are always 'in play' and the self, caught up in this play, is an ever-changing self, caught up in the narratives and meanings through which it leads its life (Lovlie, 1992). As de Lauretis puts it: 'the process is continuous, unending or daily renewed. For each person therefore subjectivity is an ongoing construction, not a fixed point of departure or arrival, from which one then interacts with the world' (quoted in Gunew, 1990: 28). Thus, there is no non-linguistic or non-historical position, no originary point, where persons can gain a privileged access to the world or to themselves. As Flax (1993) argues, subjectivity is a discursive effect, a character in a story as much as the 'author' of the story. Representations of the self, instead of being seen as 'truth', need to be seen more usefully as stories, often very powerful stories, which perform a variety of social functions, including the construction of selves with appropriate characteristics.

In being positioned through narratives we get a sense of ourselves, but this sense is always changing. When we tell stories about our experience, these are not stories simply about ourselves as entities that exist independently of the story, although they may appear to be. They are not stories about or emanating from essential selves, but stories that help in the construction of selves. Subjectivity is never a once-and-for-all construction, and the experience that meaning can have is never permanently fixed. Human beings have many stories to tell and many different ways in which they can be recognised and give meaning to themselves through them. Subjectivity is therefore always shifting and uncertain and has to be continually 're-formed'. At any one point in time, experience can take on a specific meaning but there is no guarantee that the question of its meaning is thereby forever settled.

Experience can be invested with a multiplicity of meanings, identity conducted through many possible stories. Even within any one articulation, the meaning of experience is never permanently fixed: thus, the text of experience is always open to reinterpretation. As O'Reilly (1989) points out, experience always has a quality of incoherence – it may come with pre-determined meanings but this is never the last word, since experience can always be 'reread'. One could put it this way – experience always says less than it wishes to say, there is always more that can be read into it, it never reaches the destination of total clarity and definitiveness. As 'readers' we can never make it completely present. There is a sense in which experience is always out of control, always brimming over from the social contexts within which it is represented. This is perhaps why mechanisms that seek to accredit or recognise prior learning in totalising experience, to make it decidable and to bring it under control, always end up being oppressive.

As we have seen, experience in adult education discourse has mainly signified freedom from regulation in the service of personal autonomy and/or social empowerment. *Autonomy*, empowerment, *self-expression*, self-realisation are key signifiers. Other hitherto more submerged signifiers such as '*application*' and '*adaptation*' now also have a key significance. The meaning of experience will vary according to different discursive practices, as too will the particular significance given to learning deriving from experience. Although experiential learning has become central to the theory and practice of education in the postmodern moment, as a pedagogy it is inherently ambivalent and capable of many significations. There is a need to stop seeing experiential learning in purely logocentric terms, as a natural characteristic of the individual learner or as a pedagogical technique, and more in terms of the contexts, sociocultural and institutional, in which it functions and from which it derives its significations. In itself, therefore, it has no unequivocal or 'given' meaning – it is inherently neither emancipatory nor oppressive, neither domesticating nor transformative. Rather, its meaning is constantly shifting between and across these polarities. It is perhaps most usefully seen as having a potential for emancipation *and* oppression, domestication *and* transformation, where at any one time and according to context both tendencies can be present and in conflict with one another. Accordingly, it offers a contestable and ambiguous terrain where different socio-economic and cultural assumptions and strategies can be differentially articulated. As a field of tension, it can be exploited by different groups, each emphasising certain dimensions over others.

Experiential learning can, for example, be deployed as a pedagogical strategy both in a disciplines-based curriculum and within a competences-based curriculum. Equally, it can be deployed as part of a continued questioning of and resistance to the forms of power that situate us as subjects. But at the same time, even here, experiential learning can function both as a more effective means of disciplining the 'whole' subject rather than simply the reasoning part and as a strategy to subvert the dominance of an oppressive universalistic reason by giving 'voice' to difference. What this implies, then, is that experience is always a site of struggle, a terrain where the meaning and significance of the experience to be cultivated in learning contexts is fought over. Central to this struggle is the reconfiguration of emancipation and oppression in the postmodern moment.

References

Benhabib, S. (1992) *Situating the Self*, Cambridge: Polity Press.

Boud, D. (1989) 'Some Competing Traditions in Experiential Learning', in S.W. Weil and I. McGill (eds), *Making Sense of Experiential Learning*, Milton Keynes: SRHE/Open University Press.

Boud, D., Cohen R. and Walker, D. (1993) 'Introduction: Understanding Learning from Experience', in D. Boud, R. Cohen and D. Walker (eds), *Using Experience for Learning*, Milton Keynes: SRHE/Open University Press.

Brah, A. and Hoy, J. (1989) 'Experiential Learning: A New Orthodoxy?', in S.W. Weil and I. McGill (eds), *Making Sense of Experiential Learning*, Milton Keynes: SRHE/Open University Press.

Candy, P. (1987) 'Evolution, Revolution or Devolution: Increasing Learner Control in the Instructional Setting', in D. Boud and V. Griffin (eds), *Appreciating Adults Learning*, London: Kogan Page.

Flax, J. (1990) *Thinking in Fragments*, Oxford: University of California Press.

Flax, J. (1993) *Disputed Subjects*, London: Routledge.

Gunew, S. (ed.) (1990) *Feminist Knowledge: Critique and Construct*, London: Routledge.

Knowles, M. (1978) *The Adult Learner: A Neglected Species*, Houston, Tex.: Gulf Publishing.

Knowles, M. (1985) *Andragogy in Action*, San Francisco, Calif. Jossey-Bass.

Lovlie, L. (1992) 'Postmodernism and Subjectivity', in S. Kvale (ed.), *Psychology and Postmodernism*, London: Sage.

Michelson, C. (1996) 'The Usual Suspects: Experience, Reflection and the (En)gendering of Knowledge', *International Journal of Lifelong Education*, 15: 438–454.

O'Reilly, D. (1989) 'On Being an Educational Fantasy Engineer', in S.W. Weil and I. McGill (eds), *Making Sense of Experiential Learning*, Milton Keynes: SRHE/Open University Press.

Richards, B. (1989) *Images of Freud*, London: J.M. Dent.

Rogers, C.R. (1967) *On Becoming a Person*, London: Constable.

Rogers, C.R. (1983) *Freedom to Learn in the '80s*, Columbus, Ohio: Charles E. Merrill.

Rose, N. (1994) *Governing the Soul: The Shaping of the Private Self*, London: Routledge.

Shotter, J. (1989) 'Social Accountability and the Social Construction of "You" ', in J. Shotter and K.J. Gergen (eds), *Texts of Identity*, London: Sage.

Shotter, J. (1993) *Conversational Realities*, London: Sage.

Weedon, C. (1987) *Feminist Practice and Post-structuralist Theory*, Oxford: Basil Blackwell.

Chapter 6

Promoting reflection in professional courses

The challenge of context

David Boud and David Walker

Introduction

One of the key ideas and features of all aspects of learning from experience is that of reflection. Dewey (1933) expressed an early view that 'while we cannot learn or be taught to think, we do have to learn how to think well, especially acquire the general habit of reflecting'. Since Dewey's time many writers in the field have emphasised the importance of reflection: Kolb (1984) has drawn attention to the role of reflection in Lewin's experiential learning cycle, Schön (1983, 1987) has introduced the concept of the reflective practitioner into current discourse, and many others have taken the idea of reflection and explored it in the context of theory and practice in experiential learning. Reflection has also been a central feature of our own work for many years (e.g. Boud *et al.*, 1985; Boud and Walker, 1990). Different aspects of reflection have been explored, in particular reflection-in-action and reflection-on-action. Reflection has been used differently depending on the tradition from which the writer or practitioner has come. More recently the notion of critical reflection has become the centre of attention, driven partly by the interests of critical social scientists (Walker and Boud, 1992) and by practitioners who regard the idea of 'normal' practice as problematic (e.g. Brookfield, 1995).

Over the past ten years or so we have seen the translation of ideas of reflection and reflective practice into courses and programmes for the initial training and continuing education of a wide variety of practitioners, particularly in professions such as teaching (e.g. Zeichner and Liston, 1987; Clift *et al.*, 1990; Calderhead and Gates, 1993; Smith and Hatton, 1993; Loughran, 1996), nursing (e.g. Parlmer *et al.*, 1994; Johns and Freshwater, 1998) and social work (e.g. Yelloly and Henkel, 1995; Gould and Taylor, 1996), where field experience and academic study need to be closely integrated. With this has come the challenge of incorporating ideas about reflection, which in some

This is an edited version of an article previously published in *Studies in Higher Education*, 1998, 23(2): 191–206.

cases are only partially understood, into teaching contexts that are not conducive to the questioning of experience – that is, situations that do not allow learners to explore 'a state of perplexity, hesitation, doubt' (Dewey, 1933), 'inner discomforts' (Brookfield, 1987), 'disorienting dilemmas' (Mezirow, 1990), uncertainties, discrepancies and dissatisfactions that precipitate, and are central to, any notion of reflection.

More recently, in parallel with increasing acceptance of reflective practice as an organising framework for professional preparation, there has been a questioning of Schön's views on reflective practice. Greenwood (1993) argues that he neglects the importance of reflection before action and Eraut (1995) suggests that there is little evidence of reflection-in-action in the crowded setting of classrooms. The unreflexive nature of Schön's accounts of his ideas is a concern of Usher *et al.* (1997), who also raise doubts about his methodology as it applies to practice, and draw attention to its insufficiently contextualised nature.

While we are sympathetic to the focus on learning through experience in reflective practice and are committed to the inclusion of reflective processes and theorising about reflection within professional courses, we believe that there are now many examples of poor educational practice being implemented under the guise and rhetoric of reflection. Unfortunately, it is impossible to assess readily the extent of this. However, evidence from our own observations of staff development activities devoted to reflection and reflective practice, and reports from experienced teachers across many professional areas enrolled in higher degree study, suggest that reality falls very far short of the rhetoric.

What are the problems?

The problems that we have encountered cover a broad range, from inexperience in how to conduct experience-based learning activities to basic misunderstandings of the nature of learning and reflection. Activities in which these problems arise include various different classroom tasks, the keeping of diaries and journals, the debriefing of workshops and placements and drawing on the life experience of students. None of these are problematic *per se*; it is the ways in which they are used that give rise to difficulties. The following are some examples that we have encountered.

Recipe following. In this form of practice, class activities typically take students through a sequence of steps of reflection and require them to reflect on demand. Elements of models of reflection are turned into checklists that students work through in a mechanical fashion without regard to their own uncertainties, questions or meanings. For example, nursing students might be asked to 'reflect' on a clinical experience in response to a predetermined set of questions to which 'answers' are expected. While there are many circumstances in which a list of reminders can be useful, in the case of reflection there is the great risk that acts of reflection become ritualised, without reference to context or outcomes. This leads to false expectations of what reflection is (it is linear, about external knowledge and unproblematic) and what learning outcomes can be expected of reflective activities (those that can be found in course statements and competency standards). When combined with a teacher- rather than a learner-centred approach to education, rule following turns 'reflection' into a process to be memorised and applied unthinkingly. The one characteristic of the references to reflection cited in this article is that they eschew the following of simple formulae to encourage reflection. Where stages or elements are given, authors are careful to point out that these are illustrative or conceptual elements, not an operational process. There is a challenge to teachers in turning ideas about reflection into tangible processes that can be commended to learners, but many are not meeting this challenge.

Reflection without learning. While reflection is important, not all planned reflective processes lead to learning.[1] Inadequate, inappropriate, or badly used reflective activities can become an obstacle. Just leaving time for reflection does not mean that the time will be used in a productive way. In many cases students may be able to use such time as an opportunity to take breath in a crowded curriculum, but they may not be able to use it to reflect or learn in ways that are meaningful to them. It is important to frame reflective activities within the learning context in which they are taking place. Without some direction reflection can become diffuse and disparate so that conclusions or outcomes may not emerge. Without a focus on conceptual frameworks, learning outcomes and implications, reflection for learners can become self-referential, inward looking and uncritical. There is inevitably a tension between guidance that leads to the problems of recipe following (identified above) and a lack of structure that can lead to a loss of focus. There are no reflective activities that are guaranteed to lead to learning, and conversely there are no learning activities guaranteed to lead to reflection. It is often in the presentation of appropriate reflective activities that the skill of the teacher is manifest and that students are assisted in their learning. The common strategy of asking students to take time out to make reflective notes is only likely to prompt reflection if the course in which it is used is one that encourages students to make their own meanings. In a different setting it could simply lead to 'spotting the examination question' or 'appearing to satisfy the teacher'.

Belief that reflection can be easily contained. There is often a pretence, or a naive assumption, that reflection can be restricted to matters outlined by the teacher within the teacher's comfort zone. In fact, the very nature of reflective activities is such that they may lead to serious questioning and critical thinking, involving the learners in challenging the assumptions of teachers or the learning context in which they are operating. For example, clinical placement for nursing students or teaching practice for education students can generate considerable distress, provoke students to query their vocation and throw up ethical dilemmas related to the practice of experienced professionals that cannot be resolved by making notes and having a discussion. It is not surprising then that students may not accept the boundaries of reflection within a subject that teachers take for granted. Reflective activities may lead students to focus on personal distress, oppressive features of the learning environment, the programme of study, resources provided, assessment practices and so on. There is no way that these can be barred, and facilitators of reflection need to be aware that any activity can tap into such issues. If the learning context is not supportive of a least some wider exploration, intolerable tensions between staff and students can result, and some students may be left in situations detrimental to them.

Not designing for a formal learning context. Even when a recipe-following approach is avoided, there can still be a problem of a mismatch between the type of reflection proposed and where it is used. The context of learning is often taken to be non-problematic in educational institutions. For example, asking students to explore their misconceptions or to reveal their uncertainties (a reflective task), in a situation in which they will be assessed in terms of understanding of the subject matter (a non-reflective requirement) on the basis of what they write, undermines the teacher's goal of encouraging reflection – students expect to write for assessment what they know, not reveal what they don't know. Assessment used in this way not only shows a poor understanding of the relationship between assessment and learning and the link between assessment tasks and learning outcomes, but also a limited appreciation of how to establish a climate conducive to reflection. Another example of a mismatch between reflection and assessment is in the use of reflective journals. The expectation that they will be read by an assessor leads some students to censor their reflections so much that they fail to engage with their felt experience and avoid learning. In circumstances where it is judged necessary to assess students' reflection skills (a goal that might itself be questioned – see, for example, Sumsion and Fleet (1996)), reflective writing should be judged in terms of criteria for the recognition of reflective writing (e.g. Hatton and Smith, 1994), not in terms of standard academic writing conventions.

Intellectualising reflection. Because emotions and feelings are often downplayed in educational settings, it is common for reflection to be treated as if it were an intellectual exercise – a simple matter of thinking rigorously. However, reflection is not solely a cognitive process: emotions are central to all learning. Recognition of affective dimensions of learning means teachers taking responsibility to create a climate in which the expression of feelings is accepted and legitimate. Unless learners are able to express themselves in conditions of trust and security, and know that the expression of emotion is not likely to lead to negative consequences for them, then the use of many forms of reflection may be inappropriate. This is a particular dilemma in professional courses in, for example, teaching and nursing, where expressions of feelings may lead staff to believe that a student may not be able to cope in a practice context, and lead to doubts about whether the student should be permitted to enter the profession. One of the most common outcomes of intellectualising reflection is, ironically, that of leaving students in emotional disarray. Denying the power and influence of emotion leaves staff with no strategies for dealing with it when it inevitably arises. Of course, allowing for emotional disclosure creates its own challenges.

Inappropriate disclosure. Because it is difficult and often inappropriate to focus reflection tightly, there is always the potential for learners to disclose matters that may be very confronting for staff: matters of great personal sensitivity, confidential information, unethical behaviour or even knowledge of crimes. In situations in which students do not feel constrained and are comfortable, they can include material that embarrasses staff and reveals information about others upon which their supervisors may feel professionally obliged to act. Dilemmas of breaking confidentiality, undermining colleagues, whistle-blowing and privacy can arise. At other times, learners may be asked to disclose too much of their inner life, their relationships or work with others. The use of personal journals that are handed in and discussed with staff is a risky strategy. Unless they are carefully planned with these dilemmas in mind and students are guided in how to use them, they can become a forum in which students reveal more than they or their teachers can handle.

Uncritical acceptance of experience. While most teachers who use reflective activities would shrink from encouraging students to accept experience without question, there are some more radical practitioners who tend to reify felt experience as if it possessed a special truth that would be damaged by questioning. They see reflection as a bulwark against the conformity of the curriculum and a means of celebrating naive experience against other influences. Whilst sensations and feelings provide important data for learning, they do not provide unambiguous messages: they are always influenced by our presuppositions, framed by theory – be it formal or informal – and subject to multiple interpretations. As Bryant et al. (1996) argue, experience cannot be separated from knowledge, it needs to be interpreted as a social practice; it is not coherent, complete or masterable.

Going beyond the expertise of the teacher. While it impossible to predict the full range of possibilities in any given situation, it is necessary for teachers to be well prepared for the most common issues that are likely to emerge. Unfortunately this is rarely the case, and teachers have been deterred from using some forms of reflection in their courses because of unfortunate disclosures with which they could not cope. Some of these instances can be avoided through appropriate design of activities or staff development that extends facilitative expertise. There are reasonable expectations of learners that if they are encouraged to disclose information about themselves, then teachers will help them deal with the issues that are raised: teachers may not share the same assumption. However, a more unfortunate situation can arise if staff begin to work with issues that are beyond their expertise. Disturbed perhaps by what they have unwittingly elicited, or feeling that they cannot leave the student in the emotional state that they have inadvertently provoked, they may endeavour to work further with the issues raised to the detriment of the student. Teachers must be aware of what they can and cannot handle, work within their capacities and develop networks with other kinds of practitioners (e.g. counsellors) to whom they can refer when they do not have expertise.

Excessive use of teacher power. The use of reflective activities can lead to staff gaining far greater influence over the lives of students. Worryingly, for a minority of staff this may be part of their attraction. More is known about students' experience than previously and this can be enormously beneficial in facilitating learning; teaching can be better related to students' experience and misconceptions more readily addressed. However, in less benign environments this can be severely detrimental. When learners are required to provide personal information to staff, there is greater potential for the misuse of power. Problems of teacher power are compounded by the fact that many teachers are simply not conscious of what they are doing and would be offended if it were suggested to them that they were even exercising power over students. A degree of mature awareness (Maslow, 1968) beyond that possessed by many teachers may be needed if reflective processes are to be used ethically.

The question that these examples pose is why have some of these ideas been interpreted in such educationally destructive, naive or negative ways? Is it because there are problems with the basic ideas upon which these practitioners are drawing, or with the ways in which they have been presented? Or is it because there is a problem in educational practice to which the use of such approaches draws attention? Our view is that these aspects require attention. However, in this chapter we focus on the last question. We explore the nature of context and how it influences the use of reflection in courses in higher and professional education.

Context and reflection

Consideration of the context in which reflective action is engaged is a seriously underdeveloped aspect of discussion of reflection. The context to which we are referring is the total cultural, social and political environment in which reflection takes place. This broader context is so all-pervasive that it is difficult to recognise its influence. It is, however, mirrored in and is in turn modified by particular local settings within which learning occurs: the classroom, the course and the institution. Context influences teachers and learners in a variety of ways in their everyday interactions as well as in learning outcomes and processes. Included here are influences on teachers, in terms of what goals they pursue for what ends, their own competence in handling teaching–learning situations and the resources they deploy; on learners, in terms of what they aspire to and how their expectations are framed; on learning outcomes, in terms of what teachers and learners accept as legitimate goals and what outcomes are valued over others; and on learning activities, in terms of what processes are acceptable in any given situation. There is a need to acknowledge these influences if the boundaries that they set are to be utilised or challenged, as is the case when reflective activities are used.

Some exponents of reflection, particular those Morrison (1996) identifies as adopting a politically oriented model, encourage students to focus on their own context and settings and change them (e.g. Smyth, 1996). However, it is far less common to extend such reflection to an analysis by learners of the context in which the reflective activity itself is taking place.

In an earlier model of reflection and learning from experience (Boud and Walker, 1990), we gave considerable emphasis to what we referred to as the learning milieu. The learning milieu, as we conceived of it then (following Parlett and Hamilton, 1977), represented the totality of the human and material influences that impinge on learners in any particular situation. These include co-learners, teachers, learning materials, the physical environment and everything that was to be found therein. Whilst these influences are undoubtedly important and provide some of the key resources for change, a conception of milieu that focuses on these alone is far too limited a notion to describe adequately the context of learning and its effects. Context is perhaps the single most important influence on reflection and learning. It can permit or inhibit working with learners' experience.

Varieties of views on context

Any view of context now must take account of the considerable theoretical contributions in recent years of, for example, critical social science, poststructuralism and postmodernism, which have drawn attention to the ways in which our constructions of what we accept as reality are constituted. The context in which we operate has many features that are taken for granted and are normally invisible on a day-to-day basis. These features have a profound influence over who we are, what and how we think and what we regard as legitimate knowledge. These features include *inter alia* the language we use to name the world (we cannot hold concepts or draw meaning from experiences for which we do not have language); the assumptions we hold about ourselves and others (what we believe we can and cannot learn); what is acceptable and not acceptable for us to do and what outcomes it is reasonable for us to seek in any given situation; which social groups are dominant or oppressed (who is heard and who is acted upon); who has resources and what they are; and many other economic, political and cultural considerations. These wider features of the context of learning reach deeply into the ways in which we view ourselves and others. They impinge on our identity and influence the ways in which we relate to others.

This broader social, political and cultural context influences every aspect of learning. It is not possible to step aside from it, or view it 'objectively', as it permeates our very being. It is reflected in our personal foundation of experience, which, although constructed from unique experiences, is also formed by the context in which we have developed. Context is subject to rereading and multiple readings: while it may be experienced as 'given', it is always available for reinterpretation. Institutions embody through their rules and modes of operation cultural assumptions that are or were dominant in particular aspects of society; they exemplify particular readings of context in their operation.

The ways in which context is represented in or challenged by institutions are of particular importance. As with individuals, institutions do not operate independently of their context, but there is some potential for administrators and teachers in key positions within them to counter, or at least draw attention to, particular features that may be antithetical to some kinds of learning. For example, leaders may initiate within the institution ground rules that emphasise inclusiveness and treat individuals according to their specific contributions and relevant differences rather than attributes (such as gender and race) unrelated to the work at hand. This can give staff within educational institutions more scope to create microcontexts, which operate as enclaves that have features separate from dominant cultural influences and which are conducive to particular kinds of reflective activity. Of course, many reflective activities – even the notion of reflection itself – are steeped in particular cultural practices and it may be necessary to draw attention to these in order to avoid establishing a new mystique and terminology that acts on some groups to exclude rather than include them.

Managing the influence of context

We believe that it is necessary to be optimistic about the extent to which the formation of such separate microcontexts is possible. There are far more opportunities for challenging undesired aspects of the broader context than are often acknowledged, and there are many examples within higher education of radical questioning of dominant values and practices that could be cited. Whilst it is vital to take account of context and plan teaching and learning activities on the basis on how context frames and influences possibilities, it is especially important that the power of context should not be used as an excuse to do nothing or to reinforce the status quo. Aspects of context change and can be changed, some obviously more so than others.

Because context is so embedded within situations, teachers and learners need to find ways of managing and working with it. It is never possible to set it aside. Context can be foregrounded though, and the ways in which it is manifest in any particular teaching and learning setting made the subject for exploration.

Teachers and learners also need to take personal responsibility for creating microcontexts and alternative readings of contexts that permit a wider range of exploration and learning than might otherwise be possible, and avoid blaming contextual factors for their own reluctance to seize the opportunities that exist in any situation. They should, however, be mindful that some forms of context (for example, that of some forms of competency-based learning) may operate precisely to limit possibilities for alternative ways of operating.

Limitations of individual conceptions

Individualistic conceptions of reflection fail to take account of the subtle and powerful ways in which context legitimises and frames particular forms and approaches to reflection, and defines those outcomes from reflection that are accepted as valid. There are many circumstances in education and training in which it is inappropriate for teachers to be encouraging particular reflective activities as the local context is such that it is not likely that useful outcomes will result; for example, promoting the use of reflective journals when formal assessment is based on competitive, cognitively oriented examinations, or encouraging the exploration of personal identity when anti-discriminatory practices are not well established within an institution. It is important to identify the conditions that may be required for productive reflection to occur.

Many discussions of reflection imply that it is a universal process that can be considered independently of context. However, if reflection is regarded as universal it more easily lends itself to abuse than if it is construed as a cultural practice located in a particular time and place. Reflection might therefore take on a variety of forms or processes, dependent on a wide range of factors. Factors to be considered might include class, race, gender, and so on as well as many local forms of difference. It may be necessary to contextualise not only the content of reflective activities, but also the process itself

– as suggested earlier. It is tempting to locate reflection as part of the set of teaching innovations that emphasise autonomy and self-direction. However, to do this is to run the risk of limiting the idea and its applications and to position it as part of an individualist discourse. Michelson (1996) takes this argument further and suggests that a consequence of this kind of positioning is to give reflection an inappropriately masculinist character.

Creating the local context: conditions under which reflection might be promoted

An image may help to illustrate our use of context here. When people gather together in an organisation, certain dynamics take over so that the organisation itself begins to influence the attitudes and behaviour of those who constitute it. People are drawn into it, and often act in a way that is contrary to what they might do alone. They can be carried along with the organisational ethos, caught up in a bigger purpose, and taken over by its character and behaviour. Creating a local context is like making a space in the organisation for groups of members to operate apart from immediate pressures to perform. It can establish a different atmosphere within which people can resist the draw of organisational requirements, and can act out of different attitudes and values. It can act as a kind of oasis, which provides an environment different from that which surrounds it. This is a space in which conditions are created deliberately rather than just accepted from the larger context; some of these conditions may be in contradiction to the larger context. The metaphor also suggests that while it may be possible to find a space for other activities within the wider setting, such a space is still within the organisation and ultimately subject to its influences.

While institutional contexts supportive of systematic reflection are not as common as is frequently assumed, the local context within which a particular group is situated must be one in which there are norms that counter negative features of the wider social context (e.g. one group norm might be that patterns of oppression are not accepted as legitimate and are questioned). It is this local context that is the focus of learning, and it needs to provide what is best to foster the learning process. One of the most important steps in the creation of the local context is to filter the negative influences of the larger context, for example, by developing ground rules for a class that make unacceptable remarks by students that might be taken as 'putting down' other members of the group. However, it is sometimes easier to counter negative influences than it is to create positive ones, especially when models for good practice are hard to find. For example, it is easier to filter expressions of racism through banning offensive statements than it is to establish a climate of safety in which members of minority groups feel valued and supported. For the latter to occur, trust is essential, but it can only be built progressively, never assumed.

There are a number of factors to be considered in establishing conditions for reflection in the light of an awareness of context. These include what teachers are and are not able to do, the need to build trust and the problematic nature of so doing, the need to create situations in which learners are able to make their own meaning rather than have it imposed on them, the ways in which disciplines and professions frame what is possible in the higher education setting, consideration of whose interests are being pursued in reflective activities and the importance of creating and respecting boundaries between the institutional imperatives of learning and the personal domain of the learner.

Limitations on teachers

It is especially important to recognise that the influence of the sociopolitical, or even institutional, context on teachers can have serious consequences for the local context. Teachers may be too captive to the larger context to relate to the experience of participants and thus fail to engage them in meaningful reflection. They themselves may be unaware of the power of context and so operate in naive ways that ignore many of the important dynamics that affect learners: they may not be sensitive to some of the traps. They may collude with the dominant culture and guide reflection in order to avoid engagement with issues of power and control. Reflection on creating the local context may help teachers become more aware of previously unrecognised forces and the ways they are limited by them.

The influence of power and knowledge can never be avoided, though, and it would be simplistic to imply that a reflective space can be treated by the good intentions of a teacher alone. Teachers need to be sensitive to whether particular reflective practices have been misused in this local context and have thus created a negative response from participants – for example, through the intrusive use of journals or demands for disclosures from students inappropriate to the course. Sometimes particular practices may have been employed by a dominant group to the disadvantage of others. Such practices need to be avoided. Also, it is important to check that participants respect reflective processes of the kind that may be introduced, or at least are neutral to them.

Building trust

A good reflective space or microcontext requires a level of trust commensurate with the levels of disclosure that might reasonably be expected. Trust inevitably involves risk however; respect for participants and norms of confidentiality need to be actively worked towards and agreed to. Participants need to be able to express themselves intellectually and emotionally, and know that such expression, and discussion of it, is legitimate and accepted.

Barriers that prevent open interaction and reciprocal communication need to be addressed. This may involve identifying differences of power or status among participants (i.e. when some hold public or implied positions of authority over others) and differences in levels of contribution by members of the group (i.e. ensuring that some members are not silenced). Oppressive behaviour (e.g. remarks directed to others because of visible or implied differences that are not related to the content of discussion) may need to be confronted and such behaviour worked through should it occur. The teacher should be aware that participants may have a history of seeing others in the group as barriers to their learning. Difference is always a challenge: in some cultures the expression of thoughts and feelings to relative strangers is problematic. Particular ways of promoting openness may in themselves act as barriers to disadvantage some learners.

Permitting the making of meaning

Suggestions for activities need to be sensitive to the unique characteristics of the group and acknowledge that the outcomes desired by members may differ from expectations of the institution with which the activity may be associated or the teacher involved. The intent of participants must be accepted to a significant extent in order that they can find their own meaning within the learning situation. Their intent may not at first be apparent to themselves or to others. Their articulated points of view are to be respected even if they are also to be challenged. It is important to introduce activities in ways that provide an understandable rationale for their use, allowing participants consciously to opt in or opt out without direct or implied coercion, and indicating that time will be available for debriefing. The processes selected need to take account of emotions and work with them as appropriate to the task and context. It is only when the need for learners to make their own meaning in ways that connect with their unique experience is accepted that learners can feel free to reflect within the limits of the activity proposed.

Framing by disciplines and professions

Everything we do is framed and situated. This framing rarely occurs through our own volition but is part of the world we experience as given. Framing imposes assumptions, it legitimises practices and it provides a language for describing and analysing what we do. The processes of framing are not ones of which we are usually conscious. Of particular significance in professional education is the framing imposed by particular disciplinary and professional contexts within which teachers and students operate. Disciplines and professions define what counts as legitimate knowledge and acceptable practice by their members. The invisibility of this framing offers a major challenge for teachers in working with students, as staff are normally enculturated into their discipline or profession and take it for granted. While this framing of context forms major barriers to the construction of microcontexts for teaching and learning, it needs to be subject to critique and challenge by teachers working together concertedly over time. Examples of successful challenges can be found in the ways in which gender assumptions about access to professional education have been successfully challenged in many professional areas, and how traditional notions of the route of initial training through low level non-academic work have been overturned in a number of the health professions.

Whose interests are being pursued?

The broader context in which reflective activities take place must, then, always be considered. 'Who establishes the activity for whom?' is often the basic question to be considered. When there are differences of power between individuals or groups, as is inevitably the case in teaching and learning, there are many opportunities for one party unwittingly to oppress the other. For example, if reflection is initiated by a teacher who is a member of a particular dominant social group, for those who are not members of the group there is the risk that participation in reflection will merely add to oppressive activities that exist, rather than exposing or confronting them. The most likely outcome will be compliance, in which participants go through the motions of reflection without revealing (sometimes even to themselves) what are fundamental learning issues. For example, a student may attribute his or her inability to function well to a personal lack of confidence rather than a failure on the part of their teacher adequately to address and confront their own (low) expectations about what it is possible for that particular student to achieve.

Under other less oppressive circumstances resistance from participants may be evident. Indeed, resistance is often a positive feature, though sometimes inconvenient for teachers, as it can indicate that power dynamics are being subverted. However, unless the institution or organisation in which the activity is promoted is credibly committed to anti-oppressive practices for all social groups (for example, being known to be active in dealing with issues associated with sexism, racism and other dominant group practices), then a sufficient climate of trust and safety – to offset the inherently risky and disruptive nature of reflection itself – may not be possible to enable effective reflection to occur.

Boundaries of reflection

It is necessary to establish a common discourse for reflection within the domain of knowledge that is being considered. The range and class of activities that will be the object of reflection should be agreed. Without this there is potential to enter inadvertently areas that are beyond the normal contract between teacher and learner and thus to face tricky ethical dilemmas. There is a need for boundaries on what outcomes of reflection are to be shared with others and these boundaries should be clear from the start. The boundary between professional space and private space is not fixed, but needs to be clarified in any given setting in order to avoid a particular version of what Habermas (1987) has referred to as 'colonisation of the life-world'; that is the intrusion of institutions – work, profession, educational institution – into the domain that has been regarded as personal and in the hands of the individual to share.

If boundaries of reflection are defined by ideas and concepts in the discipline being studied, this should be explicit and attention given to developing a shared vocabulary and understanding of central concepts. For example, students may be expected in class to say what they know about the topic in the language of concepts that are publicly accepted, rather than explore uncertainties that may exist within their own frame of reference. If the boundaries are to include the professional practice of the learner (as in a work placement), then this should be agreed also. Moreover, if learning with an emancipatory focus that might involve exploring personal and social relationships is the *raison d'être* (e.g. Mezirow, 1990), then this too must be part of what is accepted by all parties as legitimate. Of course, it is also in the disruption of such boundaries that possibilities for different understandings occur.

When discourse crosses one or more of these boundaries without becoming questioned and contracts of acceptable behaviour renegotiated, then trouble will arise and ethical dilemmas will quickly emerge. The respecting of boundaries is of particular significance in educational institutions where the shift in discourse from public knowledge to personal reflection is problematic for both staff and students. For example, in religious education it needs to be clear whether the focus of attention in any particular situation is on understanding the particular theological tradition being studied or exploring personal crises of faith. The contracts of understanding between staff and student would differ in each case. Teachers may have to mediate between the expectations of the cultural or institutional context and that of learners to establish a clear contract that defines the boundaries for this local context. This does not mean that insights from personal experience or from understanding a particular tradition are not available to be drawn upon in either case. However, it does imply that self-disclosure of affective responses should not be required without prior agreement.

Perceptions of context

It is sometimes comfortable to assume that it is possible to identify what the context might be in any given situation. Unfortunately, this is very rarely the case. Understanding context is always hard-won and there are always multiple readings of what it might be. Each participant will see it differently as each brings their own personal foundation of knowledge and set of life experiences with them. There will be competing views about how context is to be interpreted, and differences of perception. Context will be manifest in the behaviour and attitudes of each participant as each will have experienced, to a greater or lesser extent, forms of oppression from the wider context that bring that context into their own personal world. Context will be manifest in internal oppression of participants as they recreate the external world in their own. While context is a useful organising idea, it cannot be treated as unproblematic in conception or use.

Implications for those facilitating reflection

Teachers need to consider themselves, the learners with whom they are working, the local context in which they operate, the processes they use, and the expected outcomes as defined by each party (including external ones, for example, the institution or accrediting body). They need to create a microcontext within which the kinds of reflection acceptable to learners and consistent with the values of learners and teachers can occur and that does not reproduce those aspects of the dominant context that impose barriers to learning.

Of the many factors that are important, the following indicate some that *teachers* may need to take into account.

In focusing on context

- Their awareness of what elements of the cultural, institutional or disciplinary context may need to be filtered or confronted in this local context, or may be used to advantage in the learning event (i.e. a particular session in a course).
- How they can cope with the demands of the institution within which they operate.
- Their own power and the ways in which this might impact on learners singularly and collectively.

Reflection by teachers and learners before the learning event is as important as reflection during, or after, it. Understanding beforehand the factors that may be operating within the future learning event is necessary in order to work creatively within that event. Teachers and learners bring with them all the essential elements of the larger context: they are imbued with the assumptions and practices of their culture, the demands and expectations imposed by the educational institution, and the attitudes and ways of operating that dominate the particular discipline. Periodically, and in each new situation, teachers need to explore specifically how the subjects they are dealing with, and the learners they are working with, are affected, both positively and negatively, by this larger context. In particular, the larger context constructs the teacher as having specific power. The teacher needs to be aware of this and ensure that it is used productively within the learning event. Reflection on the larger context in relationship to the subject and the learners can help the teacher work on how to cope with these operating forces and develop strategies that will counter them, or use them creatively.

In focusing on learners

- Their assumptions about the particular learning event, their own intent and how this may relate to the intent and expectations of learners.
- How they can elicit from learners responses appropriate to the learning and reflective processes of the given activity.
- The prior experience of learners, both with regard to the substantive learning outcomes that are sought and the particular processes of reflection that are being contemplated.
- How they can respect learners and their agendas and take these as the focus rather than other agendas of the culture, institution or themselves.

Learners carry with them assumptions and practices of the larger context. However, their personal experience of their culture, their institution and the particular discipline may have affected them in different ways. It could have given them particular expectations and demands and affected how they approach the various processes of the learning event. It may be necessary, for example, to find an opportunity in any part of a course to introduce particular activities that elicit learners' assumptions about a learning event, and their intent or expectations of it. The planning for the event needs to respect these elicited assumptions and intents, give them priority, and relate them creatively to the assumptions and intent of the culture, institute or teacher. It is especially important to elicit and work in accord with emotional responses that learners bring to the event because these are often the most powerful influences affecting how learners engage in the event. While some of these insights may be known to the teacher from previous experience, they will probably need to be verified and filled out at an early stage.

In focusing on processes

- How they can construct a learning environment in awareness of the influence of dominant groups and intervene appropriately within it to counter oppressive behaviour on the part of learners towards each other.
- How they can create appropriate reflection processes for this context that will assist the learner to come to meaningful learning.

- How to avoid mechanistic processes that do not respond to unique circumstances and particular learners involved.
- How they can establish patterns of reciprocal communication and create a place of trust and respect in which reflection and exploration can flourish.
- The need to establish agreements about what is and is not legitimate in the particular activity and about the appropriate roles of learners and teacher, and to respect and reinforce such agreements.

There is a uniqueness in each learning event that needs to be respected. To repeat the same approaches, processes and practices with every group of learners does not respect the variation in experience that necessarily exists. If teachers are sufficiently sensitive to the climate in the group, activities can be initiated to draw out some of the feeling of participants, and even reveal aspects of the dynamics of power. This can help teachers build appropriate ways of relating that respect the different approaches and further foster an atmosphere of trust and respect. It may be necessary to set ground rules. These are determined by the purpose and particular composition of the group rather than by the subject to be worked with. If the group is divided, distracted and discontented, it is unlikely that fruitful learning will be achieved. It is only when the teacher has begun to work with these issues of the group that it will be clear what reflective processes and modes of use are likely to engage members of the group in meaningful learning.

This list of factors is quite daunting, but it is hard to envisage a list that is substantially smaller yet which takes into account the issues that were portrayed earlier. It points to the need for increasing sophistication of teachers in professional education, and for opportunities for them to develop these skills over time.

If we return to the problems of use and abuse of reflection introduced earlier, we can illustrate this approach with a few examples. *Recipe following* is inappropriate because it does not take account of the uniqueness of the learners, their prior experience, the particular context in which they are operating nor the need to address any unhelpful dynamics of power or oppression which may intrude. *Reflection without learning* can indicate similar inappropriate approaches, and also the inability of the teacher to offer appropriate reflection processes for this context. *Belief that reflection can be easily contained* conflicts with all the evidence about learning that we have. It ignores the power of the larger context and the personal history of the learner. *Failure to design for context* is a particular outcome of the failure to recognise the importance of context as outlined in this article. *Intellectualising reflection* can be a lack of recognition that the emotional is important in learning, or a sign of teachers' inability to handle the emotional aspects of the learning process. *Going beyond the expertise of the teacher* may indicate the inability of the teacher to reflect on his or her own preparedness and ability to enter into this learning situation. *Inappropriate disclosure* may indicate the inability of the teacher to frame the reflective process or to contract appropriately with learners. *Excessive use of teacher power* arises from many aspects of the context and it may be related as much to teachers' own perceived powerlessness in an institution as from their failure to recognise the primacy of the learner.

Conclusion

Reflection can obviously occur even when circumstances are less than ideal – the capacity for humans to learn in the least auspicious conditions is quite remarkable. Some form of learning can occur in almost any situation. However, there is limited scope for critical reflection if the microcontext is not created to counter many of the factors that can readily inhibit it. If conditions of the kind discussed above are not generally found then misuse and abuse can flourish. It is necessary for teachers to be clear about whether they are really interested in fostering reflection and whether they are prepared to take a sufficiently contextualised view of it into account. If they are, they must confront themselves, their processes, and their outcomes. An honest self-appraisal conducted in conjunction with peers is one of the hallmarks of an effective promoter of reflection. Indeed, such an appraisal is needed when teachers are working with any processes which have the potential to blur the differences between the personal and professional lifeworlds.

Note

1   Learning in this chapter is interpreted broadly. It includes reconceptualisation and reframing of situations as well as more conventional outcomes which can be readily assessed.

References

Boud, D., Keogh, R. and Walker, D. (1985) Promoting reflection in learning: a model, in: D. Boud, R. Keogh and D. Walker (Eds) *Reflection: turning experience into learning*, pp. 18–40 (London, Kogan Page).
Boud, D. and Walker, D. (1990) Making the most of experience, *Studies in Continuing Education*, 12(2), pp. 61–80.
Brookfield, S.D. (1987) *Developing Critical Thinkers: challenging adults to explore alternative ways of thinking and acting* (San Francisco, CA, Jossey-Bass).
Brookfield, S.D. (1995) *Becoming a Critically Reflective Teacher* (San Francisco, CA, Jossey-Bass).
Bryant, I., Usher, R. and Johnston, R. (1996) *Adult Education and the Postmodern Challenge* (London, Routledge).
Calderhead, J. and Gates, P. (Eds) (1993) *Conceptualizing Reflection in Teacher Development* (London, Falmer Press).

Clift, R.T., Houston, R.W. and Prignach, M.C. (Eds) (1990) *Encouraging Reflective Practice in Education: an analysis of issues and programmes* (New York, Teachers College Press).

Dewey, J. (1933) *How We Think: a restaurant of the relation of reflective thinking to the educative process* (Lexington, MA, D.C. Heath).

Eraut, M. (1995) Schön shock: a case for reframing reflection-in-action, *Teachers and Teaching*, 1, pp. 9–22.

Gould, N. and Taylor, I. (Eds) (1996) *Reflective Learning for Social Work: research, theory and practice* (Aldershot, Ashgate Publishing).

Greenwood, J. (1993) Reflective practice: a critique of the work of Argyris and Schön, *Journal of Advanced Nursing*, 18, pp. 1,183–1,187.

Habermas, J. (1987) *The Theory of Communicative Action. Vol. 2. Lifeworld and System: a critique of functionalist reason*, tr. Thomas McCarthy (Cambridge, Polity Press).

Hatton, N. and Smith, D. (1994) Reflection in teacher education: towards definition and implementation, *Teaching and Teacher Education*, 11, pp. 33–49.

Johns, C. and Freshwater, D. (1998) *Transforming Nursing through Reflective Practice* (Oxford, Blackwell Science).

Kolb, D.A. (1984) *Experiential Learning* (Englewood Cliffs, NJ, Prentice-Hall).

Loughran, J. (1996) *Developing Reflective Practice: learning about teaching and learning through modelling* (London, Falmer Press).

Maslow, A.H. (1968) *Toward a Psychology of Being* (Princeton, NJ, Van Nostrand).

Mezirow, J. (1990) *Fostering Critical Reflection in Adulthood: a good to transformative and emancipatory learning* (San Francisco, CA, Jossey-Bass).

Michelson, E. (1996) Usual suspects: experience, reflection and the (en)gendering of knowledge, *International Journal of Lifelong Education*, 15, pp. 438–454.

Morrison, K. (1996) Developing reflective practice in higher degree students through a learning journal, *Studies in Higher Education*, 21, pp. 317–332.

Palmer, A., Burns, S. and Bulman, C. (Eds) (1994) *Reflective Practice in Nursing: the growth of the professional practitioner* (London, Blackwell Scientific).

Parlett, M.R. and Hamilton, D.F. (1977) Evaluation as illumination: a new approach to the study of innovatory programmes, in: D. Hamilton, D. Jenkins, C. King, B. MacDonald and M. Parlett *Beyond the Numbers Game: a reader in educational evaluation*, pp. 6–22 (London, Macmillan).

Schön, D.A. (1983) *The Reflective Practitioner* (London, Temple Smith).

Schön, D.A. (1987) *Educating the Reflective Practitioner* (San Francisco, CA, Jossey-Bass).

Smith, D.L. and Hatton, N. (1993) Reflection in teacher education: a study in progress, *Educational Research and Perspectives*, 20, pp. 13–23.

Smyth, J. (1996) Developing socially critical educators, in: D. Boud and N. Miller (Eds) *Working with Experience: animating learning*, pp. 41–57 (London, Routledge).

Sumsion, J. and Fleet, A. (1996) Reflection: can we assess it? Should we assess it? *Assessment and Evaluation in Higher Education*, 21, pp. 121–130.

Usher, R., Bryant, I. and Johnston, R. (1997) *Adult Education and the Postmodern Challenge: learning beyond the Limits* (London, Routledge).

Walker, D. and Boud, D. (1992) Facilitating critical reflection: opportunities and issues for group learning, *A Quarterly Experience (Australian Journal of Experiential Learning)*, 29, pp. 10–20.

Yelloly, M. and Henkel, M. (1995) *Learning and Teaching in Social Work: towards reflective practice* (London, Jessica Kingsley).

Zeichner, K. and Liston, D. (1987) Teaching student teachers to reflect, *Harvard Educational Review*, 57, pp. 23–48.

Chapter 7

Legitimate peripheral participation in communities of practice

Jean Lave and Etienne Wenger

In this chapter we recast the central characteristics of historical realizations of apprenticeship in terms of legitimate peripheral participation in communities of practice. First, we discuss the structuring resources that shape the process and content of learning possibilities and apprentices' changing perspectives on what is known and done. Then we argue that 'transparency' of the socio-political organization of practice, of its content and of the artefacts engaged in practice, is a crucial resource for increasing participation. We next examine the relation of newcomers to the discourse of practice. This leads to a discussion of how identity and motivation are generated as newcomers move toward full participation. Finally, we explore contradictions inherent in learning, and the relations of the resulting conflicts to the development of identity and the transformation of practice.

Structuring resources for learning in practice

One of the first things people think of when apprenticeship is mentioned is the master–apprentice relation. But in practice the roles of masters are surprisingly variable across time and place. A specific master–apprentice relation is not even ubiquitously characteristic of apprenticeship learning. Indeed, neither Yucatec midwives nor quartermasters learn in specific master–apprentice relations. Newcomers to Alcoholics Anonymous (AA) do have special relations with specific old-timers who act as their sponsors, but these relations are not what defines them as newcomers. In contrast, tailors' apprentices most certainly have specific relations with their masters, without whom they wouldn't be apprentices. Master tailors must sponsor apprentices before the latter can have legitimate access to participation in the community's productive activities. In short, the form in which such legitimate access is secured for apprentices depends on the characteristics of the division of labour in the

This is an edited version of a chapter previously published in *Situated Learning*, 1991, Cambridge: Cambridge University Press.

social milieu in which the community of practice is located. Thus, the midwife is learning a specialism within her own family of orientation, a form of labour different, but not separated in marked ways, from the widely distributed 'ordinary' activities of everyday life; legitimate participation comes diffusely through membership in family and community. Where apprentices learn a specialized occupation, sponsorship into a community of practice – within a community in the more general sense – becomes an issue. Intentional relations, and even contractual relations with a specific master, are common. It should be clear that, in shaping the relation of masters to apprentices, the issue of conferring legitimacy is more important than the issue of providing teaching.

Even in the case of the tailors, where the relation of apprentice to master is specific and explicit, it is not this relationship, but rather the apprentice's relations to other apprentices and even to other masters that organize opportunities to learn; an apprentice's own master is too distant, an object of too much respect, to engage with in awkward attempts at a new activity. In AA, old-timers who act as 'sponsors' reportedly withhold advice and instruction appropriate to later stages; they hold back and wait until the newcomer becomes 'ready' for a next step through increasing participation in the community (Alibrandi, 1977). In all the cases of apprenticeship discussed in this chapter researchers insist that there is very little observable teaching; the more basic phenomenon is learning. The practice of the community creates the potential 'curriculum' in the broadest sense – that which may be learned by newcomers with legitimate peripheral access. Learning activity appears to have a characteristic pattern. There are strong goals for learning because learners, as peripheral participants, can develop a view of what the whole enterprise is about, and what there is to be learned. Learning itself is an improvised practice: a learning curriculum unfolds in opportunities for engagement in practice. It is not specified as a set of dictates for proper practice.

In apprenticeship opportunities for learning are, more often than not, given structure by work practices instead of by strongly asymmetrical master–apprentice relations. Under these circumstances learners may have a space of 'benign community neglect' in which to configure their own learning relations with other apprentices. There may be a looser coupling between relations among learners on the one hand and the often hierarchical relations between learners and old-timers on the other hand, than where directive pedagogy is the central motive of institutional organization. It seems typical of apprenticeship that apprentices learn mostly in relation with other apprentices. There is anecdotal evidence (Butler, personal communication; Hass, n.d.) that where the circulation of knowledge among peers and near-peers is possible, it spreads exceedingly rapidly and effectively. The effectiveness of the circulation of information among peers suggests that engaging in practice, rather than being its object, may well be a *condition* for the effectiveness of learning.

So far, we have observed that the authority of masters and their involvement in apprenticeship varies dramatically across communities of practice. We have also pointed out that structuring resources for learning come from a variety of sources, not only from pedagogical activity. We argue that a coherent explanation of these observations depends upon *decentring* common notions of mastery and pedagogy. This decentring strategy is, in fact, deeply embedded in our situation approach – for to shift as we have from the notion of an individual learner to the concept of legitimate peripheral participation in communities of practice is precisely to decentre analysis of learning. To take a decentred view of master–apprentice relations leads to an understanding that mastery resides not in the master but in the organization of the community of practice of which the master is part: the master as the locus of authority (in several senses) is, after all, as much a product of the conventional, centred theory of learning as is the individual learner. Similarly, a decentred view of the master as pedagogue moves the focus of analysis away from teaching and on to the intricate structuring of a community's learning resources.

The place of knowledge: participation, learning curricula, communities of practice

The social relations of apprentices within a community change through their direct involvement in activities; in the process, the apprentices' understanding and knowledgeable skills develop. In the recent past, the only means we have had for understanding the processes by which these changes occur have come from conventional speculations about the nature of 'informal' learning: that is, apprentices are supposed to acquire the 'specifics' of practice through 'observation and imitation'. But this view is in all probability wrong in every particular, or right in particular circumstances, but for the wrong reasons. We argue instead that the effects of peripheral participation on knowledge-in-practice are not properly understood; and that studies of apprenticeships have presumed too literal a coupling of work processes and learning processes.

To begin with, newcomers' legitimate peripherality provides them with more than an 'observational' lookout post: it crucially involves *participation* as a way of learning – of both absorbing and being absorbed in – the 'culture of practice'. An extended period of legitimate peripherality provides learners with opportunities to make the culture of practice theirs. From a broadly peripheral perspective, apprentices gradually assemble a general idea of what constitutes the practice of the community. This uneven sketch of the enterprise (available if there is legitimate access) might include who is involved; what they do; what everyday life is like; how masters talk, walk, work and generally conduct their lives; how people who are not part of the community of practice interact with it; what other learners are doing; and what learners need to learn to become full practitioners. It includes an increasing understanding of how, when, and about what old-timers collaborate, collude and collide, and what they enjoy, dislike, respect and admire. In particular, it offers exemplars (which are grounds and motivation for learning activity), including masters, finished products and more advanced apprentices in the process of becoming full practitioners.

Such a general view, however, is not likely to be frozen in initial impressions. Viewpoints from which to understand the practice evolve through changing participation in the division of labour, changing relations to ongoing community practices, and changing social relations in the community. And learners have multiple structured relations with ongoing practice in other ways. Apprenticeship learning is not 'work-driven' in the way stereotypes of informal learning have suggested; the ordering of learning and of everyday practice do not coincide. Production activity-segments must be learned in different sequences from those in which a production process commonly unfolds, if peripheral, less intense, less complex, less vital tasks are learned before more central aspects of practice.

Consider, for instance, the tailors' apprentices, whose involvement starts with both initial preparations for the tailors' daily labour and finishing details on completed garments. The apprentices progressively move backward through the production process to cutting jobs. (This kind of progression is quite common across cultures and historical periods.) Under these circumstances, the initial 'circumferential' perspective absorbed in partial, peripheral, apparently trivial activities – running errands, delivering messages, or accompanying others – takes on new significance: it provides a first approximation to an armature of the structure of the community of practice. Things learned, and various and changing viewpoints, can be arranged and interrelated in ways that gradually transform that skeletal understanding.

When directive teaching in the form of prescriptions about proper practice generates one circumscribed form of participation (in school), preempting participation in ongoing practice as the legitimate source of learning opportunities, the goal of complying with the requirements specified by teaching engenders a practice different from that intended (Bourdieu, 1977). In such cases, even though the pedagogical structure of the circumstances of learning has moved away from the principle of legitimate peripheral participation with respect to the target practice, legitimate peripheral participation is still the core of the learning that takes place. This leads us to distinguish between a *learning curriculum* and a *teaching curriculum*. A learning curriculum consists of situated opportunities (thus including exemplars of various sorts often thought of as 'goals') for the improvisational development of new practice (Lave, 1989). A learning curriculum is a field of learning resources in everyday practice *viewed from the perspective of learners*. A teaching curriculum, by contrast, is constructed for the instruction of newcomers. When a teaching curriculum supplies – and thereby limits – structuring resources for learning, the meaning of what is learned (and control of access to it, both in its peripheral forms and its subsequently more complex and intensified, though possibly more fragmented, forms) is mediated through an instructor's participation, by an external view of what knowing is about. The learning curriculum in didactic situations, then, evolves out of participation in a specific community of practice engendered by pedagogical relations and by a prescriptive view of the target practice as a subject matter, as well as out of the many and various relations that tie participants to their own and to other institutions.

A learning curriculum is essentially situated. It is not something that can be considered in isolation, manipulated in arbitrary didactic terms, or analysed apart from the social relations that shape legitimate peripheral participation. A learning curriculum is thus characteristic of a community. In using the term 'community', we do not imply some primordial culture-sharing entity. We assume that members have different interests, make diverse contributions to activity and hold varied viewpoints. In our view, participation at multiple levels is entailed in membership in a *community of practice*. Nor does the term community imply necessarily co-presence, a well-defined, identifiable group, or socially visible boundaries. It does imply participation in an activity system about which participants share understandings concerning what they are doing and what that means in their lives and for their communities.

The concept of community underlying the notion of legitimate peripheral participation, and hence of 'knowledge' and its 'location' in the lived-in world, is both crucial and subtle. The community of practice of midwifery or tailoring involves much more than the technical knowledgeable skill involved in delivering babies or producing clothes. A community of practice is a set of relations among persons, activity and world, over time and in relation with other tangential and overlapping communities of practice. A community of practice is an intrinsic condition for the existence of knowledge, not least because it provides the interpretive support necessary for making sense of its heritage. Thus, participation in the cultural practice in which any knowledge exists is an epistemological principle of learning. The social structure of this practice, its power relations and its conditions for legitimacy define possibilities for learning (i.e. for legitimate peripheral participation).

It is possible to delineate the community that is the site of a learning process by analysing the reproduction cycles of the communities that seem to be involved and their relations. For the quartermasters, the cycle of navigational practice is quite short; a complete reproduction of the practice of quartermastering may take place every five or six years (as a novice enters, gradually becomes a full participant, begins to work with newcomer quartermasters who in their own turn become full participants and reach the point at which they are ready to work with newcomers). The reproduction cycle of the midwives', the tailors' or the butchers' communities is much longer. In AA, its length is rather variable as individuals go through successive steps at their own pace. Observing the span of developmental cycles is only a beginning to such an analysis (and a rough approximation that sets aside consideration of the transformation and change inherent in ongoing practice), for each such cycle has its own trajectory, benchmarks, blueprints and careers (Stack, 1989).

In addition to the useful analytic questions suggested by a temporal focus on communities of practice, there is a further reason to address the delineation of communities of practice in processual, historical terms. Claims *about* the definition of a community of practice and the community of practice actually in process of reproduction in that location may not coincide – a point worth careful consideration.

For example, in most high schools there is a group of students engaged over a substantial period of time in learning physics. What community of practice is in the process of reproduction? Possibly the students participate only in the reproduction of the high school itself. But assuming that the practice of physics is also being reproduced in some form, there are vast differences between the ways high school physics students participate in and give meaning to their activity and the way professional physicists do. The actual reproducing community of practice, within which schoolchildren learn about physics, is not the community of physicists but the community of schooled adults. Children are introduced into the latter community (and its humble relation with the former community) during their school years. The reproduction cycles of the physicists' community start much later, possibly only in university (Traweek, 1988).

In this view, problems of schooling are not, at their most fundamental level, pedagogical. Above all, they have to do with the ways in which the community of adults reproduces itself, with the places that newcomers can or cannot find in such communities, and with relations that can or cannot be established between these newcomers and the cultural and political life of the community.

In summary, rather than learning by replicating the performances of others or by acquiring knowledge transmitted in instruction, we suggest that learning occurs through centripetal participation in the learning curriculum of the ambient community. Because the place of knowledge is within a community of practice, questions of learning must be addressed within the developmental cycles of that community, a recommendation that creates a diagnostic tool for distinguishing among communities of practice.

The problem of access: transparency and sequestration

The key to legitimate peripherality is access by newcomers to the community of practice and all that membership entails. But though this is essential to the reproduction of any community, it is always problematic at the same time. To become a full member of a community of practice requires access to a wide range of ongoing activity, old-timers and other members of the community; and to information, resources and opportunities for participation. The issue is so central to membership in communities of practice that, in a sense, all that we have said so far is about access. Here we discuss the problem more specifically in connection with issues of understanding and control, which along with involvement in productive activity are related aspects of the legitimate peripherality of participants in a practice.

The artefacts employed in ongoing practice, the technology of practice, provide a good arena in which to discuss the problem of access to understanding. In general, social scientists who concern themselves with learning treat technology as a given and are not analytic about its interrelations with other aspects of a community of practice. Becoming a full participant certainly includes engaging with the technologies of everyday practice, as well as participating in the social relations, production processes and other activities of communities of practice. But the understanding to be gained from engagement with technology can be extremely varied depending on the form of participation enabled by its use. Participation involving technology is especially significant because the artefacts used within a cultural practice carry a substantial portion of that practice's heritage. Thus, understanding the technology of practice is more than learning to use tools; it is a way to connect with the history of the practice and to participate more directly in its cultural life.

The significance of artefacts in the full complexity of their relations with the practice can be more or less *transparent* to learners. Transparency in its simplest form may just imply that the inner workings of an artefact are available for the learner's inspection: the black box can be opened, it can become a 'glass box'. But there is more to understanding the use and significance of an artefact: knowledge within a community of practice and ways of perceiving and manipulating objects characteristic of community practices are encoded in artefacts in ways that can be more be less revealing. Obviously, the transparency of any technology always exists with respect to some purpose and is intricately tied to the cultural practice and social organization within which the technology is meant to function: it cannot be viewed as a feature of an artefact in itself but as a process that involves specific forms of participation, in which the technology fulfils a mediating function. Apprentice quartermasters not only have access to the physical activities going on around them and to the tools of the trade; they participate in information flows and conversations, in a context in which they can make sense of what they observe and hear. In focusing on the epistemological role of artefacts in the context of the social organization of knowledge, this notion of transparency constitutes, as it were, the cultural organization of access. As such, it does not apply to technology only, but to all forms of access to practice.

Productive activity and understanding are not separate, or even separable, but dialectically related. Thus, the term *transparency* when used here in connection with technology refers to the way in which using artefacts and understanding their significance interact to become one learning process.

Control and selection, as well as the need for access, are inherent in communities of practice. Thus access is liable to manipulation, giving legitimate peripherality an ambivalent status: depending on the organization of access, legitimate peripherality can either promote or prevent legitimate participation. In a study of butchers' apprentices, Marshall (1972) provides examples of how access can be denied. The trade school and its shop exercises did not simulate the central practices of meat cutting in supermarkets, much less make them accessible to apprentices; on-the-job training was not much of an improvement. Worse, the master butchers confined their apprentices to jobs that were removed from activities rather than peripheral to them. To the extent that the community of practice routinely sequesters newcomers, either very directly as in the example of apprenticeship for the butchers, or in more subtle and pervasive ways as in schools, these newcomers are prevented from peripheral participation. In either case legitimacy is not in question. Schoolchildren are legitimately peripheral, but kept from participation in the social world more generally. The butchers' apprentices participate legitimately, but not peripherally, in that they are not given productive access to activity in the community of practitioners.

An important point about such sequestering when it is institutionalized is that it encourages a folk epistemology of dichotomies, for instance, between 'abstract' and 'concrete' knowledge. These categories do not reside in the world as distinct forms of *knowledge*, nor do they reflect some putative hierarchy of forms of knowledge among practitioners. Rather, they derive from the nature of the new practice generated by sequestration. *Abstraction* in this sense stems from the disconnectedness of a particular cultural practice. Participation in that practice is neither more nor less abstract or concrete, experiential or cerebral, than in any other. Thus, legitimate peripheral participation as the core concept of relations of learning places the explanatory burden for issues such as 'understanding' and 'levels' of abstraction or conceptualization not on one type of learning as opposed to another, but on the cultural practice in which the learning is taking place, on issues of access, and on the transparency of the cultural environment with respect to the meaning of what is being learned. Insofar as the notion of transparency, taken very broadly, is a way of organizing activities that makes their meaning visible, it opens an alternative approach to the traditional dichotomy between learning experientially and learning at a distance, between learning by doing and learning by abstraction.

Discourse and practice

The characterization of language in learning has, in discussions of conventional contrasts between formal and informal learning, been treated as highly significant in classifying ways of transmitting knowledge. Verbal instruction has been assumed to have special, and especially effective properties with respect to the generality and scope of the understanding that learners come away with, while instruction by demonstration – learning by 'observation and imitation' – is supposed to produce the opposite, a literal and narrow effect.

Close analysis of both instructional discourse and cases of apprenticeship raise a different point: issues about language, like those about the role of masters, may well have more to do with legitimacy of participation and with access to peripherality than they do with knowledge transmission. Indeed, as Jordan (1989) argues, learning to become a legitimate participant in a community involves learning how to talk (and be silent) in the manner of full participants. In AA telling the story of the life of the non-drinking alcoholic is clearly a major vehicle for the display of membership. Models for constructing AA life stories are widely available in published accounts of alcoholics' lives and in the storytelling performances of old-timers. Early on, newcomers learn to preface their contributions to AA meetings with the simple identifying statement 'I'm a recovering alcoholic', and, shortly, to introduce themselves and sketch the problems that brought them to AA. They begin by describing these events in non-AA terms. Their accounts meet with counterexemplary stories by more-experienced members who do not criticize or correct newcomers' accounts directly. They gradually generate a view that matches more closely the AA model, eventually producing skilled testimony in public meetings and gaining validation from others as they demonstrate the appropriate understanding.

In the *Psychology of Literacy*, Scribner and Cole (1981) speculate that asking questions – learning how to 'do' school appropriately – may be a major part of what school teaches. This is also Jordan's conclusion about Yucatec midwives' participation in biomedical, state-sponsored training courses. She argues that the verbal instruction provided by health officials has the effect of teaching midwives how to talk in biomedical terms when required. Such talk only serves to give them 'face validity' in the eyes of others who believe in the authoritative character of biomedicine. But Jordan argues that it has no effect on their existing practice.

This point about language use is consonant with the earlier argument that didactic instruction creates unintended practices. The conflict stems from the fact that there is a difference between talking *about* a practice from outside and talking *within* it. Thus the didactic use of language, not itself the discourse of practice, creates a new linguistic practice, which has an existence of its own. Legitimate peripheral participation in such linguistic practice is a form of learning, but does not imply that newcomers learn the actual practice the language is supposed to be about.

In a community or practice, there are no special forms of discourse aimed at apprentices or crucial to their centripetal movement toward full participation that correspond to the marked genres of the question–answer–evaluation format of classroom teaching, or the lecturing of college professors or midwife-training course instructors. But Jordan makes a further, acute, observation about language, this time about the role of *stories* in apprenticeship: she points out that stories play a major role in decision making (1989). This has implications for what and how newcomers learn. For apprenticeship learning is supported by conversations and stories about problematic and especially difficult cases:

> What happens is that as difficulties of one kind or another develop, stories of similar cases are offered up by the attendants [at a birth], all of whom, it should be remembered, are experts, having themselves given birth. In the ways in which these stories are treated, elaborated, ignored, taken up, characterized as typical and so on, the collaborative work of deciding on the present case is done … These stories, then, are packages of situated knowledge … To acquire a store of appropriate stories and, even more importantly, to know what are appropriate occasions for telling them, is then part of what it means to become a midwife.
>
> (Jordan, 1989: 935)

Orr (1990) describes comparable patterns of story telling in his research on the learning of machine-repair work: technicians who repair copier machines tell each other 'war stories' about their past experiences in making repairs. Such stories constitute a vital part of diagnosing and carrying out new repairs. In the process, newcomers learn how to make (sometimes difficult) repairs, they learn the skills of war-story telling, and they become legitimate participants in the community of practice. In AA also, discussions have a dual purpose. Participants engage in the work of staying sober and they do so through gradual construction of an identity. Telling the personal story is a tool of diagnosis and reinterpretation. Its communal use is essential to the fashioning of an identity as a recovered alcoholic, and thus to remaining sober. It becomes a display of membership by virtue of fulfilling a crucial function in the shared practice.

It is thus necessary to refine our distinction between *talking about* and *talking within* a practice. Talking within itself includes both talking within (e.g. exchanging information necessary to the progress of ongoing activities) and talking about (e.g. stories, community lore). Inside the shared practice, both forms of talk fulfil specific functions: engaging, focusing, and shifting attention, bringing about co-ordination, etc., on the one hand; and supporting communal forms of memory and reflection, as well as signalling membership, on the other. (And, similarly, talking about includes both forms of talk once it becomes part of a practice of its own, usually sequestered in some respects.) For newcomers then the purpose is not to learn *from* talk as a substitute for legitimate peripheral participation; it is to learn *to* talk as a key to legitimate peripheral participation.

Motivation and identity: effects of participation

It is important to emphasize that, during the extended period of legitimate participation typical of the cases of apprenticeship described here, newcomers participate in a community of practitioners as well as in productive activity. Legitimate peripheral participation is an initial form of membership characteristic of such a community. Acceptance by and interaction with acknowledged adept practitioners make learning legitimate and of value from the point of view of the apprentice. More generally, while learning in practice, apprentice learners know that there is a field for the mature practice of what they are learning to do – midwifing, tailoring, quartermastering, butchering or being sober. The community of midwives, tailors, quartermasters, butchers or non-drinking alcoholics and their productive relations with the world provide apprentices with these continuity-based 'futures'.

To be able to participate in a legitimately peripheral way entails that newcomers have broad access to arenas of mature practice. At the same time, productive peripherality requires less demands on time, effort and responsibility for work than for full participants. A newcomers' tasks are short and simple, the costs of errors are small, the apprentice has little responsibility for the activity as a whole. A newcomer's tasks tend to be positioned at the ends of branches of work processes, rather than in the middle of linked work segments. A midwife's apprentice runs errands. Tailors' apprentices do maintenance on the sewing machine before the master begins work, and finishing details when the master has completed a pair of trousers; a lot of time in between is spent sitting beside the master on his two-person bench. For the quartermasters, the earliest jobs are physically at the periphery of the work space. In many cases, distinctions between play and work, or between peripheral activity and other work, are little marked. In all the cases of apprenticeship mentioned here, however, it is also true that the initial, partial contributions of apprentices are useful. Even the AA newcomer, while reinterpreting his or her life, produces new material that contributes to the communal construction of an understanding of alcoholism. An apprentice's contributions to ongoing activity gain value in practice – a value that increases as the apprentice becomes more adept. As opportunities for understanding how well or poorly one's efforts contribute are evident in practice, legitimate participation of a peripheral kind provides an immediate ground for self-evaluation. The sparsity of tests, praise or blame typical of apprenticeship follows from the apprentice's legitimacy as a participant.

Notions like those of 'intrinsic rewards' in empirical studies of apprentice-ship focus quite narrowly on task knowledge and skill as the activities to be learned. Such knowledge is of course important; but a deeper sense of the value of participation to the community and the learner lies in *becoming* part of the community. Thus, making a hat reasonably well is seen as evidence that an apprentice tailor is becoming 'a masterful practitioner', though it may also be perceived in a more utilitarian vein in terms of reward or even value. Similarly, for alcoholics, telling one's life story or making a Twelfth Step call (carrying the AA message of recovery to other sufferers) confers a sense of belonging. Moving toward full participation in practice involves not just a greater commitment of time, intensified effort, more and broader responsi-bilities within the community, and more difficult and risky tasks, but, more significantly, an increasing sense of identify as a master practitioner.

When the process of increasing participation is not the primary motiva-tion for learning, it is often because 'didactic caretakers' assume responsibility for motivating newcomers. In such circumstances, the focus of attention shifts from co-participating in practice to acting upon the person-to-be-changed. Such a shift is typical of situations, such as schooling, in which pedagogically structured content organizes learning activities. Overlooking the importance of legitimate participation by newcomers in the target prac-tice has two related consequences. First, the identity of learners becomes an explicit object of change. When central participation is the subjective inten-tion motivating learning, changes in cultural identity and social relations are inevitably part of the process, but learning does not have to be medi-ated – and distorted – through a learner's view of 'self' as *object*. Second, where there is no cultural identity encompassing the activity in which newcomers participate and no field of mature practice for what is being learned, exchange value replaces the use value of increasing participation. The commoditization of learning engenders a fundamental contradiction between the use and exchange values of the outcome of learning, which manifests itself in conflicts between learning to know and learning to display knowledge for evaluation. Testing in schools and trade schools (unnecessary in situations of apprenticeship learning) is perhaps the most pervasive and salient example of a way of establishing the exchange value of knowledge. Test taking then becomes a new parasitic practice, the goal of which is to increase the exchange value of learning independently of its use value.

Contradictions and change: continuity and displacement

In considering learning as part of social practice, we have focused our atten-tion on the structures of social practice rather than privileging the structure of pedagogy as the source of learning. Learning understood as legitimate peripheral participation is not necessarily or directly dependent on pedagogical goals or official agenda, even in situations in which these goals appear to be a central factor (e.g. classroom instruction, tutoring). We have insisted that exposure to resources for learning is not restricted to a teaching curriculum and that instructional assistance is not construed as a purely interpersonal phenomenon; rather we have argued that learning must be understood with respect to a practice as a whole, with its multiplicity of relations – both within the community and with the world at large. Dissociating learning from pedagogical intentions opens the possibility of mismatch or conflict among practitioners' viewpoints in situations where learning is going on. These differences often must become constitutive of the content of learning.

We mentioned earlier that a major contradiction lies between legitimate peripheral participation as the means of achieving continuity over generations for the community of practice, and the displacement inherent in that same process as full participants are replaced (directly or indirectly) by newcomers-become-old-timers. Both Fortes (1938) and Goody (1989) have commented on this conflict between continuity and displacement, which is surely part of all learning. This tension is in fact fundamental – a basic contradiction of social reproduction, transformation and change. In recent accounts of learning by activity theorists (e.g. Engeström 1987), the major contradiction underlying the historical development of learning is that of the commodity. Certainly this is fundamental to the historical shaping of social reproduction as well as production. But we believe that a second contradiction – that between continuity and displacement – is also fundamental to the social relations of production and to the social reproduction of labour. Studies of learning might benefit from examining the field of relations generated by these interrelated contradictions. For if production and the social reproduction of persons are mutually entailed in the reproduction of the social order, the contradictions inherent in reproducing persons within the domestic group and other communities of practice do not go away when the form of production changes, but go through transformations of their own. How to characterize these contradictions in changing forms of production is surely the central question underlying a historical understanding of forms of learning, family and, of course, schooling.

The continuity–displacement contradiction is present during apprenticeship, whether apprentice and master jointly have a stake in the increasingly knowledgeable skill of the apprentice, as among the tailors and midwives, or whether there is a conflict between the master's desire for labour and the apprentice's desire to learn (see Goody, 1982), as among the meat cutters. The different ways in which old-timers and newcomers establish and maintain identities conflict and generate competing viewpoints on the practice and its development. Newcomers are caught in a dilemma. On the one hand, they need to engage in the existing practice, which has developed over time: to understand it, to participate in it and to become full members of the community in which it exists. On the other hand, they have a stake in its development as they begin to establish their own identity in its future.

We have claimed that the development of identity is central to the careers of newcomers in communities of practice, and thus fundamental to the concept of legitimate peripheral participation. This is illustrated most vividly by the experience of newcomers to AA, but we think that it is true of all learning. In fact, we have argued that, from the perspective we have developed here, learning and a sense of identity are inseparable: they are aspects of the same phenomenon.

Insofar as the conflicts in which the continuity–displacement contradiction is manifested involve power – as they do to a large extent – the way the contradiction is played out changes as power relations change. Conflicts between masters and apprentices (or, less individualistically, between generations) take place in the course of everyday participation. Shared participation is the stage on which the old and the new, the known and the unknown, the established and the hopeful, act out their differences and discover their commonalities, manifest their fear of one another, and come to terms with their need for one another. Each threatens the fulfilment of the other's destiny, just as it is essential to it. Conflict is experienced and worked out through a shared everyday practice in which differing viewpoints and common stakes are in interplay. Learners can be overwhelmed, over-awed and overworked. Yet even when submissive imitation is the result, learning is never simply a matter of the 'transmission' of knowledge or the 'acquisition' of skill; identity in relation with practice, and hence knowledge and skill and their significance to the subject and the community, are never unproblematic. This helps to account for the common observation that knowers come in a range of types, from clones to heretics.

Granting legitimate participation to newcomers with their own viewpoints introduces into any community of practice all the tensions of the continuity–displacement contradiction. These may be muted, though not extinguished, by the differences of power between old-timers and newcomers. As a way in which the related conflicts are played out in practice, legitimate peripheral participation is far more than just a process of learning on the part of newcomers. It is a reciprocal relation between persons and practice. This means that the move of learners toward full participation in a community of practice does not take place in a static context. The practice itself is in motion.

Since activity and the participation of individuals involved in it, their knowledge and their perspectives are mutually constitutive, change is a fundamental property of communities of practice and their activities. Goody (1989) argues that the introduction of strangers into what was previously strictly domestic production (a change that occurred within an expanding market in West Africa in the recent past) led masters to think more comprehensively about the organization of their production activities. She points out that the resulting division of work processes into segments to be learned has been mirrored in subsequent generations in new, increasingly specialized occupations. Legitimate peripherality is important for developing 'constructively naive' perspectives or questions. From this point of view, inexperience is an asset to be exploited. It is of use, however, only in the context of participation, when supported by experienced practitioners who both understand its limitations and value its role. Legitimacy of participation is crucial both for this naive involvement to invite reflection on ongoing activity and for the newcomer's occasional contributions to be taken into account. Insofar as this continual interaction of new perspectives is sanctioned, everyone's participation is legitimately peripheral in some respect. In other words, everyone can to some degree be considered a 'newcomer' to the future of a changing community.

References

Alibrandi, L.A. (1977) The recovery process in Alcoholics Anonymous: The sponsor as folk therapist. Social Sciences Working Paper 130. University of California, Irvine.

Bourdieu, P. (1977) *Outline of a Theory of Practice*. Cambridge: Cambridge University Press.

Engeström, Y. (1987) *Learning by Expanding*. Helsinki: Orienta-Konsultit Oy.

Fortes, M. (1938) Social and psychological aspects of education in Taleland. (Supplement to *Africa* 11(4).)

Goody, E. (ed.) (1982) *From Craft to Industry*. Cambridge: Cambridge University Press.

Goody, E. (1989) Learning and the division of labor, in M. Coy (ed.), *Anthropological Perspectives on Apprenticeship*. New York: SUNY Press.

Hass, M. (n.d.) Cognition-in-context: The social nature of the transformation of mathematical knowledge in a third-grade classroom. Program in Social Relations, University of California, Irvine.

Jordan, B. (1989) Cosmopolitical obstetrics: Some insights from the training of traditional midwives. *Social Science and Medicine* 28(9): 925–944.

Lave, J. (1989) The acquisition of culture and the practice of understanding, in J. Stigler, R. Shweder and G. Herdt (eds), *The Chicago Symposia on Human Development*. Cambridge: Cambridge University Press.

Marshall, H. (1972) Structural constraints on learning, in B. Geer (ed.), *Learning to Work*. Beverly Hills, CA: Sage Publications.

Orr, J. (1990) Sharing knowledge, celebrating identity: War stories and community memory among service technicians, in D.S. Middleton and D. Edwards (eds), *Collective Remembering: Memory in society*. Beverly Hills, CA: Sage Publications.

Scribner, S. and Cole, M. (1981) *The Psychology of Literacy*. Cambridge, MA: Harvard University Press.

Stack, C. (1989) Life trajectories and ethnography. Proposal to the Group on Lifespan Research. University of California, Berkeley.

Traweek, S. (1988) Discovering machines: Nature in the age of its mechanical reproduction, in F. Dubinskas (ed.), *Making Time: Ethnographies of high technology organizations*. Philadelphia: Temple University Press.

Chapter 8

Learning from other people at work

Michael Eraut, Jane Alderton, Gerald Cole and Peter Senker

Introduction

This chapter presents findings from one aspect of the Sussex University project on the development of knowledge and skills in employment (Eraut *et al.*, 1998). This involved double interviews, 6–12 months apart, with 120 people operating at a professional, management, team leader or technician level in 12 organisations. These were medium to large organisations in the engineering, business and health care sections. The approach adopted was to find out what types of work activity our respondents were currently conducting, what types of knowledge and skill were entailed, how they had acquired the capability to do what they now did, and what factors had affected this learning process.

Learning from other people and the challenge of the work itself proved to be the most important dimensions of learning for the people we interviewed. Although some reported significant learning from formal education and training, this was by no means universal and often only of secondary importance. This confirmed our view that the dominant assumption that learning in The Learning Society comes only from recognised formal provision needs to be balanced by more empirical evidence about what, how, where and why people learn at work. There was also a need to understand more about factors affecting this informal and mainly self-directed learning and how it was situated within working contexts and personal life histories. Without such evidence the current wave of visionary literature about learning organisations is in danger of remaining at the rhetorical level.

The research literature on informal learning at work is very thin and somewhat overshadowed by practitioner literature advocating that it be given more attention and advising people on how to promote it. This is usually illustrated with success stories about organisations that have established reputations for their innovative approaches, but backed by very little evidence

This is an edited version of a chapter previously published in *Learning at Work*, 1998, Bristol: The Policy Press.

from independent evaluations. Three studies stand out. Gear *et al.* (1995) interviewed 150 professionals about a recent 'learning project'. Following Tough (1971) they defined a learning project as,

> the equivalent of at least one working day over the last three years spent developing some aspect of your professional knowledge, skills and competence to the point where you could pass some of it on to a colleague.
>
> (Gear *et al.*, 1995: 8)

Our evidence covered this semi-planned type of professional learning, but also a wide range of learning that did not meet this particular definition. Nevertheless their evidence both for informal learning and for significant learning from other people (reported by 92 per cent of their respondents) was very strong. However, they do not provide much detail about the contextual factors that gave rise to this learning. The image presented is that of an independent professional rather than that of a professional worker in a large organisation, perhaps reflecting their very different sample. This 'independent professional' ethos can also be found in a long-running programme of excellent studies by researchers into continuing medical education in North America (Davis and Fox, 1994; Fox *et al.*, 1989). This research is deeply situated in the physicians' work environment and professional lives; but again the sample is very different from our own. Finally Mumford *et al.* (undated) have recently reported research into the learning of 144 board members/directors of 41 organisations, concluding that in most organisations formal management development programmes had been relatively ineffective. Informal learning on the job was of greater importance, but learning opportunities at work were not sufficiently used.

This chapter is divided into three main sections: organised learning support; consultation and collaboration within the working group; and learning from people outside the working group.

Organised learning support

We interpret the term 'organised learning support' as referring to any form of support for people's learning that requires special organisation. The main kinds of activities reported (not necessarily in our terminology) were: apprenticeship; induction; mentoring; coaching; rotations; visits; shadowing; and reference to experts. Though never subversive these activities were not necessarily organised in any official way, and knowledge of them was often confined to the immediate work unit. It was also possible to discern different assumptions about learning underpinning the selection and transaction of modes of learning support. Thus the practices we noted resulted from the interaction between:

- the prevailing level of formality and structure in the workplace;
- the initiator(s): the learner; the organisation; the line manager; or another (usually more experienced) colleague;
- the assumptions about learning held (but not often overtly stated) by the parties involved.

Assumptions about learning

Five main approaches to the facilitation of learning could be distinguished, which operated sometimes on their own and sometimes in combination.

Induction and integration

This focused primarily on people becoming effective members of their work unit and the organisation as a whole. The emphasis is on socialisation: understanding the purposes and goals of the unit and the organisation, their own roles and others' expectations of them; and fitting into the interpersonal nexus in which their work is embedded. The management approach can vary from laissez faire and light monitoring to a succession of formal events, for example, an induction course followed by other short courses. The latter will normally be part of a whole organisation approach, which local managers may or may not follow up. It is associated not only with new employees but also with planned changes in the organisation's policy or culture.

Exposure and osmosis

These are frequently used to describe the process of learning by peripheral participation. Through observations and listening the exposed learner picks up information and know-how by a process of osmosis. The role of the manager is limited to that of enabling sufficient exposure to a diversity of contexts and situations, but otherwise remains passive. However, the learner has not only to be alert and receptive but also to be able to work out what they need to know. Shadowing and certain types of rotation and visit are the usual methods employed.

Self-directed learning

This approach assumes that the learner takes a more active role, learning from doing the work and finding out on their own initiative what they need to know. Such an active role is more likely to be adopted if the work is appropriately chosen and the learner encouraged in their learning. As with the first two approaches, managers' hopes that employees will be self-directed learners may not be realised if their attitude is perceived as permissive rather than positively supportive.

Structured personal support for learning

This involves the use of supervisors, mentors or coaches. Sometimes this is an official process; sometimes the role is assumed by a manager or a more experienced colleague; sometimes a manager asks someone to provide help and advice; sometimes the learner is encouraged to seek advice from a particular colleague or group of colleagues. Whether officially organised or not, the climate of the workplace is likely to affect significantly the quality of learning support.

Performance management

This approach is being introduced by an increasing number of organisations. It involves regular appraisal and target-setting, but its emphasis can vary from a 'stick and carrot' approach to motivation, to a developmental approach focused on learning to improve personal performance. These competing attitudes towards performance enhancement have been debated by managers and management theorists for at least 50 years. At its best, performance management facilitates learning through discussion about and provision of learning support. At its worst, the learning entailed in improving one's performance is not recognised and hence discouraged.

We shall now consider some examples of organised learning support and comment on them in the light of the above analysis.

Mentoring and coaching

Example 1

Some middle managers approached our respondent about the idea of mentoring. They discussed it, talked it through and found out more. The respondent sounded out some senior colleagues who agreed to be mentors and now they have 'regular monthly one-to-ones'. No formal time is allocated and it is not part of a senior manager's job role. Our respondent only involves people who are able and willing to be mentors, those who want to contribute something and are prepared to give up the time.

> If you say to every senior manager 'You must be a mentor for someone', they do it probably badly and probably grudgingly. And that's not of much benefit to the individual.
>
> (Senior manager, insurance company)

Example 2

Basically, they just give you some new death claims and they'll sit with you and show you what to do for the first few, then you start doing it yourself. Then they go away and you have to do it, and you pass it on to them to check it, and after a while you're just left to do it all by yourself . . . they sample your work once a month and from that they can identify any problem areas which you might have. They look to correct those.

(Insurance claims technician)

Example 3

I've been on an interviewing skills course, which was quite early on . . . in terms of developing my skills in that area I feel I was coached quite effectively . . . I sat in on a number of interviews to start with, then I was interviewing along with somebody else . . . and after that I was able to gain feedback from them as to how I had got on . . . then I just got on with it on my own, which I much prefer . . . as long as I have got the skills . . .

(Graduate trainee, personnel)

Example 4

A radiographer wanted to expand her range by doing mammography. It was agreed she would do a course to get the certificate. This involved some formal teaching, visits to other departments (surgical, path lab, radiotherapy) to find out about their involvement in diseases of the breast. In addition she works for part of the week alongside a woman who already has the certificate and a lot of experience. This women goes out of her way to show her relevant things that come up when she's not there, shows her lab reports on mammograms she has done, etc., thus building up her expertise more quickly.

Comment

Mentoring is focused on problems and situations of concern to the mentee, as well as overseeing their general progress. In Example 1, the reason for an informal, voluntary approach was explained in terms of commitment and quality, but the support itself was delivered in quite a structured way. In Example 4, training was provided by a course that had a built-in requirement for visits, but the coaching aspect was offered voluntarily by a senior colleague. The manager supported the course and arranged a rotation involving both the exposure/osmosis and the self-directed learning approaches, but the volunteer coach converted this into structured personal support for learning.

Example 2 describes a standard coaching system designed for a particular purpose, adaptive to individual rates of progress and incorporating phased withdrawal of support and follow-up monitoring. Example 3 is another case where a course provides some structure and the coaching is fairly informal but still carefully phased. We also encountered many examples where courses of this kind were not accompanied by any planned follow-up in the workplace, so learners had to work it out for themselves and were generally less clear about issues of quality.

Rotations, visits and shadowing

Example 1

> I've been doing this job for ... 18 months now, and essentially all the skills that go with this technical coordinator job, I learnt from my predecessor, and so I've taken over from somebody, and, that wasn't sort of a few weeks' handover. For a good six months or more, we were working alongside each other, and as I picked things up ... He'd been doing it for about two years previously ... I'd had contact, I'd taken over from him when he went on leave before, but that was very much, just keep it ... you know, caretaking.
>
> (Engineer)

Example 2

A senior cardiac technician in a district hospital has negotiated a day a week working in a teaching hospital. His reasons are 'keeping in touch with other technicians', working on 'more technically challenging cases' which 'keep your skills up' and taking videos of local cases to get other opinions about them.

Example 3

> I went to Korea in '85. I'd been in for half a year troubleshooting, and the managing director and I noticed that they had some very good systems for how they dealt with product introduction. They went through a [type] of pilot phase before they started in serial production – just to make sure that the serial production would not be hit by any faults on the main product, because it would put them, the whole business, in jeopardy, and again I learnt a skill there, a way of working.
>
> (Engineer)

Comment

Examples 1 and 2 show an unusually high investment in learning. Both comes from organisations where there are high risks associated with mistakes. The first concerned an important technical services role in a large organisation where technical stoppages incurred very high costs and loss of reputation. The second concerned quality of care for high risk patients. Both were officially organised, though in the second case the rotation was initiated and negotiated by the technician himself. Both assumed a mixture of learning by exposure and self-directed learning.

Example 3 is better described as a special assignment than a rotation or a visit. The significance is that what was learned had nothing to do with the purpose of the assignment, which was more to do with giving than receiving information.

Designated experts

This was a strong feature of a large telecommunications company with a substantial research and development commitment. Several respondents referred to certain people as 'technical experts' or 'technical heroes', but this designation had no official status.

> Luckily the guy that actually helped me to get the job turned out to be one of the main experts in the department . . . He's just one of these people that knows everything about everything that you need to know . . . he's a technical expert . . . And the brilliant thing is, he talks . . . I think he's a natural teacher anyway . . . I'm battling over something and he'll go up to the whiteboard and draw two circles and a line and it'll all fall into place.
>
> (Software engineer)

Learning who the experts were and how to use them was part of the integration or socialisation process, and reasonably reliable in this particular company. In other companies, however, this could be a lengthy process often involving a chain of personal contacts.

Conclusion

The examples presented in this section have been positive. Negative examples where the absence of these kinds of organised support for learning on-the-job left people struggling were too numerous to count. Learning was often much slower than it needed to be. Without further analysis, we cannot judge whether these examples are representative of even positive examples, but we are fairly confident about one distinct difference between our evidence and the prevailing perspective of the human resource development literature. Very few of our positive examples resulted from organisation-wide strategies or initiatives. Most were relatively informal and initiated by middle managers, colleagues or the learners themselves. Where there were positive examples of organisational initiatives they were more likely to be in the financial sector than in health care or engineering.

Consultation and collaboration within the working group

Groups and teams

Almost all the people we interviewed identified themselves as members (and sometimes also the manager) of a group of people, but the nature of this group and of the interactions between its members varied considerably. This is reflected in the vocabulary used to describe it. A term like 'department' or 'unit' indicates merely that a group of people occupy a common space on an organisational chart and share a common manager. It does not necessarily mean that they work in the same place or that they are the exclusive occupants of their normal workspace. Overt use of the term 'group' usually implies either collocation or a shared function with regular liaison meetings, as well as introducing an affective dimension to the discussion that indicates its significance for a person's work identity. This affective dimension is even stronger when the word 'team' is used and accepted by all members of the group, but its rhetorical use by managers is resented when the designation of a group as a 'team' is not shared. The word 'team' implies a significant degree of collaboration and interdependence, where outcomes should be judged at group rather than individual level.

When studying the impact on learning, the most important variable is the style of normal interaction in the workplace. Since departments or units can be large and dispersed or small and intimate, co-membership is not on its own a useful indicator of an actual or potential working relationship. Hence we have defined the term 'working group' to indicate a group of people who have regular contact with each other at work, some sense of shared purpose, and no stronger allegiance elsewhere in the organisation. Learning from people with whom one does not have such regular contact, even though they may happen to be in the same unit or department, is discussed later.

We also found it useful to distinguish between normal groups with a common manager and special groups to which people may be allocated for a fixed period on a part-time or full-time basis: these groups are more likely to have a leader, co-ordinator or chairperson than a manager. In normal groups we discerned three main types of learning situation: ongoing mutual learning and support; collaborative teamwork; and observing others in action when one is only a peripheral participant. Special groups, intra- or cross-departmental, are usually charged with a specific task – for example, review, audit, preparation of a decision or policy brief, problem solving – and engage in large numbers of meetings with varying amounts of independent or collaborative work in between. We also found that people learned from special assignments in which they represented their working group in an external context.

The distinction between collaborative teamwork and ongoing mutual consultation is often unclear. The most obvious examples of collaborative teamwork entail group tasks on which people work together, contributing different skills. If they have separate parts of the task to work on individually, the extent to which their individual work is discussed in the group and the relative amount of time spent individually and in groups will be critical factors. One obvious example would be a hospital operating theatre where interdependence is crucial. The members of the theatre 'team' have to learn to work together but their level of mutual consultation varies widely. We encountered several small teams of engineers with complementary skills working together on a succession of problems, and cross-professional teams such as cardiologist and cardiac technician, radiographer and consultant. People reported how such work helped them to recognise knowledge and skills that they did not themselves possess and how their knowledge of tasks and situations was broadened by their continuing contact with people who had different perspectives. The process of learning to work with other people was often mentioned as transferring to other, less intensive kinds of group situation.

Several situations were reported that raised the question of when a group becomes a team. Two factors in particular seemed to affect this: the advent of a crisis and a strength of the affective dimension. Groups of individuals working in parallel with occasional consultation could become transformed into teams when confronted with a major problem or deadline; sometimes this had a lasting effect as people began to recognise each other's contributions and group identity was strengthened.

> The team I am in is absolutely fantastic. They've worked brilliantly, everybody does everything, including Q who's my manager . . . It's like when it's contract round it's everybody get round busy, they work hard and they play hard – it's as simple as that. And as I say, everybody mucks in. It's just a good working environment, you enjoy coming to work, you know that if you've worked 11 hours one day you're not expected in at 8.30 am the following day.
>
> (Contract manager, energy supply company)

Gradual development of interpersonal support that extends beyond the workplace also contributed greatly to team feeling among certain working groups. This is more likely to happen when the work is emotionally demanding, as, for example, with a group of nurses on a ward.

> It's getting involved with the people that you're actually learning with and supporting each other, I think that's what comes through isn't it. It's where you support each other, if you see that somebody's struggling with something and you found it particularly easy or you worked it out, then you can help each other. The same thing happens when you're struggling, you can say to someone how the hell did you do that. It's give and take isn't it. That's how we tend to work on the ward as well, we support each other, you know. It doesn't have to be a nursing problem, it can be anything, it doesn't matter what it is . . . We all tend to help each other, it's very good team work on this ward, actually.
>
> (Hospital nurse)

Many wards lack this collaborative ethos; yet it does not take much deliberation to recognise that strong affective bonding among staff is likely to have a significant effect upon the quality of care.

Ongoing consultation and observation

When people spoke about collaborative teamwork, mutual learning tended to be assumed as a integral aspect of it. With other types of working group, there was more overt discussion about learning from each other. Indeed, when we began our fieldwork we were surprised by the amount of learning that occurred through mutual consultation and support. For many people this was the most important mode of learning. Often learning was triggered, almost forced upon people, by the challenge of the work itself, but even this learning was frequently facilitated by consultation with others.

> You just learn as you go along, and people are quite happy if you ask, as I have done on several occasions . . . Q said if I get one of those, he'll quite happily come and give me a hand, 'cause obviously I wouldn't be expected to know how to do that straightaway.
>
> (Newly qualified radiographer)

Typically such consultations would entail a request for quick advice, seeking another perspective on a problem, help with a technical procedure or information on whom to ask for help on a particular issue. The way in which learning from colleagues happens can be very different in a new activity from how it happens in an established one. In a start-up activity, knowledge and skills are being acquired in a multitude of ways and can flow from person to person in several directions at once. In contrast, one person may acquire a large measure of the skills and knowledge needed directly from a predecessor in an established activity, perhaps by means of mentoring.

Another mode of learning – observing others in action – was frequently cited in relation to interpersonal skills (although many of the examples cited were negative rather than positive).

I've seen customers with members of staff where they've almost locked horns across the desk because the customer and the member of staff are both, kind of stubborn, neither of them will want to back down . . . you'll never get anywhere if you're like that. And I think by watching other people you learn things yourself and pick up . . . you would see a situation and you would know that that's not a situation that you want to get yourself into.

(Personal banker)

So you can learn by other people's mistakes and I think that's where I have actually picked up a lot of things because I think, God, I wouldn't talk to somebody like that or, I wouldn't like to be spoken to like that, and I think to myself, I wouldn't dream of asking anybody to do something on the ward that I wouldn't do myself.

(Ward sister)

The role of special groups and assignments

An engineer reported learning a lot from membership of a review group.

We have a trouble reporting system, which I had to learn how to use, and then we implemented things and got processes working from here. And I just sat in on the meetings, where . . . the other expert designers corrected and reviewed test cases and other documentation for corrections, and I just used that as a good background to bounce loads of questions off.

(Software engineer)

She then went on to describe how she had identified a member of the group as a useful learning resource.

Others view him as arrogant, but he's not that at all. He goes out of his way to help people and he views his job as there to help us, because he knows so much, and he also wants to help, like, new designers and testers, because he feels that he can learn so much from them as well. . . . In the review, he's the kind of person that'll question, 'Why have you done this? Who is your audience?' The things that I'm saying that people don't do, he demands when he's in a meeting . . . [but] he's very approachable.

(Software engineer)

In contrast, a radiographer reported somewhat sceptically a move to formalise a review process that was already happening on an informal level.

She has sort of set up a monitoring programme, where every now and again we're supposed to look at the films we've done and be honest with ourselves and assess how good they are: whether they're perfect; whether they're good; or whether they're adequate. Once you've done that you're supposed to just, you know, ask another radiographer's opinion, to see if you agree, and then discuss about it . . . I think the fact that she's got the certificate gives her the enthusiasm, she sort of sees it as her area.

(Radiographer)

A ward sister described how becoming a member of the hospital ethics committee gave her many valuable cross-professional perspectives. However, a more important outcome was her development of a patient advocacy role and the confidence to speak out for patients, not only in official meetings, but to senior people round the hospital when appropriate opportunities arose.

When it comes to things like advocacy, and speaking for people who can't speak for themselves, then, I think I take that quite seriously, and people can get away with a lot, but, there's a fine line . . . and if I think something is wrong I'll say it, and whether it's to a consultant or to a very junior doctor, it wouldn't bother me, because if I had confidence in myself and knew what I was doing was right, and that whatever was going on was wrong, then I would say it. I think some of that is just becoming more assertive as you become more confident in your role and in your job . . . and just as a person . . . It must be very intimidating for a patient when you've got the consultant in the bay and the house officer, and the med. student, and the registrar, and everybody standing around the bed. They're telling you all these things they're going to do to you, and you're sitting there going, 'Yes, doctor, OK that's fine'. But then . . . it is part of my role, to say, 'Well actually, no, I don't think that's fair . . . you haven't given them a choice. You've told them, but when you left they said to me, you know, that they don't want to do this, or they're not happy with it'.

(Ward sister)

Another nurse described how her manager set up a management team to discuss issues with her senior nurses, including herself. This gave her another perspective on the work of the ward, and also enabled her to understand what was involved in working as a manager. So she was far better prepared when she became a manager herself.

An engineer commented that once a problem was publicly acknowledged and a group set up to tackle it, people who had previously kept quiet started sharing their knowledge. It was highlighting the need that triggered this different response.

Feedback within the group

Feedback from colleagues is a prominent feature of the diagnostic radiographers' environment because they are accustomed to looking at each other's pictures and commenting on them. This was done in a very relaxed way, so that comments were not taken personally, and it facilitated a great deal of group learning. They also put red dots on pictures to indicate to casualty officers where they had noticed that something was broken, thus contributing to diagnoses by often relatively inexperienced doctors without trespassing on their traditional territory.

A community nurse described several ways in which feedback from her manager had both given confidence and led to learning. For example, after she had done a special project on handling and preventing falls, he asked her to prepare some posters on it, to present them to students, then later to make them available to other nurses and doctors. He gave positive feedback on the performance of a delegated task, and, if not entirely happy, gently asked if other possibilities could have been considered.

> A couple of times he's actually said, 'Well, you know you could have done so and so', and I said, 'Oh, I never thought of that', and he says, 'Well you'll know next time', or, 'We'll talk about it' or whatever . . . He's not actually disagreed with me, he's said 'Have you thought of doing so and so?' He doesn't say, 'You shouldn't have done that', he doesn't say it like that. He'll say 'Well perhaps you could have done such and such', and I think, 'I could have done that'.
>
> (Community nurse)

An insurance company manager described how when he first came to the company he got most help from immediate peer colleagues, particularly in understanding the company culture, but now he was learning more from his subordinates than his colleagues. In a vivid example he explained how he had been to two management assessment centres in connection with a job, then:

> I got the feedback, and the first thing I did was photocopy it and take it round my team and said 'There you go, that's my feedback, how are you going to help me with this?', or, 'How can you help me with this?', or, 'Do you agree with it?'. . . You're actually getting some feedback from them, sort of validating the data really. We do it in a semilight hearted way, I mean they sort of say, 'Did you really say that in this team exercise', or whatever, and we have a chat about it.
>
> (Insurance company manager)

Another manager relied on a particular colleague for honest feedback:

> One of my colleagues, Tina, is very helpful because she provides me
> with feedback that other people don't. So in fact she is very honest with
> me . . . basically she says I think you may have upset such and such . . .
> or maybe I could have done this . . . I can actually learn from that and
> build any bridges if I need to . . . so she's very helpful.
>
> (Regional manager, bank)

Learning from people outside the working group

People outside the immediate working group can be usefully divided into
three categories: those in what one might call an extended working group,
with whom there is regular contact; people in one's own organisation with
whom contact has to be specially arranged, sometimes through a common
acquaintance; and people outside the organisation altogether. Examples of
the first category – the extended working group – included a fortnightly
meeting of personal bankers from different branches, a cross-departmental
committee and health care professionals seeing the same patients. In this
last case learning from doctors often occurred by peripheral participation in
ward rounds or clinic.

People within the organisation

Various reasons were cited for seeking help from people in parallel positions
in one's organisation. For the newly arrived or newly promoted it was often
practical help with common organisational procedures such as tendering or
preparing specifications. In one case there was also strong affective support:

> In the first few weeks of starting the F grade, Liz, our G grade, was away
> and our ward clerk was also away. When the two of them are away it
> was basically . . . you know . . . it was me. I think that was a bit scary
> but it was quite nice because I thought well if I can cope for these
> couple of weeks on my own, then I'll cope . . . You're learning as you
> go along, and if you know there's things that you've never done before
> then there's lots of people that you call on. Other F grades, other G
> grades in the hospital, will phone, and did phone and say, 'Is everything
> all right?'
>
> (Hospital nurse)

For others it was keeping abreast of the micropolitics of the organisation,
getting early information about changes of people or policies, getting advice
about when, to whom and in what way to put forward a proposal. This nearly
always took place in an informal setting, over lunch or in a bar, using
networks created by people who used to work together or met on an in-

house training course. These meetings were also used to get feedback about the work of one's own unit.

> Maybe somebody's havin' a real gripe about the way you put a new system in, and the fact that none of the users get trained adequately or something, and they're much more likely to say that off the record, over a beer or something, and have a real gripe about it.
>
> (Manager, engineering company)

In several cases critical information for one's work had to be sought elsewhere in the organisation and this often required some initiative. For example, learning where the services are located in a large and complex building is notoriously difficult. One service engineer we interviewed was constantly debriefing people about what went where. He made considerable effort to be present wherever new services were being installed, which he might later have to modify or repair. We also interviewed an installer who emphasised the need to talk to the people who designed the telecommunications equipment he was about to install. Sometimes people realised with considerable concern that an individual elsewhere in the organisation had unique knowledge that they needed:

> We've had a callout from [a company] about performance measurements . . . I've gotta get to another guy who knows about [it], and he's got to go in and look at it for me, and I'm saying to him, 'Look, you really have to sit down one day' . . . it's only one guy who knows about this application, and we've gotta sit down with him, and he's gotta show us. The only other way is to do what he did. He just tinkered around, and he's getting knowledge through tinkering around, and we could do that, but it takes too long . . . I don't have time to do that, and none of the other guys have time to do that either. So basically the quickest way of learning is to get him for a day, and say, 'Look, just take us through the basics of this, otherwise we're gonna be weeks learning this'.
>
> (Customer service engineer)

Yet another engineering example concerned cross-departmental co-operation between a designer and a manufacturer.

> I would be good at identifying the problem, the root cause of the problem – the root cause is we don't have . . . I don't know . . . enough force at this point or something like that or this bit cracks because it's not expanding, so I would identify the problem and then Mike and I would sit down and we'd bounce ideas and I'd say 'Well, look, you could do this by doing that', and he'd say, 'Well you know, it's a little bit complicated, can't we do it this way?', or, 'That wouldn't work because of this'.
>
> (Development engineer)

One company set up a special communication channel to encourage the flow of information between departments, but informal contact was still the preferred method and usually proved to be faster and more effective.

> I got to know . . . people in test plant support quite well, which is quite handy if you've got a problem and you phone them up . . . They have a number you phone if you've got a problem, and then they will phone one of the test plant support people, and then they will come out and see you . . . They try to say, do it all officially but if you happen to bump into them and you just want to ask a quick question, they might give you a quick answer . . . or they might say, 'Well phone it in, I'll come and see you in a minute'.
>
> (Development engineer)

Another informant described how he got the benefit of a course in a faster and more relevant way without having to attend it. His method was to contact the in-house expert involved, get the course materials, read for an hour or two then question the expert for a couple of hours on points of particular relevance to his work.

> Sometimes I pick up more important information because I ask the specific questions and find out the exact things, you know, go down the things which are of interest to me rather than having to [sift through general material] . . . A lot of it can seem rather obvious and straightforward and the bit that I'm particularly interested in isn't covered maybe in sufficient detail.
>
> (Telecommunications engineer)

Professional networks

In the health care sector, the working group was also extended by a rich variety of professional networks. But these networks were still largely dependent on personal contacts – A had previously worked or trained with B – often renewed by finding themselves on a course together or working for a common organisation.

> Di that works here, we trained together, and I've known her now for seven or eight years, and it's a bit like having a house sister I suppose. We're very close, but I think it's only natural that when you've been through training together and you've been through a lot of different situations that you do have that bond . . . I couldn't imagine not having friends who weren't nurses or doctors. Because you can ring them up and say if you've had a bad day, and they know what you mean . . . they know exactly how you feel, and they'll know exactly what to say . . .

and that's quite important . . . Sometimes, when you have incidents that you'd really rather forget about, and you don't want to talk about it, but you know that it'll just sit inside and fester away, if it was something that happened and you think you made the wrong decision, or whatever, then [to] people like Di and Liz, I can say, 'Look, I can't sleep, this is worrying me', or whatever, and they'll know, because they've had – not the same situation – but they'll have had a similar incident where they were really worried and couldn't sleep about it, and it's quite nice just to talk it out with people.

(Hospital nurse)

This nurse went on to note the absence of such support among junior doctors.

I think sometimes with the doctors, it seems quite different. I think they seem to have a lot less support than we do, and I feel quite sorry for them really, because they seem constantly to be in situations where they've just never had to do it before, or they have no idea what they're doing.

(Hospital nurse)

Our experience from other research suggests considerable variation in such support across organisations as well as between professions.

There was also some evidence of 'invisible colleges' in the health professions that extended beyond close personal contacts but also depended on occasional meetings for their sustenance.

We've been on conferences, we do chat to the radiologist and cardiologists, and they have an input. Our radiologist is eager to develop new ideas, so we then look into it and . . . assess whether it's worth pursuing. We might go to Brighton or Hastings if they're doing some new technique, to see if it would be beneficial for us to start, see what sort of results they're getting. But within South East Thames we might [ring up] another centre.

(Senior cardiac technician)

We've got people, people who are on courses at the moment, like the nuclear medicine course, we've had one last year and we've got one this year, and they come back with new ideas, and they need to do this experiment or do that experiment, see this or see that, they go off to other centres, come back and tell us all about it.

(Senior radiographer)

A related example from the insurance sector was an informal mentoring relationship with a former boss.

My old boss from 1995, he's moved on to become a director in the corporate pensions business, up in Kingswood, and I've kept in touch with him and used him as a sounding board on things like, 'I'm going to try this, what do you think?', because he's got a lot of experience in the area. 'What do you think of this, what do you think of that?' And personal decisions, 'What should I do about this job?' ... We get on well together and on the same sort of wavelength and I know he will be honest, so he just won't deal in platitudes and say, 'There you go, yes you're doing very well'.

(Team leader, insurance company)

Learning from suppliers and customers

The search for knowledge by some engineers is best described as entrepreneurial. We have already described a service engineer who went to great lengths to be present whenever something new was being installed, and another who 'short-circuited' a lengthy course. Others sought to extract information from suppliers and/or customers, not just market information but also technical information. One sought to get the customer perspective on technical aspects of the equipment he installed. Another described how he had begun to acquire a more customer-oriented view of production and criticised his colleagues for giving this insufficient attention in their development of new products. A third found debriefing customers and suppliers a better way of keeping up to date than reading the journals. The following excerpt from an interview vividly describes how an energetic, problem-solving engineer makes use of several different personal sources of help.

A lot of that information I learnt from my predecessor . . . what is unique to this area, how the automation works, how it thinks, and how it progresses along its list of tasks. Because we were still developing this software, the software had bugs, so you need to have a fairly good understanding of what it's trying to do, in what sequence the software's trying to do things ... I talked in depth with the two people who actually write software and provide the hardware . . . the way things work. I would be called upon when we had a problem, I would look into the problem, I may be able to solve it, or I may need to go back to . . . my predecessor, and ask for advice, and he may come and help, or he may say, 'Oh yes, I think you need . . .'. But it is very much thrown in at the deep end, hands on ... When something unusual crops up, you have to go in at the basic level and work through the system ... If it's something provided by an outside company I quite often ring up and ask for advice . . . regularly make use of outside companies who supplied equipment, always found that very useful, technical departments, much more than I have done previously in my career to be honest.

(Process engineer)

Conclusions

At a theoretical level, our research strongly supports the importance of informal learning, but it also shows how strongly it is situated in the work itself and its social and organisational context. We elicited evidence of tacit knowledge in the areas of personal relations, problem orientation, and expertise in using (or repairing) particular machines or software systems, as well as knowledge that was explicitly articulated. However, a major reason for the prevalence of learning from other people was that this knowledge was held by individuals rather than embedded in social activities. While some knowledge was firmly embedded in organisational activities, other knowledge *was* located only with a small number of individuals – often only one. Thus we can consider both a continuum from tacit knowledge to knowledge in the form of written propositions, and a continuum from knowledge that is individually situated, to knowledge that is organisationally situated.

At the level of practical policy, we suggest that informal learning may be enhanced by two complementary approaches. Individuals can be helped to become more capable learners, who can be both more reflective and more self-directed, more proactive and more able to recognise and use emergent learning opportunities. Managers can be helped to take more responsibility for the quality and quantity of learning in the units that they manage. Our research suggests that a manager's indirect impact on learning through the allocation of work, as a role model and by creating/sustaining a microculture that supports learning from peers, subordinates and outsiders, is no less important than their direct impact through advice and encouragement, appraisal and feedback.

References

Davis, D.A. and Fox, R.D. (eds) (1994) *The physician as learner*, Chicago, IL: American Medical Association.

Eraut, M., Alderton, J., Cole, G. and Senker, P. (1998) *Development of knowledge and skills in employment*, Research Report No. 5, Brighton: University of Sussex Institute of Education.

Fox, R.D., Mazmanian, P.E. and Putnam, R.W. (eds) (1989) *Changing and learning in the lives of physicians*, New York, NY: Praeger.

Gear, J., McIntosh, A. and Squires, G. (1995) *Informal learning in the professions*, Hull: School of Education, University of Hull.

Mumford, A., Robinson, G. and Stradling, D. (undated) *Developing directors: The learning process*, Buckingham: University of Buckingham International Management Centre.

Tough, A.M. (1971) *The adult's learning projects*, Toronto: Ontario Institute for Studies in Education.

Chapter 9

Beyond the institution of apprenticeship

Towards a social theory of learning as the production of knowledge

David Guile and Michael Young

Introduction

Traditionally, the idea of apprenticeship has been associated with the process of skill formation within craft and industrial production and, to a lesser extent, within certain professions. Apprenticeship in these different contexts has usually been characterized by a constellation of both legal and contractual rules and relations governing the status of employment, associated workplace entitlements and a combination of formal and informal educational processes that help to socialize workers into specific workplace and occupational cultures. We have defined these arrangements in a recent article as the 'institution of apprenticeship' (Guile and Young, 1998a). Apprenticeship as an institution, irrespective of its workplace context, is also an educational process and like formal education has been assumed to rest on a transmission model of learning. However, unlike formal education, the institution of apprenticeship is also assumed to be underpinned by the dual assumptions of *learning by doing* and a *master as the role model*, rather than any model of curriculum or formal instruction. Furthermore, it is also assumed that as a model of work-based learning, apprenticeship will produce different outcomes of learning compared with programmes based in schools and colleges.

There is gradually emerging, however, a body of literature that has suggested that the concept of apprenticeship does not have to be restricted to the range of occupations and contexts with which it has traditionally been associated (Brown *et al.*, 1989; Guile and Young, 1998a; Lave and Wenger, 1991; Teles, 1993). Once a 'situative' perspective on learning is adopted (Greeno, 1997), the idea of apprenticeship can be used to conceptualize both the process of learning and the practices, tools and resources that support learning. As we shall suggest in this chapter, apprenticeship offers a way of conceptualizing learning that does not separate it from the production of

This is an edited version of a chapter previously published in *Apprenticeship: Towards a New Paradigm of Learning*, 1999, London: Kogan Page.

knowledge or tie it to particular contexts. It can therefore be the basis of a more general theory of learning that might link learning at work and learning in classrooms, rather than see them only as distinct contexts with distinct outcomes.

Following the recent work of cultural anthropologists such as Jean Lave, we are interested in the potential of apprenticeship for conceptualizing learning as a social process. Our particular interest is in exploring how far this reconceptualization can lead to the development of new pedagogic criteria for what we have referred to elsewhere as 'reflexive learning' (Guile and Young, 1998a). The concern of this chapter, therefore, is in the main conceptual rather than substantive. Building initially upon recent developments within sociocultural activity theory (Vygotsky, 1978), we introduce the concept of the 'zone of proximal development' to argue that despite its traditional association with work-based learning, the concept of apprenticeship can also shed light on pedagogic processes of classrooms. Such an analysis, therefore, offers three possibilities, which we can only begin to point to in this chapter. First, it forms the basis of a critique of 'transmission models'; second, it can indicate similarities and differences between work-based and classroom-based learning; third, it can suggest the basis of new types of relationships between the two. We begin, however, by using Vygotsky's concept of the zone of proximal development to analyse the model of learning traditionally associated with the 'institution' of apprenticeship, before proceeding to examine two alternative conceptions of the zone of proximal development – what we will refer to as the 'societal' and the 'transformatory'. We argue that these conceptions offer a new perspective on the process of learning that relates to emerging features of learning in an era of 'reflexive modernization' (Beck et al., 1994).

Existing approaches to learning have tended to rely on behaviourist and individualist assumptions and be dependent on transmission pedagogues. They also tend to treat the concept of knowledge transfer as a decontextualized process, or associated with cognitive science accounts of learning as the stable individual mastery of well-defined tasks. However, new models of learning are emerging within social psychology (Greeno, 1997), the philosophy of education (Prawat, 1993) and sociolingusitics (Gee, 1992) that emphasize its 'situative' or social character. They focus upon the context of learning and the importance of ideas as a resource for learning, and they argue that all learners require opportunities to transform social practice and develop new ideas. Neither should be the privilege of an elite; they should be possibilities for all learners. Drawing, in particular, upon recent work in the philosophy of education, we introduce the notion of 'ideas-based constructivism' to illustrate how this shift towards a social theory of learning can be the basis for seeing knowledge production as integral to the process of learning. In addition, we draw upon ideas derived from sociocultural psychology to highlight two aspects of the potential of information and communication technology (ICT): first, if the potential for learning of ICT is to be realized, it has to be on the basis of a social theory of learning; second, ICT offers promising new ways of integrating learning with the production of knowledge and hence of overcoming the barriers between school and work-based learning. Finally, we outline the criteria that might inform such a social theory of learning and production of knowledge and offer some brief considerations about the implications of our ideas for learning in schools and colleges and the new relationships between school and college-based learning and learning in workplaces.

Apprenticeship, learning and the zone of proximal development

The concept of the zone of proximal development is central to Vygotsky's theory. He defined it as:

> the distance between the actual development level as determined by independent problem solving and the level of potential development as determined through problem solving under adult guidance or in collaboration with more able peers.

> (1978: 85)

Vygotsky was concerned with the progress that students make with their studies as they relate their 'everyday' concepts – the understanding that emerges spontaneously from interaction with other people and in different situations – to the 'scientific' concepts that they experience through textbook and the formal curriculum. Vygotsky saw scientific concepts as those ideas whose analytic purchase had been deepened over a long period of time. As Kozulin (1990) has argued, the concept of the zone of proximal development was an integral part of Vygotsky's programme to account for the complex interaction between scientific concepts and everyday concepts and hence the development of intellectual and practical expertise. He also saw it as a framework to identify the pedagogic structure(s) needed to assist learners to move beyond the stage of mastery that they were capable of on their own.

Over the years the concept has been modified, developed and given a broader interpretation within sociocultural activity theory both in the United States (Brown *et al.*, 1989; Griffen and Cole, 1985; Lave and Wenger, 1991; Rogoff, 1990; Scribner and Ciole, 1971; Wertsch, 1981) and in the Soviet Union (Davydov and Radzikouskii, 1985; Leontiev, 1978). Following the tradition of Vygotsky's own empirical research, most writers have restricted the use of the concept to understanding child development. It has, however, been applied in two quite different ways within contemporary curriculum theory. One interpretation has favoured a 'practical problem-solving' approach to teaching and learning, while the other has focused upon the important role of ideas within teaching and learning (Prawat, 1993).

It is our contention, however, that there are common processes that underlie learning in all contexts and for all ages and that Vygotsky's concept of the zone of proximal development is a useful way of highlighting similarities as well as differences between learning in formal and informal contexts. Moreover, we believe that more recent interpretations of this concept help to throw light on the complex relationship between the role of ideas, practical problem solving and the production of new knowledge that could be the basis for reconceptualizing an approach to learning in vocational education (Engeström, 1996b; Lave and Wenger, 1991). We also feel that the concept, in particular, provides a useful way of taking further some of our ideas about linking school and work-based learning (Guile and Young, 1998a). From our point of view, the appeal of Vygotsky's approach lies in the emphasis it places on the idea of mind *in* society, its associated focus on cognitive development in specific contexts and the pedagogic practices that underpin such development.

Learning and the institution of apprenticeship

As we stated earlier, apprenticeship has traditionally rested upon a transmission model of learning that was supposed to develop work-related knowledge and skill. We begin, therefore, by exploring the ideas about learning implicit in the institution of apprenticeship. It is our intention to question the traditional assumptions of apprenticeship as an institutional approach to learning that is radically different from learning in formal education. One helpful way of approaching this issue, we believe, is to distinguish between the process, the types and the outcomes of learning and the arrangements for learning.

Most studies in cognitive psychology, cultural anthropology and anthropology of education portray apprenticeship as lacking an explicit theory of instruction and not dependent upon any formal teaching (Coy, 1989; Scribner and Cole, 1971). Learning is seen as a natural process that happens over time and occurs via observation, assimilation and emulation and without any substantial intervention from more experienced others (Raizen, 1991). However, two slightly different emphases emerge within this literature. For some commentators, learning appears as a result of direct interaction between apprentices and their environment. This interaction can take the form of observation, trial and error, conditioning and so on. A different interpretation emerges from those studies that originate from sociocultural activity theory. They are more inclined to stress the idea of mediation as an integral aspect of the learning process (Scribner and Cole, 1971) and accord more importance to the interaction between experienced adults and apprentices as a process that facilitates practical participation in, and eventual understanding or mastery of, different activities.

Nonetheless, despite the existence of these slightly different interpretations of the process of learning within apprenticeship, both groups have assumed that formal and informal contexts involve different types of learning and result in different outcomes of learning. Resnick has argued that there are three broad characteristics of mental activity typical of formal education that stand in contrast to learning in informal contexts. These, she suggests, are that (1) learning in formal educational contexts is an individual process; (2) it involves a purely mental activity based on the manipulation of symbols; and (3) it results in the production of generalized concepts. Learning in *informal* contexts, in contrast, is a collaborative process; it usually involves the manipulation of tools (machinery, computers, etc.) and it leads to highly context-specific forms of reasoning and skills (Resnick, 1987).

These distinctions about the different process of learning and the forms and outcomes of learning in formal and informal contexts help to sustain the overriding and widely held belief that expertise in apprenticeship is developed through the gradual accumulation of experience under the guidance of an established master within an unspecified 'zone of proximal development'. Consequently, it tends to be assumed that the concept of knowledge developed within apprenticeship is restricted to a combination of trade or craft knowledge handed down by the master and the implicit knowledge that is part of all practical activity.

Research from other branches of social science, e.g. post-compulsory education and training and management science, however, has adopted a different perspective on the processes of work-based learning and the skill development that take place within the institution of apprenticeship. By focusing on the arrangements for apprenticeship, it has identified models of apprenticeship that embrace formal and informal learning within structured on- and off-the-job training provided by employers (Brown et al., 1994; Fuller, 1996; Gherardi et al., 1988). It has also highlighted that in practice, work contexts vary widely in the learning processes and forms of learning that they make available. Some workplaces are relatively routine and require little explicit knowledge, whereas others are highly knowledge-intensive. Also, work contexts vary according to whether the explicit knowledge involved is of a 'traditional' craft type or more associated with a developing body of 'theory' (Gott, 1995). As a consequence, a general theory of learning needs to take account not only of differences in the degree of expertise needed within specific occupations, but also of differences in the content and quality of such expertise.

In addition to the acquisition of craft-based skill through workplace learning, employers have increasingly required apprentices to acquire more formal types of knowledge to help them cope with industrial change and the demands of knowledge-intensive work. Consequently, there has been a slow realization that the emergence of new contexts for, and new demands upon, apprenticeship and the need to enhance workplace learning with more formal types of learning calls for a reassessment of the traditional assumptions about both types of learning and their relationship to apprenticeship. Among other matters, it has become apparent that the transmission model of learning traditionally associated with apprenticeship, i.e. involving learning by doing and the master as a role model, always implicitly involved a zone of proximal development, albeit an informal zone, since apprentices were being moved beyond the stage of 'mastery' they were capable of on their own (Guile and Young, 1998a). This implies greater similarity between the process of learning that occurs within apprenticeship and formal learning than had previously been accepted to be the case.

Reconceptualizing the zone of proximal development

Over the last decade researchers from many fields within social and psychological science have begun to adopt new perspectives on the process of learning. One of the main reasons for this interest has been the way in which the zone of proximal development has been reconceptualized in neo-Vygotskian theory. Cole (1985) for instance has suggested that culture and cognition create each other within the zone via a dynamic interrelationship between people and social worlds as expressed through language, art and understanding.

Accordingly, Cole laid the foundations for extending the application of the concept to human development in general, rather than restricting its use to analyses of child development. Cole's interpretation of the zone of proximal development has offered contemporary researchers a way of examining the processes through which cognition is developed among individuals and groups in different types of formal and informal context (Engeström, 1996b; Lave, 1996; Wertsch, 1984). In addition it provided a new perspective on the process of learning. Instead of focusing upon the content of formal or informal learning, it encouraged researchers to investigate how learning may occur through common processes in different contexts.

As we have recently pointed out (Guile and Young, 1998a), Cole's original argument that culture and cognition create each other within the zone of proximal development has been expanded by both Lave and Engeström. Instead of focusing upon apprenticeship purely as an 'institution', Lave, working in collaboration with Wenger, has developed it to emphasize the dynamic interrelationship between social, cultural, technological and linguistic practices. This breakthrough was made possible because Lave and Wenger extended the zone of proximal development to highlight the social and cultural basis of learning (Lave, 1996; Lave and Wenger, 1991). This approach enabled them to highlight how, over a period of time, social, cultural, technological and linguistic practices afford individuals and groups opportunities to learn. Although Engeström's work has not been directly concerned with apprenticeship, he shares with Lave an interest in overcoming the limitations of much of contemporary learning theory (Engeström, 1987, 1995; Engeström *et al.*, 1995; Lave, 1993; Lave and Wenger, 1991). Engeström also took the zone of proximal development as his starting point; however, he was interested in how people developed the capability to do something they had not previously accomplished. This led him to adopt what Lave and Wenger (1991) have described as a transformatory perspective on the zone of proximal development. His studies on the social transformation of the organization of work begin to identify how individuals and groups, through critically interrogating their work contexts, collectively produced new understandings and hence new knowledge (Cole and Engeström, 1993; Engeström, 1993, 1996b). It is our contention that taken together the contributions of Lave and Engeström and recent work in the philosophy of education provide the basis of a more comprehensive social theory of learning.

A societal perspective on the zone of proximal development

Lave and Wenger developed their 'societal' perspective on the zone of proximal development, by highlighting the historical and social dimensions of learning, and 'connecting issues of socio-cultural transformation with the changing relations between newcomers and old-timers in the context of a changing shared practice' (1991: 49). This emphasis on a historical and social perspective is important in reconceptualizing learning, especially in a period of continued social change. First, it directs attention to the distance (and potentially, the links) between the everyday activities of individuals and the historically new forms of social practice that need to be collectively generated as solutions to everyday problems. Second, it identifies learning as a social process, and by broadening the concept of 'social' beyond immediate contexts of interaction, it acknowledges the contribution that technological and other external 'resources' can make in support of such learning processes, as well as how learning is shaped by wider social forces and can shape them. This reconceptualization of the process of learning led Lave and Wenger to identify how social structures and social relationships influence the process of learning over time; the importance of relationships between one context of learning (or 'community of practice', to use their term) and another; and the opportunities available for learning within such communities, and the human and technological resources needed to support them. They come to conceive of learning in terms of 'participation [since it] focuses attention on ways in which it is an evolving, continuously renewed set of relations' (1991: 51). Furthermore they argue that participation:

can be neither fully internalized as knowledge structures [within individual minds] nor fully externalized as instrumental artefacts or overarching activity structures. Participation is always based on situated negotiation and re-negotiation of meanings in the world. This implies that understanding and experience are in constant interaction – indeed, are mutually constitutive.

(Lave and Wenger, 1991)

Viewing the relationship between learning, activity and sociocultural contexts as a mutually constitutive process within 'communities of practice' leads Lave and Wenger to challenge the idea that expertise in a given field is invariant and consists of mastery of discrete tasks and skills. This leads them to reconceptualize intelligence as a distributed process as well as an attribute of individuals. Their argument suggests that zones of proximal development are constituted by such resources as physical and cultural tools, as well as other people, and that these resources are used, or brought together to be used, to shape and direct human activity. It follows that, from their perspective, intelligence and expertise are acquired through a process of accomplishment, rather than being a matter of self-possession.

This is not to deny that individuals develop particular forms of 'knowledgeability' (i.e. forms of knowledge and skill). However, Lave and Wenger (1991) emphasize the collective basis through which individuals develop a social identity, learn new forms of social practice and become 'knowledgeable'. By 'knowledgeability' they mean the combination of knowledge and skill required to successfully operate within a 'community of practice'.

Lave and Wenger argue that learning is not a distinct mental process. It is better understood as a relational process that is generated socially as well as historically in social formations where participants engage with each other as a condition and precondition for their existence (Lave and Wenger, 1991). Thus learning becomes a matter of emerging identities developing within different 'communities of practice'. Such a perspective adds another dimension to reformulating existing ideas about skill transfer. Conventional approaches usually assume contexts are invariant. They also rely upon a narrow transmission model of teaching and play down the importance of the meaning given to skills and knowledge by learners. The assumption of such approaches is that the message to be transferred is always unproblematic and clearly understood; it follows that there is a need to address how new knowledge might be produced within the contexts between which the knowledge or skill is to be transferred. On the other hand, as recent research has shown, accomplishing the transfer of learning and crossing organizational boundaries is a complex and challenging process (Engeström and Middleton, 1996). It involves people developing the capacity to think beyond the immediate situation they find themselves in and understanding why it might be both possible and necessary to generate new knowledge.

A transformatory perspective on the zone of proximal development

As we have noted earlier, in order to address how people learn to do things that they have not previously accomplished and, in the process, generate new understandings and new knowledge, Engeström elaborated further the idea of the zone of proximal development being collective and the basis for learners to transform the situation they find themselves in (Guile and Young, 1998a). Engeström concentrates upon identifying how collaborative activity is needed to reconfigure workplace activity and the knowledge that employees have (Cole and Engeström, 1993; Engeström, 1996b). He recognizes that many existing approaches to learning assume that it involves the circulation of existing knowledge rather than the production of 'knowledgeability' and also argues that considerable variation exists in the fundamental imprint of the different groups with their different goals and circumstances, on what it might mean 'to know' on a particular occasion, in a particular context, or within the culture of a particular organization. Consequentially, he broadens his framework of analysis from a sole focus upon 'expert' definition of what is to be learned and how it is to be learned.

He emphasizes the importance of encouraging learners to identify contradictions or puzzles within their existing knowledge or workplace practices as a way of developing new knowledge. It is these 'problems' that Engeström sees as legitimate starting points for exploring and designing solutions and therefore as a basis for new learning (Cole and Engeström, 1993).

Engeström's studies of the transformation of health centres in Finland (Engeström, 1993) and learning in work teams (Engeström, 1996a) highlight the relationship between different modes of learning, the types of outcome arising from each mode and the influence of context and conditions upon each mode of learning (Guile and Young, 1998b). Although he accepts Lave and Wenger's premise that learning is a social and reflexive process that leads 'communities' to change their identities over time, he implies that learning within 'communities of practice' is likely to be a slow continuous evolution of practice rather than transformative. Nevertheless, as the health centre and work team studies demonstrate, crisis points often occur because the 'communities of practice' end up confronting conflicts or problems that are not immediately resolvable (Cole and Engeström, 1993).

Engeström's research indicates that two conditions need to be met if people are to expand their understanding and transform existing 'communities of practice'. They are, first, the context of learning must be expandable to include the existing organization, its purposes and 'tools' of work, as well as its location in the wider community. This avoids limiting the focus of learning to 'here-and-now' problems and relatively 'quick fixes'. It also enables new possibilities for the organization of work to be extensively debated and their likely implications for other related activities to be considered prior to any process of change (Engeström, 1996b). Second, if the context of practice is to be taken into account, it is vital that participants feel they are able to question, criticize or reject some aspects of accepted practice and existing wisdom.

One common thread runs through both Lave and Wenger's and Engeström's argument about the process of learning. Both view learning as a mediated activity that will benefit from access to linguistic, technological and social resources that are not necessarily part of the context of learning itself. In contrast to Lave and Wenger, who endorse the appropriation and exploitation of those resources that are already available within existing 'communities of practice', Engeström retains an explicit role for concepts and learning technologies (ICTs) that may be located externally to an organization's existing culture and environment. He recognizes the value of concepts and ideas that may be external to a community but be the basis of frameworks for reconceptualizing the felt dilemmas and contradictions within the community of practice. As Engeström's field studies indicate, unless these conditions prevail, it will not be possible for participants to construct a vision of the past and the future of their specific activity systems, nor will they be able to produce new knowledge (Engeström *et al.*, 1996).

The idea of reflexive learning

There are several conclusions that follow from our preceding argument. First, if participation in communities of practice is a critical aspect of developing 'knowledgeability' or working out the meaning of an idea in the context of its use, it raises questions about how communities of practice are established and sustained. Second, the idea that concepts and access to learning technologies (ICTs) are important in workplace learning stands in stark contrast to the traditional assumption that apprenticeship only involves a process of learning by doing with a master as the main role model. Clearly there are certain workplace situations where this model may still apply (Lave and Wenger, 1991); however, increasingly in modern workplaces, in which continuous change is the norm, this idea is less and less tenable (Hirschorn, 1986; Shaikin, 1996; Zuboff, 1988). Third, if concepts are important to the process and outcomes of learning, it suggests that the traditional emphasis in apprenticeships on developing 'tacit knowledge' and 'action-orientated' skills will be inadequate, on its own, to enable apprentices or for that matter other employees to operate effectively in future in workplaces (Gott, 1995; Zuboff, 1988). Fourth, if the first two observations are taken together, they imply that learning by doing may well be an inadequate model for describing work-based learning or apprenticeship.

Learning by doing or problem solving has been emphasized as a foundation of both apprenticeship and school-based vocational education. Moreover, as Prawat (1993) has argued, the educational benefits of extending 'learning by doing' are widely accepted in learning research. This has led,

Prawat suggests, to an emphasis upon the assimilation of knowledge through the use of existing schemata to interpret problematic situations and by a reliance on available routines. In essence, he argues, this implies an *informative*, rather than a *transformative* relationship with the world (Prawat, 1993).

The critical question from our point of view is how powerful learning experiences will lead individuals and groups to develop a more *transformative* relationship with the world that is based around collaborative activities which can be provided in formal and informal contexts. At the heart of this question is the relationship between what Vygotsky distinguished as 'scientific' concepts, i.e. those which emerge from collaborative activity between apprentices/students and more experienced adults and are immersed in disciplinary or multidisciplinary fields, and the 'everyday or spontaneous' concepts, i.e. those concepts that emerge from reflection on such everyday experiences as play, work, interpersonal interaction and so on. As different generations of sociocultural theorists have made clear, this distinction between 'scientific' and 'everyday' concepts is consistent pedagogically with both 'societal' and 'transformatory' notions of the zone of proximal development (Engeström, 1991; Wertsch, 1985). Learning becomes a process of mediating in new contexts, ideas or concepts that have been meticulously worked up and debated over a period of time in other social contexts in relation to other practical problems.

Certainly, both concepts refer to learning processes. However, as Kozulin and Presseisen (1995) have recently made clear, while the learning in a generic sense can emerge from any of the latter processes, 'learning activity', i.e. grasping the meaning of scientific concepts and using them to transform understanding and social practice, does not occur spontaneously. Consequently, from our point of view, the challenge is to redefine the relationship between theory or scientific concepts and practice or everyday concepts. Yet, as writers from such diverse fields as cognitive psychology and sociolinguistics have begun to argue over the last decade or so, not only do ideas, or 'scientific concepts', play a crucial role in directing attention to important aspects of the environment that otherwise would go unnoticed (Neisser, 1976), their transformational potential only occurs when they are discussed and applied in a social context (Gee, 1992).

The US philosopher of education Prawat introduces the concept 'ideas-based constructivism' to encapsulate this process. It is his contention that all forms of learning are enhanced when ideas or concepts that emerged from other contexts can be drawn upon to clarify thinking, knowing and, ultimately, help to transform social practice. Prawat's ideas fit in well with our distinction between the 'societal' and 'transformatory' perspectives on the zone of proximal development and the value of the concept of 'legitimate peripheral participation'. In Lave and Wenger's work, meaning is developed through immersion into and exploration of different forms of social practice and this may lead to a fuller and richer understanding of the 'ideas' that lie behind specific social practices. In the case of Engeström, 'communities of practice' should be encouraged to use ideas to transform situations by enabling participants to question, criticize or reject some aspects of accepted practice and existing wisdom.

Such a development is only likely if ideas or concepts external to a situation can be called upon to clarify thought and understanding of purposes. This raises two key questions. First, how do 'communities of practice' use ideas to serve such purposes? Second, given the rapid emergence of ICT as a resource for learning and hence access to new ideas, how do 'communities of practice' use ICT to transform thinking and practice?

Certain clues as to the answer to the first question have been provided by Engeström. He has argued very persuasively that connecting ideas to practice involves using a learning cycle that explicitly incorporates context, cognition and contradiction (Engeström, 1995). The learning cycle Engeström proposes is based upon his concept of 'expansive learning' (Engeström, 1987) and enables individuals and groups to connect the current level of their understanding about practice to emerging ideas as to how to transform practice and hence to generate new knowledge about practice. Within his learning cycle, ideas represent what Neisser (1976) has referred to as 'anticipatory phases of activity'. In other words, they direct attention to aspects of the cyclic process of questioning, modelling, revising practice, etc. and in the process become part of the cycle and help to determine how further information and/or responses, etc. are accepted and used. Unlike Kolb's (1984) much better-known 'learning cycle', which emphasizes learning either as a process of natural reflection or formalized procedures and specifically directs participants to rely on 'everyday concepts', Engeström's 'learning cycle' adopts a transformatory perspective. This encourages 'communities of practice' to find ways of connecting 'scientific' and 'everyday' concepts to achieve changes in understanding and social practice.

A partial answer is provided to our second question about the use of ICT as a resource for learning by the work of the Helsinki Centre for Activity Theory (Engeström et al., 1995, 1996). They indicate an awareness that new conceptual and technological resources must be used sensitively within 'communities of practice' if they are to complement the forms of learning already being engaged in within communities; however, they do not specifically address the use of ICT as a resource for learning and the production of new knowledge. In fact, this dual role of ICT is rarely addressed in the social and psychological sciences. One of the most imaginative contributions to our understanding of the role of ICT as a resource for learning comes from the work of Pea (Pea, 1993; Pea and Gomez, 1992). His work makes it clear that although ICTs can be used to enhance individual learning within given parameters, they can also be used to create the possibility of 'communities of practice' being extended to become *distributed communities of learning*.

These insights about the potential use of ICT need to be set in the context of our earlier discussion about reconceptualizing apprenticeship as the basis of a social theory of learning. Contrary to the assumption of traditional approaches to apprenticeship, namely that learning is implicit and informal and pedagogy is irrelevant, we have argued that it is possible to identify how pedagogic structures are embedded within workplace activity. Lave and Wenger (1991) stress the idea of situated learning that sensitizes us both to the negotiated character of learning as a social practice and to how opportunities to participate within workplace cultures influence whether and how we learn. Hence, their emphasis upon the social character of the zone of proximal development. Engeström, however, goes one stage further with his idea of 'transformative' learning, which, rather than only focusing upon the transmission of existing knowledge, acknowledges the importance of new knowledge being produced within workplace communities as part of the process of learning. The critical issue for Engeström is that although transformative learning has to be designed, design focuses on more than formal teaching and has to take into account the context as a whole. He retains a role for a theory of instruction as well as a focus on the social processes, relationships and resources that are needed to support learning. Instruction in this sense involves ensuring that the goals of learning are clear and people are encouraged to think beyond the immediate circumstances. This ensures that the zone of proximal development is collectively organized to facilitate the transformation of context, cognition and practice. Nonetheless, unless *communities* enable their members to extend the sources of information to which they have access and expand their sociocultural basis, they will not develop new forms of 'knowledgeability' nor will they begin to use ICT to produce new knowledge (Guile and Young, 1998b). As we have argued elsewhere, such activity can be described as a process of 'reflexive learning' (Guile and Young, 1998a) and is the 'micro' expression of the 'macro' process of 'reflexive modernization' (Beck *et al.*, 1994).

Conclusion

This chapter was stimulated by two issues, one theoretical and one practical. Theoretically, it arose via recent developments in sociocultural activity theory, from the possibility of using apprenticeship as a conceptual model for a social theory linking learning and production of knowledge. Practically, it is an attempt to respond to the recent policy interest in apprenticeship and the possibilities it may provide for overcoming the separation of formal and informal learning and of educational institutions and workplaces. Thus, it has tried to provide a more unified perspective on the different types of learning traditionally associated with these different contexts.

The chapter has examined some of the assumptions underlying the institution of apprenticeship and the possibilities it might offer when freed from its historic legacies, for overcoming barriers to learning opportunities in post-compulsory education and training and constituting part of a strategy for the UK becoming a learning economy.

If young people are to develop the new kinds of skills and knowledge that are emerging as essential to a learning society, they will need to be able to use ICT as a resource both to access information as well as to collaborate with others within distributed communities of practice to produce new knowledge (Lundvall, 1996). We have argued that exploiting the learning potential of ICT will involve radical changes to how we organize education and training. More fundamentally, it will involve exploring the implications of recognizing learning as a *social* process. This chapter, therefore, argues that critical to any such changes is that policy makers, users and education and training providers rethink their ideas about learning and pedagogy as well as developing a more critical approach to the potential of on-line learning. To this end, the chapter draws upon the twin notions of 'community of practice' and 'ideas-based constructivism' and suggests a transformative approach to Vygotsky's idea of the zone of proximal development as the basis for a social theory of learning. Such a theory, it argues, could provide a way of linking work-based and school- and college-based learning together as changes in work and society become *the ideas* for reflecting on changes in pedagogic practice, and the disciplines of subject-based knowledge become the *criteria* for interrogating changes in work and society.

We are not the first to suggest that the concept of apprenticeship might serve as the basis of an alternative learning paradigm for formal education and training (Brown *et al.*, 1989), or on-line learning (Teles, 1993). We draw on Prawat's distinction between 'problem-based' and 'ideas-based' approaches to learning to differentiate between our and earlier approaches. The former refer to those attempts to introduce a practical approach to problem solving as the paradigmatic context for promoting higher order thinking in classrooms and elsewhere. This, we argued, leads to an *informative* relationship with the world, since 'communities of practice' are encouraged to accept a problem as it is posed to them, by a teacher or other adult, and to use existing conventions, beliefs and practices to explain how to address them. The latter refers to our argument that learning should encourage 'communities of practice' either to identify problems that need to be solved, or where problems have been identified for them to solve, think about their relation to the problem and pose alternatives to it. Such an approach, we have suggested, implies a much more *transformative* relationship with the world. This transformative approach, we contend, can only occur when the learning process explicitly involves the use of both 'scientific' and 'everyday' concepts. Although the former may direct attention to aspects of a problem that may otherwise go unnoticed, they are ultimately only valuable when they can be used to help transform everyday problems.

Furthermore, we argued that the educative purposes of ICT have to be rethought in relation to both the changes occurring in work as a result of the introduction of ICT, and in relation to the new potential for learning ICT generates. The recognition that both 'ideas' and ICT are equally important resources for 'communities of practice' led us to argue that such 'communities' must have a stake in the development of new practices if they are to establish their own future identities, develop their capacity for lifelong learning and the production of new knowledge and hence contribute to the creation of a learning society. Accordingly, we suggested that our concept of *reflexive learning* encapsulated the process whereby 'communities of practice' can connect ideas to practice. We suggested this might happen in two ways. First, through the use of a 'learning cycle' that specifically incorporated context, cognition and context; second, by using ICT to create the possibility of a 'community of practice' being extended to become a *distributed learning community*.

References

Beck, U., Giddens, A. and Lash, S. (1994) *Reflexive Modernization*, Polity Press, Cambridge.

Brown, A., Evans, K., Blackman, S. and Germon, S. (1994) *Key Workers: Technical training and mastery in the workplace*, Hyde, Bournemouth.

Brown, J., Collins, S. and Duguid, P. (1989) Situated cognition and culture of learning, *Educational Researcher*, 18 (1): 32–42.

Cole, M. (1985) The zone of proximal development: where culture and cognition create each other, in *Culture Communication and Cognition: Vygotskian perspectives*, ed. J. Wertsch, Cambridge University Press, New York.

Cole, M. and Engeström, Y. (1993) A socio-historical approach to distributed cognition, in *Distributed Cognition*, ed. G. Saloman, Cambridge University Press, Cambridge.

Coy, M. (1989) *Anthropological Perspectives on Apprenticeship*, SUNY Press, New York.

Davydov, V.V. and Radzikouskii, L.A. (1985) Vygotsky's theory and the activity orientated approach in psychology, in *Culture Communication and Cognition: Vygotskian perspectives*, ed. J. Wertsch, Cambridge University Press, New York.

Engeström, Y. (1987) *Learning by Expanding*, Orienta-Konsultit Oy, Helsinki.

Engeström, Y. (1991) Towards overcoming the encapsulation of school learning, *Learning and Instruction*, 1 (1): 243–261.

Engeström, Y. (1993) Developmental studies on work as a testbench of activity theory, in *Understanding Practice*, ed. S. Chaicklin and J. Lave, Cambridge University Press, Cambridge.

Engeström, Y. (1995) *Training for Change*, International Labour Office, London.

Engeström, Y. (1996a) *Innovative Learning in Work Teams: Selected papers on expansive learning*, Centre for Activity Theory and Developmental Work Research, Helsinki.

Engeström, Y. (1996b) Developmental work research as educational research: looking ten years back and into the zone of proximal development, *Nordisk Pedagogik: Journal of Nordic Educational Research*, 16: 131–143.

Engeström, Y., Engeström, R. and Karkkainen, M. (1995) Polycontextuality and boundary crossing, *Expert Cognition Learning and Instruction*, 5: 319–337.

Engeström, Y. and Middleton, D. (eds) (1996) *Cognition and Culture at Work*, Cambridge University Press, Cambridge.

Engeström, Y., Viorkkunen, J., Helle, M., Pihlaja, J. and Poiketa, R. (1996) The change laboratory as a tool for transforming work, *Lifelong Learning in Europe*, 2: 10–17.

Fuller, A. (1996) Modern apprenticeships: process and learning. Some emerging issues, *Journal of Vocational Education and Training*, 48 (3): 229–249.

Gee, P. (1992) *The Social Mind: Language, ideology and social practice*, Bergin and Garvey, New York.

Gherardi, S., Nicolini, D. and Odella, F. (1998) Towards a social understanding of how people learn in organizations: the notion of a situated curriculum, *Management Learning*, 29 (3): 273–297.

Gott, S. (1995) Rediscovering learning: acquiring expertise in real-world problem solving tasks, *Australian and New Zealand Journal of Vocational Education Research*, 3 (1): 6–20.

Greeno, J.G. (1997) On claims that answer the wrong question, *Educational Researcher*, 26 (1): 5–17.

Griffen, P. and Cole, M. (1985) Current activity for the future, in *Children's Learning in the Zone of Proximal Development*, ed. B. Rogoff and J. Wertsch, Jossey-Bass, San Francisco, CA.

Guile, D. and Young, M. (1998a) Apprenticeship as the social basis of learning, *Journal of Vocational Education*, 50 (2): 173–192.

Guile, D. and Young, M. (1998b) The concept of learning and learning organizations (unpublished).

Hirschorn, L. (1986) *Beyond Mechanization*, MIT Press, Harvard, MA.

Kolb, D. (1984) *Experiential Learning: Experience as the source of learning and development*, Prentice Hall, Englewood Cliffs, NJ.

Kozulin, A. (1990) *Vygotsky's Psychology: A biography of ideas*, Harvard University Press, Cambridge, MA.

Kozulin, A. and Presseisen, B.Z. (1995) Mediated learning experiences and psychological tools: Vygotsky's and Feurestain's perspective in a study of student learning, *Educational Psychologist*, 30 (2): 65–75.

Lave, J. (1993) The practice of learning, in *Understanding Practice*, ed. S. Chaiklen and J. Lave, Cambridge University Press, Cambridge.

Lave, J. (1996) Teaching as learning, in practice, *Mind Culture and Society*, 3 (3): 9–27.

Lave, J. and Wenger, E. (1991) *Situated Learning*, Cambridge University Press, Cambridge.

Leontiev, A.N. (1978) *Activity, Consciousness and Personality*, Prentice Hall, Englewood Cliff, NJ.

Lundvall, B.A. (1996) *The Social Dimension of the Learning Economy*, DRUID Working Paper No. 96.1, Aalborg University, Denmark.

Neisser, U. (1976) *Cognition and Reality*, Freeman, San Francisco, CA.

Pea, R.D. (1993) Distributed intelligence, in *Distributed Cognition*, ed. G. Saloman, Cambridge University Press, Cambridge.

Pea, R.D. and Gomez, L. (1992) Distributed multimedia learning environments, *Interactive Learning Environments*, 2 (2): 73–109.

Prawat, R. (1993) The value of ideas, *Educational Researcher*, 31 (7): 5–16.

Raizen, S. (1991) Learning and work: the research base, paper presented at the United States Department for Education and The Overseas Education Centre for Development Conference, Phoenix, Arizona: Linkages in Vocational Technical Education and Training, April.

Resnick, L. (1987) Learning in and out of school, *Education Researcher*, 16 (9): 13–20.

Rogoff, B. (1990) *Apprenticeship in Thinking: Cognitive development in social contexts*, Oxford University Press, New York, pp. 3–25.

Scribner, S. and Cole, M. (1971) Cognitive consequences of formal and informal learning, *Science*, 82 (1): 553–559.

Shaiken, H. (1996) Experience of the collective nature of skill, in *Cognition and Culture at Work*, ed. Y. Engeström and D. Middleton, Cambridge University Press, Cambridge.

Teles, L. (1993) Cognitive apprenticeship in global networks, in *Global Networks*, ed. L. Harrison, MIT Press, Cambridge, MA.

Vygotsky, L.S. (1978) *Mind in Society*, Cambridge University Press, Cambridge.

Wertsch, J. (1981) *The Concept of Activity in Soviet Psychology*, M.E. Sharp, Armonk, NY.

Wertsch, J. (1984) Children's learning in the zone of proximal development, in *New Directions for Child Development*, ed. B. Rogoff and J. Wertsch, Jossey-Bass, San Francisco, CA.

Wertsch, J. (ed.) (1985) *Culture Communication and Cognition: Vygotskian perspectives*, Cambridge University Press, Cambridge.

Zuboff, S. (1988) *In the Age of the Smart Machine*, Heinemann, Oxford.

Chapter 10

The technology of learning in a social world

Terry Mayes

The pedagogy of on-line learning

The rapid developments in technology-mediated learning (or just 'on-line learning' or even the currently fashionable 'e-learning') are often accompanied by claims about its effectiveness in enhancing the process of learning itself, as well as its new efficiency in overcoming barriers of place and time in educational provision. The question is raised: are we seeing the development of a new pedagogy? Do we need an entirely new way of thinking about 'e-learning' that distinguishes it from the kind of learning that takes place in conventional educational settings? In fact, over the last two or three years almost every sector of education and training will have developed some of the methods associated with the new technology of learning. Almost every existing university, for example, will have some ongoing activity that involves creating new courses for the Internet, or web-based versions of existing courses. Most of these developments in the traditional university sector are attempting to apply existing methods and quality procedures to the new conditions of learning and teaching. This is not necessarily the case with all e-university developments, some of which are emerging from areas that have no tradition, or a very different tradition, of quality assurance. These include corporate universities, for-profit higher education companies, publishing and new media companies, and educational brokers.

There are probably as many aspects to the pedagogy underlying e-learning as there are different kinds of teaching and learning in schools, universities, training labs or home-learning, since the term simply implies that some Internet or web technology is involved. Since a computer can play some role in almost any kind of teaching, then e-learning can be associated with any kind of pedagogical approach, ranging from problem-based learning to simulator training. Nevertheless, the new language in which e-learning is largely discussed at the policy level emphasises the *delivery of learning*. The implicit assumption is that learning itself is significantly enhanced by the

Newly commissioned work.

new technology, rather than just the educational procedures, such as giving access to course notes or transmitting the tutor's comments. This view is understandable since there are clearly powerful new capabilities for accessing, structuring and presenting information. The ability to create virtual worlds for exploration, for example, is so striking that it is hard not to think of it as a new educational paradigm. Nevertheless, we have been here many times before (see Mayes, 1995). For most of the twentieth century technological developments were repeatedly greeted with predictions of a revolution in educational method. In his book *Teachers and Machines*, Larry Cuban (1986) has traced the history of attempts to use technology in the classroom. Some of the illustrations in that book show, to our modern eyes, wonderfully inappropriate and quaint attempts to use technology. In one example, a photograph entitled 'the aerial geography lesson' shows a class of children sitting in orderly rows of pre-war school desks, with a schoolmistress earnestly pointing to something on a geography globe at the front. What makes the photograph amusing is that the 'classroom' is in fact the cabin of an airborne aeroplane, and the photograph appears to illustrate that the technology of flight has simply been used pointlessly to transport a conventional classroom into the air. It is tempting to conclude that new technologies have failed to revolutionise education because they are always used to support existing pedagogy, rather than to help to develop new forms of teaching and learning. In fact, despite the repeated raising of expectations, no new technology has ever led to major change in education. This should not surprise us. Real change in the way education is provided, especially to learners who may not previously have had the opportunity to benefit, need not involve either new technologies or new pedagogical approaches at all. The development of the Open University provides a good example. Although it was originally conceived of as the 'University of the Air', and was strongly associated with the use of broadcasting as an innovative teaching method, its success has been based more directly on the application of sound conventional principles of carefully designed learning assignments and individual feedback from locally-based tutors. Perhaps we have already a perfectly good understanding of what is needed for effective learning to occur in any domain. The real challenge is to find cost-effective ways of offering this to large numbers of learners. By this argument, the main opportunity for on-line education is, after all, not pedagogy but *delivery*. Not the 'delivery of learning' (a phrase that conveys the misleading idea that learning is directly dependent on learning materials) but the delivery of new opportunities for learning. Technology may be directed towards change in the way education and training is organised: where and when learning occurs, how resources can be accessed, how learning can be assessed. It is not new pedagogies that we need. We need new ways of providing existing pedagogy efficiently and flexibly.

The main aim of this chapter is to offer a way of thinking about how technology can support the learning cycle, the goal–action–feedback loop that provides a basic model for all learning. We need to understand first how learning technology can support this fundamental pedagogy in which individual learners are given guidance about the performance of learning tasks at the right level of difficulty, and then given individualised feedback on their performance. In educational or training situations where this individualised support can be provided by personal tutors then there is no necessary advantage to be gained from on-line technology at all. The real challenge, of course, is to provide real support for learning in situations where there are too many learners and too few tutors, where the cost of tutors cannot be met, or where tutors and learners are unable to meet face-to-face, or where learners simply cannot access the resources for learning.

At a theoretical level it is probably true to say that never before has there been so much agreement about the pedagogical fundamentals (Jonassen and Land, 2000), resulting in what I shall refer to as the 'pedagogical consensus'. There has been a widespread rejection of a view of learning in which knowledge is 'acquired' (Anderson *et al.*, 1987), in favour of a constructivist view in which learning is primarily developed through activity (Papert, 1990). A second shift has been away from a focus on the individual, towards a new emphasis on social contexts for learning (Glaser, 1990). In particular we have seen, in the work of Lave (1988), Lave and Wenger (1991) and Suchman (1987), a very influential account of learning as 'situated', and thus only properly understood within a social or organisational context. This theoretical consensus, then, emphasises the importance of learning through performing real tasks, made meaningful to the individual through the social context in which they are performed, and providing the learner with the opportunity for feedback and reflection. Of course, much of the pedagogical debate focuses on the crucial question of how to translate such a broad theoretical account of learning into precisely-specified effective educational methods. Here, we focus on the role of technology. How and where can it make a real difference?

A framework for the design of learning technology

The conceptual framework I have adopted for approaching the pedagogy of on-line learning is one that attempts to illustrate how each stage of learning needs to be supported by a different kind of technology (Mayes and Fowler, 1999). The main value of this analysis is to emphasise where the support most needs to be directed in the learning cycle. This offers us a pedagogical rationale for designing the technology, and incidentally makes it obvious where we shouldn't waste our resources. The framework describes what in the pedagogical consensus are the three main elements of a learning process – conceptualisation, construction and dialogue. It also incorporates the idea of a learning cycle – acknowledging that learning is not a one-off process (a view unfortunately encouraged by the nature of our assessment methods) but involves continuous (even lifelong) revisiting and tuning of concepts and skills.

The three components of learning can be thought of as stages, although not necessarily ordered in the way traditional stage models of learning have suggested (Fitts and Posner, 1967). The stages describe the processes or modes of learning that, according to the consensus, all successful learning must involve. *Conceptualisation* is the process of coming to an initial understanding through contact with, and exploration of, a new exposition of some kind. *Construction* involves some activity in which the new understanding is brought to bear on a problem, and the required feedback about performance is gained. The third, consolidating, stage involves the full integration of the new understanding with the learner's general framework of knowledge (if we are considering the learning of a motor skill, we would use a different terminology here, but the same principles will apply). This is the stage at which aspects of expertise begin to appear, and the learner begins to use the new understanding, or practice the new skill, in the context of real application. This we have referred to as the *dialogue* stage, emphasising here the crucial role of discussion and reflection as the new understanding becomes applied to performance. Recently, Fowler and Mayes (1999) have considered different terms for this third stage in order to give more emphasis to the motivational and social dimension. This third stage can be viewed as a process of externalising the learning and relating it to its context of application. It may be that the term *contextualisation* more accurately describes this mode of learning. In contextualisation we see those aspects of apprenticeship and peer learning that set the social context for learning coming into play. Here, too, we see scope for an expression of individual differences. Since the emphasis now will be on real-world learning, the *use* of the knowledge or skill acquired through a long period of construction, then the learner will now move close to achieving the goals that motivated the learning in the first place, and the learning dialogues will become both more personalised and more focused on the context of application.

Let us consider these three stages of conceptualisation, construction and contextualisation and ask how technology might support each stage.

Conceptualisation

The most straightforward role for technology is to present the subject matter. However, the advances in multimedia have led us into the trap of thinking that this is where technology can make most impact on learning. Certainly, bringing the learner into convenient contact with the subject matter is a necessary precondition for learning. Also, presenting the subject matter in a way that makes it easy to understand is important. Yet, as the learner interacts with information presented, what is meaningful to the learner, and thus what is learned, depends far more on what the learner already knows, and why the learner is trying to understand this material in the first place, than on the extrinsic properties of the presentation. Nevertheless, to the extent that the initial presentation of subject matter allows new concepts to be created and explored then it is supporting conceptualisation. This presentation of subject matter is *primary courseware*. At its best this kind of use for technology can directly enhance understanding, in interactive graphical programs for geometry or logic, say, or for visualisation in organic chemistry. Underlying the design of primary courseware should be assumptions about the level of understanding of the learners it is intended for. As in the approaches to programmed instruction in the 1960s, or to hypertext in the 1980s, it is possible to offer the learner choices in the level of detail given, which can go some way towards achieving individualised instruction. But in general this kind of courseware is only effective in adjunct mode, as a supplement to real teaching. It cannot satisfy the need for activity, feedback and dialogue.

Construction

What role can technology play in the learners' performance of learning tasks? The most straightforward approach to this simply comprises descriptions and instructions for the learning tasks, and some tools to help the learner perform them. In fact, it is perfectly viable to run an effective on-line course without creating any new materials for it at all. The emphasis in on-line learning should always be first on the tasks the learners are asked to perform, rather than on the way they are going to access subject matter. The on-line environment can refer learners to existing websites, or to conventional printed sources. We have referred to the task-support environment as secondary courseware. Aspects of this kind of support are starting to appear in integrated or managed learning environments. One range of tools, mindtools or cognitive tools (Kommers *et al.*, 1992) has been designed specifically to encourage users to think conceptually about the subject matter being manipulated. However, secondary courseware involves any use of the computer to produce output when the task is primarily for learning. Integrated together, primary and secondary courseware provides both information and tools for learners to develop concepts and to test their understanding through carrying out tasks that use the concepts – by writing, by self-assessment, by carrying out experiments in virtual labs, by designing artefacts, analysing, classifying, reporting, and so on across the range of educational activities. Barab and Duffy (2000) have used the metaphor of the 'practice field' (a term from American sport) in discussing the need for learning tasks to be meaningful, and by implication for the learners to be motivated to carry them out. Ideally, these practice fields must be situated authentically, that is, they should bear an obvious relation to real-world tasks, and thus should make the connection between conceptual knowledge and its application. Examples of practice fields are problem-based learning (Savery and Duffy, 1996), anchored instruction (Cognition and Technology Group at Vanderbilt, 1990, 1993) and cognitive apprenticeship (Collins, Brown and Newman, 1989).

For learning to occur, of course, the system must allow feedback about the learners' performance on these tasks. An absolutely key question is whether the feedback can be automated. Can it be accomplished through self-assessment, or automated through the indexing of performance, or provided through 'canned' answers to anticipated questions? Or is it dependent on further advances in artificial intelligence? To extend the metaphor of the practice field – if feedback can be built in automatically to the practice routine in some way then it is not necessary to have a coach permanently present and the required feedback can be contained within the courseware. Some of the new on-line universities are attempting to achieve just this solution, which tackles head-on the key problem – that individual tutors for every student are too expensive. 'Cardean University', a subsidiary of UNext.com, has been launched recently with the claim that 'most questions will have been anticipated, leading to near-automatic guidance' (The Australian: Higher Education, 2000). This begs the crucial question of whether the kind of feedback that can be built into courseware can adequately substitute for dialogue with a tutor.

Contextualisation

The third stage in our learning cycle, the contextualisation stage, refers to the stage at which the learner tries to make use of, and interpret, newly acquired knowledge beyond the confines of a practice field. Feedback is crucial here, but this will take the form of dialogue, rather than straightforward answers to 'have I understood?' kinds of questions. *Tertiary courseware*, in the sense we use the term here, includes all the resources that might support such dialogue. These resources would include the tools that support direct one-to-one synchronous discussion, as well as the structuring of discussion around threads in conferencing environments, or even a database of frequently-asked questions that are compiled from previous dialogues. It should offer the new learner access to what Cumming (1993) has referred to as the 'discussion layer', and the resources would extend beyond the tools for active discussion by the current learners to databases of discussions from previous learners. It might consist of videoclips of tutorial discussion, or examples of previous learners' coursework, with the feedback from the tutor included. The concept of tertiary courseware is to offer a new kind of resource that, instead of providing direct explanations of subject matter, tries to capture the essence of being an active member of a community of learners of that subject matter, providing access to the questions, comments and dialogues of previous learners. On-line learning can offer something that has never before been possible in classroom education: that is, the possibility of recording all the individual dialogues that take place between tutors and students, or between peer learners. Using technology we can capture these, structure them in some kind of database, and make them available to new learners. This might offer at least part of the classroom experience, where much learning occurs as a consequence of simply observing and overhearing other learners. Following Bandura (1986), we have referred to this as *vicarious* learning.

The social learner

As we have noted, the social perspective on learning has received a major boost from the reconceptualisation of all learning as 'situated'. This can be seen as a necessary correction to theories of learning in which the cognitive and the social had become disconnected. Underlying both the situated learning and constructivist perspectives is the assumption that learning must be personally meaningful, and that this has very little to do with the informational characteristics of a learning environment. Activity, motivation and learning are all related to a need for a positive sense of identity (or positive self-esteem), shaped by social forces. Learning, as a deliberate activity, might be driven by the need for self-esteem in a number of ways. In some cases, in raising self-esteem we may learn the practices of a group that actively resists the educational process.

With the concept of a community of practice comes an emphasis on the individual's relationship with a group of people rather than the relationship of an activity itself to the wider practice, even though it is the practice itself that identifies the community. This provides a different perspective on what is 'situated'. For Wenger (1998) it is not just the meaning to be attached to an activity that is derived from a community of practice: the individual's identity is shaped by the relationship to the community itself. To understand the process, we need to examine 'learning to become'. Social psychologists, such as Turner (1991), make an important distinction between personal and social identity, a distinction that has been developed into an approach known as self-categorisation theory. What the social identity literature seems to tell us is that the salience of a personal or social identity in a specific situation is crucial, but very hard to predict without knowing a very great deal about all the possibly relevant individual history. What we can say is that where social identity becomes relatively more salient than personal identity there is a depersonalisation of the self. The individual now becomes defined more by a group or community and their motivation to learn is now derived from the need to carry out the activities of the group. Almost by definition, they are given a reason to learn. But what and how they are motivated to learn will now depend crucially on the nature of the community to which they aspire. This is where we need to consider more carefully the relationship between a community of practice and the kind of learning that it requires.

There are perhaps three levels at which it is useful to think of learning being situated. At the top level is the social-anthropological or cultural perspective, represented by the work of Lave and Wenger, which emphasises the need to learn to achieve a desired form of participation in a wider community. The essence of a community of practice is that, through joint engagement in some activity, an aggregation of people come to develop and share *practices*. This is usually interpreted as a stable and relatively enduring group, scientists for example, whose practices involve the development of a constellation of beliefs, attitudes, values and specific knowledge built up over many years. Yet a community of practice can be built around a common endeavour that has a much shorter time span. Greeno *et al.* (1998) gives examples of communities of practice that more closely resemble the groups studied in the social identity literature (e.g. Ellemers *et al.*, 1999). Some examples are a garage band, an engineering team, a day care co-operative, a research group or a kindergarten class. One characteristic of these groups is that they allow a greater scope for interplay between the psychological (or personal) and the social in determining practice than do the long-established communities. The influence of individuals, and of individual relationships, is likely to be greater.

However, for long-term stable communities there are two different ways in which the community will influence learning. First, there is the sense most directly addressed by Wenger – someone aspires to become a legitimate participant of a community defined by expertise or competence in some field of application. The learning in this case is the learning of the practice that defines the community. This is the learning involved in becoming an accredited member of a community by reaching a demonstrated level of expertise, and then the learning involved in continuous professional development. This may be formal, as in medicine, or informal, by being accepted as a wine buff or a political activist. The second sense is that of a community of learners, for whom the practice is learning *per se*. That is, a very broad community identified by a shared high value placed on the process of continuous intellectual development. This sounds fanciful but actually reflects a basic goal of education: to create a community of lifelong learners. It is possible to detect an irony in current policy, which aims to encourage the development of lifelong learning by developing new forms of educational provision aimed largely at adult learners who have failed to identify with such a community through their experience of schooling.

At the second level of situatedness is the *learning group*. Almost all learning is itself embedded in a social context – the classroom, or the tutorial group, or the virtual CMC-mediated discussion group or even the year group. The learner will usually have a strong sense of identifying with such groups, and a strong need to participate as a full member. Such groups can have the characteristics of a community of practice but here the practice is the learning itself, in a particular educational or training setting. Or rather it is *educational* practice, which may or may not be centred on learning. While there have been many studies of learning in informal settings (e.g. Resnick, 1987), there are comparatively few ethnographic studies of real groups in educational settings to compare with the many studies of group dynamics in work organisations (see Greeno et al., 1998). Yet every student and every teacher knows that there are characteristics of these groups or communities that are powerful determinants of the nature of the learning that actually occurs in educational institutions. Successful students are those who learn how to pass assessments, not necessarily those who have the deepest interest in the subject matter. There are, of course, many aspects of student behaviour that are determined by social goals that have little or nothing to do with the curriculum, but much to do with peer esteem.

The third level is the level of individual relationships. Most learning that is motivated by the above two levels will actually be mediated through relationships with individual members of the communities or groups in question. The social categorisation of these individuals will vary according to the context and nature of particular dialogues. Sometimes their membership of a group will be most salient, in other situations their personal characteristics will be perceived as more important. Such relationships will vary according to the characteristics of the groups involved, the context within which they operate, and the strength of the relationships.

Ultimately almost all learning will be motivated at some level by the desire to raise self-esteem by becoming a legitimate member of a community of practice. It provides the fundamental motivational rationale for attempting to learn in the first place, provided the group is valued, and thus can enhance self-esteem. Unfortunately unless we can say more about *why* self-esteem might be influenced by identifying with particular communities, groups or relationships, then this social identity account has the feel (to me) of a circular argument. For our present purpose we must be content with the view that the concept of social identity get us much closer to understanding motivation to learn, and gives us a clearer framework for approaching the design of learning environments than do accounts based solely on information flow.

Supporting social identity through vicarious learning

How can these different levels of social or personal identity be supported through the design of a learning environment? In their review of attempts so far to introduce the concept of community into educational practice (e.g. Brown and Campione, 1990; Scardamalia and Bereiter, 1993), Barab and Duffy conclude that these attempts do not yet convincingly capture the essence of development of self through participation in a community. These attempts are more readily interpreted as versions of problem-based learning practice fields. As a result of this conclusion that the idea of community has not yet been fully exploited, Barab and Duffy pose the following questions:

> If educators move towards a learning-as-participation-in-community approach, what communities are included? Is this a trade school or professional school approach? How can the breadth of learning experiences be provided that our children need if they must be members of all the communities in order to have the necessary experiences?
>
> (Barab and Duffy, in Jonassen and Land, 2000: 35)

One answer is to pursue the approach of vicarious learning. Mayes *et al.* (2001) report the results of experiments with a system called *Dissemination*, which compiled tertiary courseware from the recordings of students and tutors engaged in a specially devised set of 'task-directed discussions'. In an experiment comparing subjects who were offered this material in addition to conventional courseware they found that those students who chose to use the vicarious resources tended to model in their own performance the tasks, language and approaches used in the discussions they had viewed vicariously. One implication was that the experience of watching other students learn helped the new learners to model the basic task of learning more effectively.

A possible approach to Barab and Duffy's questions might be based on considering more carefully the ways in which vicarious learning might be effective. For each level of situatedness the tertiary material should reflect the social dimension that is most salient. Ideally, the learner should be able to choose the most appropriate. Thus the community of practice level might provide the learner with real-world examples of practice and the dialogues should illustrate the link between what is currently being learned in a practice field and the real-world application in a community of practice. What would be observed here would be the learning that brings a peripheral member of a community into full membership. At the next level, the level of the learning group itself, the vicarious material would focus on the difficulties of learning successfully in the particular course or educational context being currently experienced by the learner. This kind of vicariousness involves the observation of a learner who can be identified as a peer in the context of a particular learning task. Finally, individual learning relationships might be supported by previous dialogues from a named teacher, or from a particular expert, or even from an identified peer. (At this level we start to raise some potentially awkward ethical issues. It must be axiomatic that any dialogue or other work that is to be used vicariously must only be done so with the permission of the original participants.)

It is, of course, possible to try to classify the social dimension in finer grain than the three broad levels identified above. In an initial attempt to study the characteristics of learning relationships, Fowler and Mayes

(1999) classified them according to the nature of the learning experience as explorative, formative and comparative learning relationships. An *explorative* learning relationship is about discovery. This relationship is often very descriptive (discovering the 'what' more than the 'why'), although some level of explanation will be involved. A *formative* learning relationship focuses more on the building of understanding through guided activity, and this is achieved through a constructive approach – the building and testing of hypotheses about the world, and about the nature of practice. The third kind of learning relationship, *comparative*, characterises a relationship that occurs once a level of expertise has been achieved or when an individual becomes accepted as more than a peripheral member of a community of practice. It is a relationship that allows the learner to identify their state of knowledge with others, or to align their practice with that of a community or organisation. The primary purpose of a comparative relationship is not necessarily to acquire new knowledge, but to position and adjust existing knowledge by comparison with other knowledge states. Fowler and Mayes (1999) have reported an initial attempt to examine learning relationships empirically on groups of 16 year olds in the UK, Portugal and Finland. Overall, the results demonstrated that the influence of a particular kind of learning relationship deepened on the stage of learning reached. However, the results also showed a complex interplay between cultural and contextual factors that directly influences the interpretation of the characteristics of a learning relationship. The support roles played by parents, teachers and peers are themselves highly influenced by social and cultural variables. Although this analysis of learning relationships is currently too simplistic, it is looking in the right place. For insight into the learning opportunities offered by the new technology, the main focus should certainly be on the relationship of the learner to other people, rather than to information.

To summarise, this chapter has attempted to show how the design of learning environments needs to follow from a consideration of the stage of learning to be supported. It has then considered how technology might support the fundamental motivation to learn, which derives from the need to achieve self-esteem through identifying with a community of practice. An approach based on vicarious learning was described, proposing a new kind of courseware, focusing on allowing the learner to identify with the dialogues of other learners, rather than the traditional focus on direct engagement with the subject matter.

The last word should go to Carl Bereiter (2002) who strikes a cautionary note that should echo loudly across the global network of e-learning:

> Constructivism, learning by discovery, learner-centred education, computer-assisted instruction . . . computer conferencing, knowledge building: each one comes accompanied by a little demon who whispers in the ear. 'You won't have to worry about learning anymore. It will take care of itself. Stop teaching. Just let it happen.'

Acknowledgements

I am very pleased to acknowledge the contributions made to the ideas discussed here by colleagues with whom I have collaborated over several years. I would especially like to thank Chris Fowler, John Lee, Finbar Dineen, Jean McKendree, Carmel Smith, Patrick McAndrew, Jim Gallacher and Christina Knussen.

References

Anderson, J.R., Boyle, C.F., Farrell, R. and Reiser, B.J. (1987). Cognitive principles in the design of computer tutors. In P. Morris (Ed.), *Modeling Cognition*, New York: Wiley.

The Australian: Higher Education (2000) *The Australian: Higher Education*, 5th July 2000.

Bandura, A. (1986). *Social Foundations of Thought and Action*. Englewood Cliffs, NJ: Prentice-Hall.

Barab, S.A. and Duffy, T.M. (2000). From practice fields to communities of practice. In D.H. Jonassen and S.M. Land (Eds), *Theoretical Foundations of Learning Environments*. Mahwah, NJ: Lawrence Erlbaum.

Bereiter, C. (2002). *Education and mind in the knowledge age*. Mahwah, NJ: Lawrence Erlbaum.

Brown, A.L. and Campione, J.C. (1990). Communities of learning and thinking, or a context by any other name. *Contributions to Human Development*, 21: 108–126.

Cognition and Technology Group at Vanderbilt (1990). Anchored instruction and its relation to situated cognition. *Educational Researcher*, 19: 2–10.

Cognition and Technology Group at Vanderbilt (1993). Anchored instruction and situated cognition revisited. *Educational Technology*, 33: 52–70.

Collins, A., Brown, J.S. and Newman, S.E. (1989). Cognitive apprenticeship: Teaching the craft of reading, writing and mathematics. In L.B. Resnick (Ed.), *Knowing and Learning: Essays in honour of Robert Glaser*. Hillsdale, NJ: Erlbaum.

Cuban, L. (1986). *Teachers and Machines: The Classroom Use of Technology since 1920*. New York: Teachers College, Columbia University.

Cumming, G. (1993). A perspective on learning for intelligent educational systems. *Journal of Computer Assisted Learning*, 9: 229–238.

Ellemers, N., Spears, R. and Doosje, B. (Eds) (1999). *Social identity: Context, Commitment, Content*. Malden, MA: Blackwell.

Fitts, P.M. and Posner, M.I. (1967). *Human Performance*. Belmont, CA: Brooks-Cole.

Fowler, C.J.H. and Mayes, J.T. (1999). Learning relationships: From theory to design. *Association for Learning Technology Journal (ALT-J)*, 7(3): 6–16.

Glaser, R. (1990). The reemergence of learning theory within instructional research. *American Psychologist*, 45(1): 29–39.

Greeno, J.G., Eckert, P., Stucky, S.U., Sachs, P. and Wenger, E. (1998). Learning in and for participation in work and society. International conference (US Dept of Education and OECD) on 'How Adults Learn'. April, Washington DC.

Jonassen, D.H. and Land, S.M. (Eds) (2000). *Theoretical Foundations of Learning Environments*. Mahwah, NJ: Lawrence Erlbaum.

Kommers, P., Jonassen, D. and Mayes, J.T. (1992). *Cognitive Tools for Learning.* Berlin: Springer-Verlag.

Lave, J. (1988). *Cognition in Practice.* Cambridge: Cambridge University Press.

Lave, J. (1997). The culture of acquisition and the practice of understanding. In D. Kirshner and J.A. Whitson (Eds), *Situated Cognition: Social, Semiotic and Psychological Perspectives.* Mahwah, NJ: Lawrence Erlbaum.

Lave, J. and Wenger, E. (1991). *Situated Learning: Legitimate Peripheral Participation.* Cambridge: Cambridge University Press.

Mayes, J.T. (1995). Learning technologies and Groundhog Day. In W. Strang, V.B. Simpson and D. Slater (Eds), *Hypermedia at Work: Practice and Theory in Higher Education.* Canterbury: University of Kent Press.

Mayes, J.T. and Fowler, C.J.H. (1999). Learning technology and usability: A framework for understanding courseware. *Interacting with Computers*, 11: 485–497.

Mayes, J.T., Dineen, F., McKendree, J. and Lee, J. (2001) Learning from watching others learn. In C. Steeples and C. Jones (Eds) *Networked Learning in Higher Education.* London: Springer Verlag.

Papert, S. (1990). An introduction to the 5th anniversary collection. In I. Harel (Ed.), *Constructionist Learning.* Cambridge, MA: MIT Media Laboratory.

Resnick, L.B. (1987) Learning in school and out, *Educational Researcher*, 16: 13–20.

Savery, J. and Duffy, T.M. (1996). Problem-based learning: An instructional model and its constructivist framework. In B. Wilson (Ed.), *Constructivist Learning Environments: Case Studies in Instructional Design.* Englewood Cliffs, NJ: Educational Technology Publications.

Scardamalia, M. and Bereiter, C. (1993). Technologies for knowledge-building discourse. *Communications of the ACM*, 36: 37–41.

Suchman, L. (1987). *Plans and Situated Actions: The Problem of Human–Machine Interaction.* Cambridge: Cambridge University Press.

Turner, J.C. (1991). *Social Influence.* Milton Keynes: Open University Press.

Wenger, E. (1998). *Communities of Practice: Learning, Meaning and Identity.* Cambridge: Cambridge University Press.

Chapter 11

Sustainable literacies and the ecology of lifelong learning

Mary Hamilton

This chapter rests on a theory of literacy as social practice. The discussion is a development on from that in Barton (1994: 34–52), where contemporary approaches to literacy are discussed within the framework of the metaphor of ecology. The essence of this approach is that literacy competence and need cannot be understood in terms of absolute levels of skill, but are *relational* concepts, defined by the social and communicative practices with which individuals engage in the various domains of their life world. It sees literacy as historically and socially situated. As Brian Street (1995) puts it, it is a shift from literacy as an autonomous gift to be given to people, to an ideological understanding of literacy that places it in its wider context of institutional purposes and power relationships. The focus shifts from literacy as deficit or lack, something people haven't got, to the many different ways that people engage with literacy, recognising difference and diversity and challenging how these differences are valued within our society. This involves us in looking beyond educational settings to vernacular practices and informal learning, and to the other official settings in which literacies play a key role. Learning does not just take place in classrooms and is not just concerned with methods. This approach has come to be known as the New Literacy Studies (NLS).

Those of us working with this new approach advocate a broader understanding of what is included when we talk about literacy, suggesting that we should look beyond texts themselves to what people do with literacy, with whom, where, and how. That is, we focus attention on the cultural practices within which the written word is embedded – the ways in which texts are socially regulated and used. This leads us to consider the differentiated uses of literacy in varying cultural contexts. It leads us to consider not just print literacy but other mass media including visual and oral ways of communicating, and especially the way that the use of these media, using both old (print) and new (electronic) technologies, is interlinked. Writing becomes

This is an edited version of a paper originally prepared for the Global Colloquium on Supporting Lifelong Learning, 2000, Milton Keynes: The Open University.

as central as reading, and other ways of interacting with print culture are identified. In sum, the New Literacy Studies encourages us to be reflective about the everyday practices that we are all part of, to ask questions, rather than to assume that we already know what literacy is.

Despite the progress in theorising a different approach to literacy, there is still a long way to go in making the NLS credible as an approach within education policy and practice. In a number of countries (including Australia, South Africa and North America) standardised curricula and assessment systems are being introduced in an atmosphere of anxiety about falling literacy standards and the presumed effects of popular culture and the new communication media. These trends move us away from strategies that would be in tune with the NLS. They point backwards to more traditional and prescriptive methods for teaching and learning writing and reading, and attempts to separate print literacy from other media, especially those that prevail in popular cultural forms. The adult basic skills strategy in England and Wales includes a national curriculum for adults that is designed to fit seamlessly with school achievement as part of a National Literacy Strategy (DfEE, 2000).

These developments in adult education, however, are also taking place within a broader strategy of lifelong learning that I believe promises a different vision of what literacy might be, a vision that is much closer, potentially, to the new understandings embodied in the New Literacy Studies. To elaborate on this potential for developing sustainable lifelong learning in relation to literacy, I will address three issues:

1   The empirical research agenda: the need to develop a more extensive research base on the detail of literacy learning and use in local communities. This research should focus not just on individual learning histories, but also on literacy practices within and between groups and communities.
2   The need to clarify underpinning notions of learning and knowing (both at the individual and the group level) that are at work in the NLS and how these relate to forms of knowing currently privileged by educational institutions.
3   The need to pay much more serious attention to the institutional processes whereby 'truths' about literacy become translated into policy and practice – the intersection between policy and learning theory.

In what follows, I discuss these three areas starting from the perspectives offered by a recent ethnographic study published with David Barton as *Local Literacies* (Barton and Hamilton, 1998). This is prefaced by a brief explanation of key components in the theory of literacy as social practice.

Literacy practices, literacy events and texts

The notion of *literacy practices* offers a powerful way of conceptualising the link between the activities of reading and writing and the social structures in which they are embedded and which they help shape. The reference to practices, then, is not just the superficial choice of a word but the possibilities that this perspective offers for new theoretical understandings about literacy. Literacy practices are the general cultural ways of utilising written language that people draw upon in their lives. In the simplest sense literacy practices are what people do with literacy. However practices are not observable units of behaviour since they also involve values, attitudes, feelings and social relationships (see Street, 1993: 12; Barton and Hamilton, 1998: 6–13; and Hamilton, 2000). This includes people's awareness of literacy, constructions of literacy and discourses of literacy, how people talk about and make sense of literacy. These are processes internal to the individual; at the same time, practices are the social processes that connect people with one another, and they include shared cognitions represented in ideologies and social identities. Practices are shaped by social rules that regulate the use and distribution of texts, prescribing who may produce and have access to them. They straddle the distinction between individual and social worlds, and literacy practices are more usefully understood as existing in the relations between people within groups and communities rather than as a set of properties residing in individuals.

The other basic concepts that this approach draws on are those of *the literacy event* (or moment), which are activities where literacy has a role, and the *written texts* that are central to these activities. Events are observable episodes that arise from practices and are shaped by them: they are the material 'traces' of literacy practices. The notion of events stresses the situated nature of literacy, that it always exists in a social context. It is derived from ideas developed in sociolinguistics for the analysis of spoken language as 'the social event of verbal interaction' rather than the formal linguistic properties of texts in isolation. Unlike spoken language, social interactions involving literacy extend across time and space. This means that the term 'literacy event' has to be interpreted more broadly than just involving face-to-face interactions (see Hamilton, 2000). Many literacy events in life are regular, repeated activities, and these can often be a useful starting point for research into literacy. Some events are linked into routine sequences and these may be part of the formal procedures and expectations of social institutions like workplaces, schools and welfare agencies. Some events are structured by the more informal expectations and pressures of the home or peer group. Written texts are a crucial part of literacy events and the study of literacy is partly a study of texts and how they are produced and used. These three components, practices, events and texts, provide the bedrock of a social theory of literacy. The approach can be summarised in the form of a set of six propositions about the nature of literacy:

- Literacy is best understood as a set of social practices; these can be inferred from events that are mediated by written texts.
- There are different literacies associated with different domains of life.
- Literacy practices are patterned by social institutions and power relationships, and some literacies are more dominant, visible and influential than others.
- Literacy practices are purposeful and embedded in broader social goals and cultural practices.
- Literacy is historically situated.
- Literacy practices change and new ones are frequently acquired through processes of informal learning and sense making.

Developing an ethnographic research base

The NLS has begun to gather detailed ethnographic data on the ecology of literacy in everyday life. However, we still do not have enough data either to begin to identify the range of literacies with which people are engaged, or to begin drawing out commonalities and varieties of practice across social groupings of different kinds We are still talking in very general terms about the roles of literacy in society. We have to further deepen and problematise the notion of 'community'.

This has been the focus of the 'Local Literacies' project, a detailed study, lasting several years, of the role of literacy in the everyday lives of people in Lancaster, England. The study (reported in Barton and Hamilton, 1998 and elsewhere) used in-depth interviews, complemented by observations, photography and the collection of documents and records. It included a door-to-door survey in one neighbourhood of Lancaster and detailed case studies of people in 12 households in the neighbourhood, observing particular literacy events, and asking people to reflect on their practices. Alongside the case studies were 30 interviews of people in what we called access points for literacy, such as bookshops, libraries and advice centres. There were also interviews of 20 adults who had identified problems with their reading and writing and had been attending courses at the Adult College. More than a year after the main part of the study in a phase called the Collaborative Ethnography project we took back transcripts of interviews and drafts of our interpretative themes to 10 of the people for further discussion.

A recurrent theme in the Lancaster interviews concerns people's experiences of situations in their day-to-day life that had motivated them to develop a specialised expertise. These experiences launch them into new areas of learning in which they muster all the resources they can find, including literacy. Often these activities involve encounters with social institutions, dealing with professionals, ways of communicating, acting and understanding that were quite alien to people's previous experience. To interact with these institutions and to have access to the knowledge they control, literacy is a key tool. As well as these short-term responses to urgent practical needs, people have preoccupations and pastimes that they pursue over lengthy periods: quests for information about family history, correspondences and leisure activities of various sorts. These lead to a wide variation in what people know about, and it is revealing to look across a community to investigate the types of vernacular knowledge that exist – as Luis Moll has done in his research with Mexican-American households in the United States. Moll (1994) refers to funds of knowledge in communities, which are the practical exchanges and responses to needs for information and resources shared across families, between siblings, neighbours, friends. Moll found funds of knowledge in areas such as agriculture, economics, construction, religion, arts and repair. In Lancaster the areas of vernacular knowledge that we have identified include home economics and budgeting, repair and maintenance, childcare, sports, gardening, cooking, pets and animal care, and family and local history. Some people had also developed knowledge of legal, political, health and medical topics.

Ian Falk refers to these funds of knowledge and the processes whereby they are created and circulated within a community as a part of 'social capital': 'networks, norms and trust that facilitate co-ordination and co-operation for mutual benefit' (see Falk and Harrison, 1998: 613; Falk and Balatti, 1999). From his research with community-based groups in Australia, Falk has begun to identify the informal processes whereby knowledge is created and circulated, such as organising forums for discussion of issues; working collectively in groups; encouraging wide participation among community members, including volunteers; making routes for people to develop and move into new positions; 'passing the torch on' to subsequent generations of activists; dividing tasks up into short, recognisable and achievable goals and stages; and making results of activities publicly visible and celebrated (Falk and Harrison, 1998: 619).

Developing notions of 'vernacular' and 'institutional' literacies

How can we better describe the learning that takes place outside of formal institutions where it is more fluid, and where roles/subject positions, goals and procedures are not necessarily settled or named? One of the main organising ideas that we used in the 'Local Literacies' study was a distinction between dominant (institutionalised) and vernacular (self-generated) literacies. This has a parallel with James Gee's notion of 'primary' and 'secondary' Discourses and raises some of the same issues (Gee, 1990). Vernacular and institutional literacies are not independent and for ever separated categories of activity but they are in dialogue and the boundaries between them are permeable and shifting.

We defined dominant literacies as those that are associated with formal organisations, such as those of the school, the church, the workplace, the legal system, commerce, medical and welfare bureaucracies. They are part of the specialised discourses of bounded communities of practice, and are standardised and defined in terms of the formal purposes of the institution, rather than in terms of the multiple and shifting purposes of individual citizens and their communities. In dominant literacies there are professional experts and teachers through whom access to knowledge is controlled. To the extent that we can group these dominant literacies together, they are given high value, legally and culturally. Dominant literacies are powerful in proportion to the power of the institution that shapes them.

Vernacular literacies are essentially ones that are not regulated or systematised by the formal rules and procedures of social institutions but have their origin in the purposes of everyday life. They are not highly valued by formal social institutions though sometimes they develop in response to these institutions. They may be actively disapproved of and trivialised and they can be contrasted with dominant literacies, which are seen as rational and of high cultural value.

Vernacular literacies are more common in private spheres than in public spheres. Often they are humorous, playful, disrespectful, sometimes deliberately oppositional. When questioned about them, people did not always regard them as real reading or real writing. Some vernacular literacies are deliberately hidden: these include those that are personal and private, where reading or writing are ways of being alone and private, ways of creating personal space. There are also secret notes and letters of love, abuse, criticism and subversion, comics, scurrilous jokes, horoscopes, fanzines, pornography – some but not all of which will be revealed to the researcher's gaze. These findings link in with a range of other research that explores the informal literacies of different age groups. See, for example, Mahiri, 1999, who has documented the uses of literacy in the popular culture of black youth in California; Falk and Harrison, 1998; Falk and Balatti, 1999; Lankshear and Knobel, 1999; Princeloo and Breier, 1996.

In our project we found vernacular literacies involved in a range of everyday activities, which we roughly classified as (1) organising life; (2) personal communication; (3) private leisure; (4) documenting life; (5) sense making; and (6) social participation. In all of these areas, we found examples of people becoming expert, consciously carrying out their own research on a topic of interest to them.

A number of points can be made about the nature of vernacular literacies based on the data from the Lancaster study. First, vernacular literacy practices are learned informally. They are acquired in homes and neighbourhood groups, through the everyday perplexities and curiosities of our lives. The roles of novice or learner and expert or teacher are not fixed, but shift from context to context and there is an acceptance that people will engage in vernacular literacies in different ways, sometimes supporting, sometimes requiring support from others. Identities shift accordingly.

Second, the vernacular literacy practices we identified are rooted in action contexts and everyday purposes and networks. They draw upon and contribute to vernacular knowledge, which is often local, procedural and minutely detailed. Literacy learning and use are integrated in everyday activities and the literacy elements are an implicit part of the activity, which may be mastering a martial art, paying the bills, organising a musical event or finding out about local news. Literacy itself is not a focus of attention, but is used to get other things done. Everyday literacies are subservient to the goals of purposeful activities and are defined by people in terms of these activities.

Where specialisms develop in everyday contexts they are different from the formal academic disciplines, reflecting the logic of practical application. Vernacular literacies are as diverse as social practices are. They are hybrid in origin, and often it is clear that a particular activity may be classified in more than one way since people may have a mixture of motives for taking part in a given literacy activity. Preparing a residents association newsletter, for instance, can be a social activity, it can be part of leisure or political activity, and it may involve personal sense making. They are part of a 'Do-It-Yourself' culture that incorporates whatever materials and resources are available and combines them in novel ways. Spoken language, print and other media are integrated; literacy is integrated with other symbolic systems, such as numeracy, and visual semiotics. Different topics and activities can occur together, making it hard to identify the boundaries of a single literacy event or practice. This is in contrast to many school practices, where learning is separated from use, divided up into academically defined subject areas, disciplines and specialisms, and where knowledge is often made explicit within particular interactive routines, is reflected upon, and is open to evaluation through the testing of disembedded skills.

As a starting point the distinction between 'vernacular' and 'institutional' knowing has been useful but it needs to be further developed, especially in terms of the dialogic relationship between the two, how the one influences and articulates with the other. One way forward is to look to other strands of theorising that are concerned to understand the process of 'knowing' as mediated, situated, provisional, pragmatic and contested. These strands include activity theory (Lave and Wenger, 1991; Wenger, 1998; Engeström, 1993) where learning is seen in terms of initiation into a community of practice involving apprentice-like relationships between expert and novice members of that community; feminist theory that foregrounds the role of personal experience and the 'knowing subject' in creating theory (Ramazanoglu and Holland, 1997); and organisational learning theory, including 'actor network' theory (as reviewed by Blackler, 1995; Law and Hassard, 1999) that focuses on the interconnected institutional systems and environments within which knowing is achieved.

Casting an eye over these related areas reveals that the New Literacy Studies is just one part of a growing recognition that 'knowing' is not simply the product of individualised skills and understandings but a relational, social process. Neither is knowing simply a cognitive matter but it simultaneously involves other modes of engaging with the world. We can, for example, identify at least the following (adapted from Blackler, 1995):

- *embodied* knowing, which is experiential and action-oriented, dependent on people's physical presence, on sensory processes, physical cues, and may be only partially explicit;
- *symbolic* knowing, which is mediated by conceptual understandings that are explicit, propositional and encoded through a variety of semiotic technologies – spoken language and other symbol systems, print and electronic communications;
- *embedded* knowing, which is procedural, shaped or engrooved by practical routines that are configurations of material, technological and social symbolic resources through which knowing is accomplished;
- *encultured* knowing, which involves the shared understandings that are achieved through social relationships and initiation into communities of practice.

Some of these modes of knowing are more explicit, abstract and portable, some are much more closely tied to physical localities and individual subjectivities, and they of course vary enormously in the relatively value that is accorded to them in different contexts. However, they are all present and affect eventual outcomes.

A further elaboration of learning is needed to explore the features of different 'communities of practice', the processes that go on within them and the resources they draw on (including the physical and material environment), and how people engage with them.

Within the communities we have studied, technical literacy skills are unevenly distributed and people may participate in literacy practices in many different ways. However, as the Lancaster research has shown, what counts as 'expert' and what is 'novice' is problematic outside of an institutional setting. People move flexibly in and out of being 'learners' in different roles, notions of exchange and identity are strongly linked. The notion of apprenticeship does not fit all situations and we need a more fluid conceptualisation of the relationships experienced outside of institutional settings. Stephen Reder's notion of practice engagement theory (Reder, 1994) may point a way toward this more fluid characterisation. He identifies three aspects of literacy practices – the technologies of reading and writing, the functions of these activities, and the social meanings carried by them – and suggests that people may engage with any or all of these three aspects in shifting, and often unequal ways. Reder's formulation could be integrated with the different modes of engagement identified above.

Creating 'truths' about literacy

So far this chapter has discussed ways of developing a fuller notion of vernacular literacies, based on a detailed database of ethnographic research. But to make use of this notion of vernacular knowing and literacy we also need to understand more about how institutions produce and privilege certain kinds of knowing as 'real knowledge', how they produce and recognise 'experts', and how in this process they devalue or redefine the vernacular for their own purposes – a process that Wenger (1998: 57) refers to as 'reification'. Much more thought needs to be given to the nature of lay expertise and its relationship to identity and to professional expertise and competence, and the tensions between these. What is acceptable as 'expertise' in informal and in institutional settings? What are the significant dimensions of expertise in each case that contribute to a person's credibility (e.g. richness of their knowledge base, institutional affiliations, ability to communicate effectively, breadth of perspective, ability to make links between formal and informal networks).

In this section I offer some thoughts about how such an enquiry might proceed. This part of the chapter is more speculative, as it projects a research agenda, rather than reporting on work already done.

To achieve an understanding of how institutional truths about literacy are created, I suggest that we need to focus less on what the teachers and learners are doing (or need to do) and more on what the administrators, assessors, quality inspectors and government agencies and policy makers are doing in relation to literacy and lifelong learning. That is, our attention and analytic effort has to move to the intersection between policy and learning theory. We should be concerned to make links between the theoretical insights offered by the NLS and the public discourses of literacy that inform educational policy and practice – and which in turn enter into popular understandings about literacy.

To give a specific example, we should be doing more to contest the solidifying international 'regimes of truth' that are developing through standardised assessment and testing – which are, in their turn, organising national and local knowledge about what literacy is. Surveys such as the International Adult Literacy Survey (IALS) (OECD, 1997) organise our knowledge about literacy and the 'literate subject'. They are based on a particular set of social relations and institutions that have both national and international dimensions, residing in government, academic and media domains. The surveys draw on a particular discipline – the psychometric measurement tradition – which is dedicated to the search for universal certainties about the relation between literacy, economy and society. They use an information processing model of literacy and attempt to identify levels of literacy skill that are independent of the context of use – the literacy counterpart of the labour skills supposedly possessed by the flexible worker. Darville (1999) and Hamilton and Barton (2000) have argued that these surveys fit well within the globalising project of the new capitalism. They are redefining literacy to fit in with the projected needs of an ideal, consumer-oriented citizen who is responsive to multiple new contexts for literacy use. They justify a vision of what literacy should be, rather than being based on people's lived experiences, and create new divisions, defining people as being with or without the correct kinds of literacy. These activities continue to be developed with large sums of research money provided by the governments of OECD countries. I would argue that this is not a democratic project, but an institutional vision that has little to do with supporting people to use and control literacy for their own purposes. It is important that we reveal the institutional underpinnings and aspirations for IALS, rather than treating the findings from surveys like this as indisputable facts about contemporary life.

Theoretical tools are already available for exploring the ways in which institutions exercise and realise power: from Foucault (1982); from Bernstein (1996) on how knowledge is re-framed within a pedagogical discourse when it is imported into an educational context; and from Wenger (1998) on the characteristics of institutional communities of practice. Methodological tools are also available (for example in actor network theory) that would enable us to trace the threads of an initiative such as the IALS through its creation and dispersion from research contexts to media, policy and practice (see Law and Hassard, 1999). These would help us analyse how literacies are embedded in the institutional relationships and processes that give them their meaning and how vernacular literacies are defined in relation to dominant, legitimated practices.

Supporting literacies through lifelong learning policy

The fact that some literacies are supported, controlled and legitimated by powerful institutions implies that others are devalued. Many of the literacies that are influential and valued in people's day-to-day lives, that are widely circulated and discussed are also ignored by educational institutions: they do not count as 'real' literacy. Neither are the informal social networks that sustain these literacies drawn upon or acknowledged. A social practice approach to literacy demonstrates the changing demands that people experience at different stages of their lives and offers convincing evidence of the need for lifelong learning systems that people can access at critical points. Whilst community resources and funds of knowledge exist, they also have their limitations. They are often unevenly distributed and can be supported by various kinds of educational response. From this perspective, formally structured learning opportunities are one important component of lifelong learning, but they are only one aspect of a solution to sustaining literacies. The focus needs to be wider. Literacy/lifelong learning funds could be used to:

- increase the physical spaces available for people and groups to meet/exchange ideas/display/perform;
- strengthen access points for literacy: libraries/cyber cafes/bookshops/advice centres etc. so that citizens can access information they are searching for through print, video, electronic forms etc., engage in virtual or actual meetings with experts;
- strengthen open local government structures that facilitate consultation and access to existing routes for change/citizen action;
- support local media that help circulate and publicise news, events, space for debating issues, ideas;
- provide structured opportunities to learn both content and process skills and link up with others interested in the same issues.

In developing this strategy, we have to pay serious attention to the social relationships that frame literacy in schools, colleges, classrooms and other learning groups, and the power dimensions of these relationships in terms of the ability to make decisions, confer value, demonstrate expertise. So long as these relationships remain unexamined and untouched, there is very little possibility that literacies can be sustained within a system of lifelong learning.

References

Barton, D. (1994) *Literacy: An Introduction to the Ecology of Writing*, Oxford: Blackwell.

Barton, D. and Hamilton, M. (1998) *Local Literacies: Reading and Writing in One Community*, London: Routledge.

Bernstein, B. (1996) *Pedagogy, Symbolic Control and Identity: Theory, Research, Critique*, London and Washington DC: Taylor and Francis.

Blackler, F. (1995) Knowledge, Knowledge Work and Organizations: An Overview and Interpretation, *Organizational Studies*, 16(6): 1,021–1,046.

Darville, R. (1999) Knowledges of Adult Literacy: Surveying for Competitiveness, *International Journal of Educational Development*, 19: 273–285.

DfEE (Department for Education and Employment) (2000) *Skills For Life: The National Strategy for Improving Adult Literacy and Basic Skills*, Nottingham: DfEE Publications.

Engeström, Y. (1993) Work as a Testbed of Activity Theory, in S. Chaiklin and J. Lave (eds) *Understanding Practice: Perspectives on Activity and Context*, pp. 65–103, Cambridge: CUP.

Falk, I. and Balatti, J. (1999) Social Capital, Literacy Ecologies and Lifelong Learning. Paper presented at the seminar Literacies Amidst Global Transformation: Workplace and Community Literacies, University of Wisconsin, Madison.

Falk, I. and Harrison, L. (1998) Community Learning and Social Capital: Just Having a Little Chat, *Journal of Vocational Education and Training*, 50(4): 609–627.

Foucault, M. (1982) The Subject and Power, in H. Dreyfus and P. Rabinow, *Michel Foucault: Beyond Structuralism and Hermeneutics*, Chicago: University of Chicago Press.

Gee, J. (1990) *Social Linguistics and Literacies: Ideology in Discourses*, London: Falmer Press.

Hamilton, M. (2000) Expanding the New Literacy Studies: Using Photographs to Explore Literacy as Social Practice, in D. Barton, M. Hamilton and R. Ivanic (eds) *Situated Literacies*, London: Routledge.

Hamilton, M. and Barton, D. (2000) The International Adult Literacy Survey: What Does it Really Measure? to appear in *The International Review of Education*, 46(5): 377–389.

Lankshear, C. and Knobel, P. (1999) The New Literacy Studies and the Study of New Literacies. Paper presented at the seminar Literacies Amidst Global Transformation: Workplace and Community Literacies, University of Wisconsin, Madison.

Lave, J. and Wenger, E. (1991) *Situated Learning: Legitimate Peripheral Participation*, Cambridge: Cambridge University Press.

Law, J. and Hassard, J. (eds) (1999) *Actor Network Theory and After*, Oxford: Blackwell.

Mahiri, J. (1999) Literacy's Lost Ones: Cultural Models of Learning and African American Youth. Paper presented at the seminar Literacies Amidst Global Transformation: Workplace and Community Literacies, University of Wisconsin, Madison.

Moll, L. (1994) Mediating Knowledge Between Homes and Classrooms, in D. Keller-Cohen (ed.) *Literacy: Interdisciplinary Conversions*, Creshill, NJ: Hampton Press.

OECD (1997) *Literacy Skills for the Knowledge Society*, Paris: OECD.

Princeloo, M. and Breier, M. (eds) (1996) *The Social Uses of Literacy: Theory and Practice in Contemporary South Africa*, Cape Town: Sached Books.

Ramazanoglu, C. and Holland, J. (1997) Tripping Over Experience: Some Problems in Feminist Epistemology. Paper presented at International Conference, Transformations: Thinking Through Feminism, Lancaster University UK, July.

Reder, S. (1994) Practice-engagement Theory: A Sociocultural Approach to Literacy Across Languages and Cultures, in B. Ferdman, R.-M. Weber and A.G. Ramirez, *Literacy Across Languages and Cultures*, New York: State University of New York Press.

Street, B. (ed.) (1993) *Cross-cultural Approaches to Literacy*, Cambridge: Cambridge University Press.

Street, B. (1995) *Social Literacies*, London: Longman.

Wenger, E. (1998) *Communities of Practice: Learning, Meaning and Identity*, Cambridge: Cambridge University Press.

Chapter 12

Academic writing in new and emergent discipline areas

Mike Baynham

Introduction

> The student who is asked to write like a sociologist must find a way to
> insert himself into a discourse defined by this complex and diffuse
> conjunction of objects, methods, rules definitions, techniques and tools
> ... In addition he must be in control of specific field conventions, a set
> of rules and methods which marks the discourse as belonging to a certain
> discipline. These vary even within disciplines: a reader response critic
> will emphasize one set of textual elements, a literary historian another,
> and the essays produced will contain these differences.
>
> > (Ball *et al.*, 1990: 357)

So pity the poor nursing student, who is required to write at times like a
sociologist, at others like a philosopher, yet again like a scientist and finally
as a reflective practitioner! Much of the literature on disciplinarity assumes,
even when it is discussing phenomena of heterogeneity, blurring and crossing (see Klein, 1993), the lineaments of traditional disciplines. In a set of
interrelated studies conducted at the University of Technology, Sydney
(Baynham *et al.*, 1995; Lee *et al.*, 1995; Gordon *et al.*, 1996; Lee, 1997) we
were particularly interested in discipline areas where complex combinations
of disciplinary influences intersect, in the 'new' discipline areas of the 'new'
university.

A basic assumption is that, in order to understand the problematic of
the novice writer, we need to understand the disciplinary contexts within
which they are required to write, or more specifically the disciplines they
are writing themselves into. But I would also like you to keep in your mind's
eye the image of the harassed first-year nursing student, hurrying from lecture
to tutorial, backpack full of photocopied journal articles, notes and guide-
lines for an essay on the sociology of nursing, a clinical report, a case study,

This is an edited version of a chapter previously published in *Student Writing in Higher
Education*, 2000, Buckingham: Open University Press.

a reflective journal. They are certainly living disciplinary and textual heterogeneity.

Recent advances in the understanding of disciplines and disciplinarity (see Messer-Davidow et al., 1993) emphasize that, rather than being neat homogeneous discourse communities, academic disciplines are radically heterogeneous and constituted in difference. Nowhere is this more apparent than in the emergent 'practice-based' disciplines of the new university. Disciplinary heterogeneity and difference have significant implications for student academic writers who can be understood as writing themselves into a 'disciplinary politics', by which I mean the internal tensions and conflicts over such issues as what counts as knowledge, what should be where in the curriculum and how it should be valued, where boundaries within and between disciplines should be drawn. Students are learning to take up writing positions in the context of this diversity and its accompanying tensions. In this chapter I will explore the implications of this approach in the areas of nurse education and adult education, drawing out implications for both research and pedagogy in academic literacies.

I will begin by identifying three perspectives on the theorization of academic writing. The first, a 'skills-based' approach to the teaching of academic writing, assumes that there is a generic set of skills and strategies that could be taught and then applied in particular disciplinary contexts. The second, 'text-based', linguistic approach assumes a relatively homogeneous discipline, with text types to be discovered, analysed and taught. The third, 'practice-based', approach proposed here investigates student writing as both text and practice, arguing that, most crucially, the student writer is learning to take up disciplinary positions in a discourse 'community'. Where the disciplinary positions are conflictual, overlapping or indeed blurred, the student academic writer will be working within the disciplinary politics that is produced.

This chapter will be illustrated with data from a series of related studies that investigated the discipline-specific aspects of student writing in new and emergent disciplines, focusing in particular on the ways in which the disciplinary practices and politics are crucial to an understanding of student writing (understood as both product and process) and the ways in which students learn to construct powerful writing positions in text.

A concept like 'writing position' cannot be fully or richly understood without a discipline-internal awareness of what counts as knowledge and what counts as an authoritative disciplinary position, and this includes the awareness of internal diversity and conflict, as realized in the politics of the discipline.

So where does this leave the student writer? In the concluding section of this chapter I will argue that academic writing pedagogy must make the concerns of disciplinarity, disciplinarization and consequent writing positions central – in other words, as Graff (quoted in Klein, 1993) suggests, we must 'teach the conflicts'.

Three perspectives on academic writing

The *skills-based approach* to the teaching of academic writing underpins the traditional 'study skills' approach to teaching academic writing and assumes that there is a generic set of skills and strategies, such as 'essay-writing' or 'referencing', that can be taught and then applied in particular disciplinary contexts. Using a skills-based approach, students are typically provided with pre-sessional courses or ongoing support sessions in study preparation, often in mixed disciplinary groups, with the implication that they can take the skills they learn and apply them in their particular disciplinary context. A major criticism of this approach is that it tends to ignore the discipline-specificity of writing requirements.

The *text-based approach* draws on the resources of linguistic analysis, in particular register (see Halliday and Martin, 1993) and genre analysis (Swales, 1990; Freedman and Medway, 1994), to understand the discipline-specific nature of writing tasks. Register analysis can characterize the language of history or science, while genre analysis focuses on the text types that are required – for example, the history essay, the laboratory report, the case report. There is now plenty of evidence of the language demands of particular discipline areas that can be used to design discipline-specific curricula to support academic writing. One problem with the text-based approach, however, is that it often assumes a relatively homogeneous discipline, with text types to be discovered, analysed and taught. To talk glibly about 'the language of science or history' can gloss over significant differences within disciplines which, as we shall see, are increasingly identified by studies of disciplines and disciplinarity themselves.

The *practice-based approach* emphasizes the social and discursive practices through which a discipline constitutes itself. A lot of the pioneer work in this regard has been carried out in the study of scientific communities (Latour, 1987; Bazerman, 1988; Myers, 1990). Such studies look at how fields are constituted and maintained, how novices are socialized into the practices that are constitutive of the field. Messer-Davidow *et al.* (1993) present a collection of such studies across a broad range of discipline areas, including accounting, social sciences, economics, art history and medicine. From a practice perspective, we are interested in how students as novices are brought into the typical discursive practices of the discipline, whether it be literary criticism, ethnographic fieldwork or participating in laboratory experiments.

In shifting the emphasis on to the ways in which disciplines are constituted it is, however, important not to lose touch with the sharply focused specificity that text-based studies provide. Language is, after all, a major means (if not necessarily the only means) by which disciplinary knowledge is constituted, reproduced, contested and added to, and learned. We need precise linguistic accounts of the linguistic means that are deployed in specific disciplinary contexts, but we also need to recognize the complexity and specificity of these contexts. So combining both the text and the practice perspective (texts and practices) has a powerful potential.

New and emerging discipline areas

The authors reviewed so far have been concentrating on the disciplinary shape of traditional university disciplines. In this chapter, however, I will be presenting case studies of student writing practices in new and emerging areas, where the focus is not on the traditional discipline, but rather on the formation of professions, nurses, adult educators, engineers, what might be called 'practice-based' disciplines.

These new and emerging areas will typically draw on a range of disciplines. Let us take adult education as an example. The adult education theorist Griff Foley (1995: 15) identifies a range of disciplines, including sociology, psychology, geography, philosophy and economics, which impact on adult education as a field of study. Knowledge from these disciplines is, of course, not imported raw but is 'recontextualized', in Bernstein's (1990) sense. Within adult education as a field of study there are different schools of thought, with different versions of what counts as knowledge, or even the boundaries of the field (Foley, 1995: 14). These involve major epistemological cleavages, for example, around positivist, interpretative and post-positivist accounts of knowledge and action. All of this adds up to the disciplinary terrain on to which the student adult educator is introduced. To paraphrase Ball *et al.*, when the adult education student is asked to 'write like an adult educator' this will be the terrain he/she will learn to inhabit. By mapping out the major dimensions of this terrain, we can develop an account of the 'disciplinary politics' that the student is writing him/herself into. To illustrate this, I would like to consider nursing education as a case study.

The data I will present below were taken from a study of student academic writing practices in three discipline areas – nursing, information studies and women's studies – at the University of Technology, Sydney, a new Australian university (in the sense that it was formed in the 1989 restructuring of higher education in Australia) whose mission statement identifies it as providing education for the professions. The data collected included interviews with students and lecturers/markers, support materials for the courses and examples of student writing. Below, first-year nursing students and their lecturers talk about writing and the disciplinary issues of nursing. I will also discuss issues arising in a first-year essay-writing task for a subject 'Professional Responsibilities in Nursing', which focuses on the changing social roles of the nursing profession.

Nursing education: a case study

One of the significant issues in nursing education has been the shift, over the last decade or so, from a 'practice-oriented' to a 'professionalized' conception of nursing (see Gray and Pratt, 1989, 1995). This has coincided with the shift of nursing training/education out of the hospitals and into the universities. So one aspect of the disciplinary politics of nursing is precisely this shift from practice-oriented to professionalized concepts of nursing. Another tension that is central to nursing education is that between practical knowledge and theorized knowledge. Like adult education, nursing draws on a heterogeneous disciplinary base, most strikingly in the contrast between the science-based, clinical subjects and the ethical subjects. Underlying these subjects are very different conceptualizations of what counts as knowledge, the clinical subjects being underpinned by the positivist scientific paradigm, the ethical subjects by an interpretative or post-positivst perspective on what counts as knowledge. The shift into academia of nursing training/education produces in turn processes of disciplinization, where nursing is pressured to constitute itself as a 'proper' discipline. (Again there are interesting parallels with adult education as a field of study.) As Webb (1992: 747) suggests:

> Nursing is a relatively young academic discipline. Like other disciplines which have attempted to establish respect and credibility, such as psychology and sociology, nursing has sought to do this by imitating longer-established disciplines and in particular the traditional or physical sciences.

Underpinning all of this is what might be termed the 'gender politics' of nursing, the construction of nursing as a handmaiden profession in relation to its other, the medical profession. This disciplinary politics of nursing (see Table 12.1) constitutes the context into which nursing students are writing themselves.

In the following extracts, nursing lecturers and a nursing student discuss some of these tensions:

Table 12.1 The disciplinary politics of nursing

Practice-based	vs.	Professionalized
Practical knowledge	vs.	Theorized knowledge
Homogeneous disciplinary base	vs.	Heterogeneous disciplinary base
Clinical subjects (positivist)	vs.	Ethical subjects (interpretative/critical)

Processes of disciplinization: nursing as a 'proper' discipline; nurse educators as 'proper' academics
Gender politics of the nursing profession: 'doctors and nurses'

There is a big gap between those working in theoretical areas and those in practical areas which is nowhere near being breached and it will be a long time before it's breached. This puts students in an interesting position. It is probably less problematic now but 4–5 years ago when our students went out to practise after graduation they were treated very badly because they were seen to be trained in an institution that was inappropriate for training nurses, by people who were too distant from nursing and in areas that were irrelevant to nursing. Now because there is an increasing number of university-trained nurses practising, that has started to dissipate but the tension underneath this has not been resolved. This is largely to do with the political climate in the hospitals; there is a dominant natural sciences medical approach to health care and there is an issue of how nurses fit into that. It's very complicated. If there is so much to be sorted out it would be hard to envisage any sort of discipline unity or clarification as to what is appropriate in the discipline for a long time.

(Lecturer interview)

I think those tensions reflect the tension for nursing because the universities seem to be teaching people about all these airy-fairy things and out in the real world they're saying they can't even fill a catheter but that's not true. What we do teach them is about real nursing but it's more than that, and I think that the faculty has to understand that people in the practice area have legitimate concerns which must be addressed by us, and I think the practice must address the fact that nursing has got to develop a profession. The only way you can develop a profession is developing thinking people. That's the tension for nursing.

(Lecturer interview)

Another lecturer speaks more explicitly about the tensions between the scientific and humanities-based components of the curriculum:

The major tension I would have to face is that I started in the K. programme which was very much a humanities programme and we did things like important skills to develop a student's thinking, their critical writing skills, there is much less emphasis on how to nurse. When I came over to this campus there was very much a focus on the nursing things, the science and the nursing, and there was less emphasis about ethics and law and critical thinking and the humanities, the meaning of caring, the meaning of being a person. So the assignments that I had to mark were really bad. I thought, I can't believe that these people are in the third year of their programme and they cannot write, they cannot think, they cannot critique other people's work. So that was a real dilemma for me and I think that was the tension for the faculty, we had this terrible battleground between one group of people feeling that one campus wasn't teaching how to nurse and the other wasn't teaching how to think. Over several years we've got a common understanding but there's still tension there.

(Lecturer interview)

So how do students experience the disciplinary tensions between nursing as a science-based curriculum and its ethical, humanistic dimensions? The following student expresses her surprise about the range of what counted as an appropriate topic in nursing journals:

When I started to look for articles, I found there were more than I thought. I thought that, being in the nursing field, journals would focus on hypertension, neck problems, new drugs, etc., but I was surprised they have a lot of articles based on hazards happening in the workforce, nurses' perception of hazards, nurses' fears about dealings with AIDS patients, things like autonomy, authority, where does your responsibility stop and what are the boundaries. It was good.

(Student interview)

The same student identifies confusing differences between the kinds of writing that are expected of her in different parts of the programme:

But for medical, surgical, if you have to write about care for a person with AIDS, you either know or you don't know. This semester we had a case on cardiac failure and that was another one where you have to go and read how the heart works, how it pumps, where does it go wrong and why does the patient present with such and such and you have to learn. I did learn from that assignment. But for this assignment, I felt that for me it was good because I spent time thinking about it, I didn't do much reading, I didn't learn very much but certain things did catch my attention, especially the need for nurses to prove that we are people with nurses, we're not just handmaidens, which I always felt. I felt that it was never being argued enough about but I know now that's not true, but it hasn't really made me a better nurse.

(Student interview)

In this section I have tried to sketch some of the broad parameters and tensions within which nursing students are writing. My argument is that the tension between positivist and critical hermeneutic versions of what counts as knowledge, the shift towards professionalization of nursing, the emphasis on nursing as a 'proper' academic discipline are constitutive of the contexts within which the students are writing. I will illustrate this in the next section with an example from a first-year undergraduate writing task.

'Professional responsibilities in nursing' essay topic

The 'professional responsibilities in nursing' subject comes from the first year of the undergraduate nursing course. As suggested above, it focuses on the changing social roles of the nursing profession and encapsulates in many ways the tensions we have been exploring in the nursing education curriculum, particularly in relation to the professionalization of nursing. The writing task demanded of the students is an expository essay that explicitly invites the students to address the professionalism issue:

> Nurses will not be able to properly fulfil their professional responsibilities until they have greater autonomy and authority – discuss.

Students taking up writing positions: voicing in the nursing essay

Drawing on notions of 'authoring', 'authority' and 'authorization' of truth statements (see Lindstrom, 1993), I will examine a range of ways in which student writers authorize statements, including through the incorporation of the voices of others into their essays. Unsurprisingly, the most commonplace strongly authorized statements in the essays tend to be supported by appeals to the literature (theorized knowledge). Others – still highly valued, as it turns out – produce appeals to experience (practical knowledge), 'what nurses think and do', rather than 'what the literature tells us that nurses think' in support of their developing argument. Both strategies interpolate the voices of others into the text – on the one hand the voices of established academic sources, on the other the voice of experience.

Yet, as we shall see, it is a mistake to set up a simplistic opposition between weakly authorized statements invoking experience and strongly authorized statements invoking theorized knowledge. From other highly valued essays we will examine data showing how the student writers can produce strongly authorized statements by appealing to experience, apparently flouting the 'academic' requirement of appealing to theorized knowledge. I would suggest that an explanation for this apparent anomaly lies in the disciplinary politics of nursing itself, in its emergence as a discipline, in the pull of different constructions of nursing, specifically between nursing as a field of practice and nursing as a professionalized and thus theorized discipline.

Here are some examples of the two contrasting ways in which the student writers authorized statements in their essays. The first is an authorization based on experience of what nurses typically do:

> Lack of sufficient autonomy and authority is seen when a nurse has to have a physician authorize a pathology test when the nurse suspects the patient has a urinary tract infection. Some physicians who trust

experienced staff will leave blank signed forms for nurses to fill out if they see the need arising (S. White, Registered Nurse, personal communication, 6 October 1994). In this instance the nurse needs more autonomy and authority so they can fill in a form and send a sample to the laboratory thereby saving precious time and also initiating treatment quicker which will eventually benefit the patient. When nurses see that a patient is being sufficiently hydrated and has no further need of an intravenous drip, they have to inform the doctor who will then authorize the removal of the cannula. Nurses are sufficiently educated to make these judgements but due to lack of autonomy and authority are unable to do so.

(Kirsten)

Kirsten's statements about nurses' need for autonomy and authority, in which greater autonomy and decision making on the part of nurses are shown to be improving care for the patient, are authorized by examples from experience, not from the research literature. Interestingly, this effect is significantly reinforced when the writer uses the 'personal communication' referencing convention to authorize a particular statement, based on experience from the field rather than from an academic source. Immediately following this, Kirsten authorizes a statement by sourcing it to an academic reference:

According to Kiereini (1980) nurses have been making independent decisions regarding management of their patients without wanting to accept accountability for their decisions.

So Kirsten's essay uses a mix of these two strategies, which seems to be successful, as her essay is well received. The marker's comments are interesting, however. While giving the essay a better than average B grade, the comment is:

The weakness in your argument lies in a lack of support for claims . . .

In contrast to Kirsten's essay, which draws on both the authorization-from-experience and the academic sourcing strategy, other essays, such as Sue's (graded A) and Lorraine's (graded B), rely almost entirely on the academic sourcing strategy. Virtually every statement they make can be traced back to an academic source:

Ironically, Beaumont (1987) states that *some* nurses themselves are reluctant to receive responsibility and accountability for their actions, as they are 'low risk takers' and fear mistakes. However, a study done by Kramer and Schmalenberg (1988, cited in Collins and Henderson, 1991: 25), [claims] that nurses preferred to work in an environment which encouraged autonomous practice. Furthermore, Schoen (1992) confirmed their claims and concluded that a number of research including her own, have discovered a positive link between autonomy and job satisfaction.

(Sue)

In Sue and Lorraine's essays, what nurses say/think/feel/do is constructed purely through the filter of the research literature. Nurses are present in the text only as reconstituted or recontextualized into a body of research.

So how do these authorization strategies operate in the less successful essays? We will look at Deirdre's essay (graded E), and Karen's essay (graded C–).

In Karen's essay we find examples both of the academic sourcing strategy, with quoted statements attributed to sourced authors, and the attributed appeal to experience:

In the health care system the doctors have the most autonomy and authority and this 'male dominated profession used the path to professionalism to ensure themselves of financial security and autonomy' (Short and Sharman 1987: 199) . . .

. . . Nurses believe that this is not true and that doctors should be educated to have a greater appreciation of nursing theory and practice, that decision making processes should be reviewed and that changes in hospital administration could ease tension between nurses and doctors.

(Karen)

Deirdre's E grade, according to the subject outline, 'represents a performance which reflects little understanding, or gives little evidence of a serious attempt to meet the expectations of the assigned task'. Her essay starts with the following:

Many nurses have seen the achievement of a professional standing as an important goal in advancing the interests of nurses and health care consumers. In particular, it has been said that it will increase nurses' autonomy and status, and therefore their capacity to achieve the aims of nursing and fulfil their professional responsibilities.

The marker's comments are as follows:

You have quoted this word for word from the subject outline without acknowledgement. This is plagiarism.

Deirdre's apparent adoption of the impersonalized unattributed academic voice is destabilized because the reader/marker can in fact trace it back to an attributable source that is rather close at hand, the subject outline.

Later on in the essay, Deirdre shifts further into the personalized experiential voice by switching to the pronoun 'we':

> So even though nurses must still take orders from doctors, we display professionalism through choosing appropriate care, professionalism, using our knowledge to choose what care will give them the best benefits, while providing emotional care.

Ivanič and others (Ivanič and Simpson, 1992) have raised the issue of such pronoun choices as resistances to the impersonalizing academic conventions. It is beyond the scope of this chapter to explore why this writer made these choices, but it is clear that the shift into 'we' is a significant shift into an experiential voice. The issue, surely, is one of informed choice. As writers we can consciously take risks, use strategies that flout dominant conventions based on informed choice. We can also produce docile, conventional texts. But this is based on awareness of the options. A writer who has not been made aware of the options is not in a position to make an informed choice.

Deirdre's appropriation of wordings that are bound to spring to the attention of the reader/marker who probably wrote them is perhaps indication enough of her unfamiliarity with key underlying conventions of academic writing. That plagiarism is a complex issue and that what counts as plagiarism is itself a social construct is well documented (Scollon, 1995) but again is beyond the scope of this chapter. I will conclude this case study by looking at an essay that raises the question of docility and risk in writing.

Mark's essay: thematizing the argument

Mark's essay is one of the most highly rated by the marker (A–) yet it does not rely heavily on the docile academic sourcing strategy that we saw in Sue and Lorraine's essays:

> Due to the fact that the nursing profession is so diverse and becoming even more so, until nurses unite, establish their practice at different levels and situations, their levels of autonomy and authority will be undermined. 'Increasingly, nurses are taking responsibility for their practice and gaining a new autonomy in their work' Reid (1993: 30) and Flint (1993: 66) agree 'everyone in a professional role, whether lawyer, doctor, teacher, or midwife, must be able to practice autonomously and use his or her professional judgement'. This brings in the argument that some nurses want to take greater control of their workload and duties, and to be accountable for them, whilst some want to take minimum

control. However, in direct conflict to these ideas, is the dominance that doctors have over nurses. Leach (1993) discusses that, with few exceptions, nurses work under medical control. The medical profession controls admissions, discharges and what goes on in between, even if the patient had been admitted for purely nursing care.

Instead, what Mark seems to do is thematize the argument, concentrating not on what the research literature tells us nurses think/feel/do or on what experience tells us, but on the implications of the argument (between autonomy and subordination, between different sections of the nursing profession, between doctors and nurses). Mark seems to take up a confident summative voice. Where Deirdre appears to take up this voice, in the first paragraph of her essay, the effect is destabilized because the reader/marker recognizes a verbatim appropriation from the subject outline. Where Mark quotes it is to back up or elaborate an argumentative position that he has already introduced. The strategy is therefore quite different from that of Sue or Lorraine in which the text is constructed almost entirely from sourced material.

'Teach the conflicts'

In this chapter I have somewhat complicated the picture of student academic writing practices within new and emergent discipline areas along the lines suggested by Goggin (1995). The skills-based approach to the teaching of academic writing assumes that there is a generic set of skills and strategies that can be taught and then applied in particular disciplinary contexts. The text-based approach assumes a relatively homogeneous discipline, with text types to be discovered, analysed and taught. I am suggesting, in line with writers such as Ball et al. (1990), that, most crucially, the student writer is learning to take up disciplinary positions in discourse and that this needs to be taught explicitly.

Where the disciplinary positions are conflictual, overlapping or indeed blurred (see Geertz, 1975, cited in Klein, 1993) the student academic writer will be working within the disciplinary politics that is produced. So where does this leave the student writer? In this section I argue that academic writing pedagogy must make the concerns of disciplinarity, disciplinarization and consequent writing positions central – in other words, as Graff (quoted in Klein, 1993) suggests, we must 'teach the conflicts'.

As I suggested earlier in the nurse education case study, a major conflict is between, on the one hand, the practice-oriented account of nursing and the experiential ways of knowing that it makes authoritative and, on the other hand, the professionalized, disciplinary account of nursing, with its consequent impersonalization and generalization of the nursing subject. We have seen how these conflicts work within the texts examined earlier, producing at one moment highly valued, if docile, texts in the impersonalized disciplinary voice (Sue and Lorraine's). Other similarly valued essays (Kirsten and Mark's) draw on the strategy of authorization from experience, though running the risk of the critical marker's comment. The less successful essays (Karen and Deirdre's) appear to fail both in making authoritative statements in the impersonalized disciplinary voice and in the generalized experiential voice of 'what nurses think'. Mark's essay seems to thematize the conflict itself between the experiential/practice-based account and the impersonalized disciplined account of nursing. While appearing somewhat unconventional, i.e. not docile, in terms of the conventions of academic writing, it is highly valued by the marker.

It is worth noting that the tensions and conflicts between the experiential/practice-based voice and the impersonalized disciplinary voice and the consequent availability of writing positions are a major theme of the work of Ivanič and others (see Ivanič and Simpson, 1992) on critical language awareness approaches to the teaching and learning of academic writing, as they are in Ball et al. (1990). Here they map very specifically on to the shift of nursing into the academy with its consequent professionalization and disciplinization. This would suggest that the disciplinary politics of nursing is not in itself limited to nursing alone, in that it draws on issues that are clearly broader than nursing such as the positivist/critical hermeneutic discourses as well as theory–practice divides.

'What every student needs to know' about academic writing is precisely the ways in which taking up or rejecting writing positions involves taking up or rejecting disciplinary positions. This is not a pedagogy to be offered instead of a focus on the technical aspects of academic writing (of course someone needs to talk Deirdre through the social meanings of plagiarism, to give her the skills to quote and reference effectively). It provides a complementary layer in which the student academic writer can explore the writing/disciplinary/subject positions that are available along with the areas of blurring, overlap and conflict that create difficulties and choices in taking up an authoritative position in writing.

Conclusion: intrinsic and embodied readings

An underlying theme of this chapter has been, in a sense, how lecturers/markers read student writing and how students read the circumstances within which they are required to write. Here I take 'reading' in a broader pedagogical sense: how we read these texts as people concerned with the teaching of academic writing. I want to suggest that there are two broad ways of characterizing this: first, the idea of intrinsic reading or an intrinsic reading; second, the idea of embodied reading and embodied readings. What do I mean by this?

An intrinsic reading is one which reads the pedagogical issues of student texts in terms of skills or technologies. Learner writers in this version will have greater and lesser degrees of skill in, for example, incorporating word-ings and meanings into text. They will to a greater or lesser extent have available to them the linguistic technologies to do so. An embodied reading is one that reads the text as an embodiment of the disciplinary politics within which it is produced, and as an embodiment of the processes of subject production at work as learner writers engage with the writing demands of the discipline. In this chapter I argue that such embodied readings are an essential basis for academic writing pedagogy.

References

Ball, C., Dice, L. and Bartholomae, D. (1990) Developing discourse practices in adolescence and adulthood, in R. Beach and S. Hynds (eds) *Advances in Discourse Processes* Vol. XXXIX. Norwood, NJ: Ablex.

Baynham, M., Beck, D., Gordon, K. and San Miguel, C. (1995) Constructing a discourse position: Quoting, referring and attribution in academic discourse, in K. Chanock (ed.) *Integrating the Teaching of Writing in the Disciplines*. Melbourne: LaTrobe University.

Bazerman, C. (1988) *Shaping Written Knowledge: The Genre and Activity of the Experimental Article in Science*. Madison: University of Wisconsin Press.

Bernstein, B. (1990) *The Structuring of Pedagogic Discourse*. London: Routledge.

Foley, G. (ed.) (1995) *Understanding Adult Education and Training*. Sydney: Allen & Unwin.

Freedman, A., Adam, C. and Smart, G. (1994) Wearing suits to class: Simulating genres and simulations as genre. *Written Communication*, 11(2): 193–226.

Freedman, A. and Medway, P. (eds) (1994) *Learning and Teaching Genres*. Portsmouth, NH: Heinemann/Boynton Cook.

Geertz, C. (1975) *The Interpretation of Cultures: Selected Essays*. London: Hutchinson.

Goggin, M.D. (1995) Situating the teaching and learning of argumentation within historical contexts, in P. Costello and S. Mitchell (eds) *Competing and Consensual Voices: The Theory and Practice of Argument*. Clevedon: Multilingual Matters.

Gordon, K., Baynham, M., Lee, A. and San Miguel, C. (1996) Academic writing and disciplinary politics: What every student needs to know. Paper presented at Knowledge and Discourse conference, University of Hong Kong, 18–21 June.

Gray, G. and Pratt, R. (1989) *Issues in Australian Nursing*. Melbourne: Churchill Livingstone.

Gray, G. and Pratt, R. (eds) (1995) *Scholarship in the Discipline of Nursing*. Melbourne: Churchill Livingstone.

Halliday, M. and Martin, J. (1993) *Writing Science*. London: Falmer Press.

Ivanič, R. and Simpson, J. (1992) Who's who in academic writing? in N. Fairclough (ed.) *Critical Language Awareness*. London: Longman.

Klein, J.T. (1993) Blurring, cracking and crossing: Permeation and the fracturing of discipline, in E. Messer-Davidow, D.R. Shumway and D.J. Sylvan (eds) *Knowledges: Historical and Critical Studies in Disciplinarity*. Charlottesville: University Press of Virginia.

Latour, B. (1987) *Science in Action: How to Follow Scientists and Engineers Through Society*. Cambridge, MA: Harvard University Press.

Lee, A. (1997) Working together? Academic literacies, co-production and professional partnerships. *Literacy and Numeracy Studies*, 7(2): 65–82.

Lee, A., Baynham, M., Beck, D., Gordon, K. and San Miguel, C. (1995) Researching discipline specific academic literacy practices: Some methodological issues, in A.C. Lynn Zelmer (ed.) *Higher Education: Blending Tradition and Technology. Research and Development in Higher Education*, 18: 464–482.

Lindstrom, L. (1993) Context contests: debatable truth statements on Tanna (Vanuatu), in A. Duranti and C. Goodwin (eds) *Rethinking Context: Language as an Interactive Phenomenon*. Cambridge: Cambridge University Press.

Messer-Davidow, E., Shumway, D.R. and Sylvan, D.J. (eds) (1993) *Knowledges: Historical and Critical Studies in Disciplinarity*. Charlottesville: University Press of Virginia.

Myers, G. (1990) *Writing Biology*. Madison: University of Wisconsin Press.

Scollon, R. (1995) Plagiarism and ideology: Identity in intercultural discourse. *Language in Society*, 24: 1–28.

Swales, J. (1990) *Genre Analysis: English in Academic and Research Settings*. Cambridge: Cambridge University Press.

Webb, C. (1992) The use of the first person in academic writing: Objectivity, language and gatekeeping. *Journal of Advanced Nursing*, 17: 747–752.

Chapter 13

Pedagogies for lifelong learning

Building bridges or building walls?

Miriam Zukas and Janice Malcolm

Situating lifelong learning

Lifelong learning pedagogies do not, as yet, exist in the UK. We have a stratified and segmented educational system in which there is little connection between those sectors that might be regarded as contributing to the virtual concept of lifelong learning. There is little conceptual connection between adult and further education, higher education, training and professional development. Even within obvious areas for overlap such as work-related learning, each sector has tended to develop its own subspecialism. The notion of lifelong learning implies some continuity within the system; we argue that, so far, lifelong learning pedagogies are marked by disjunctions. Where we might have expected to see conceptual bridges, we (and our studies) experience pedagogical walls.

These claims may seem overstated but one example demonstrates the point. Adult education and higher education in the UK still retain their identities as 'separate spheres' even when adult education is provided through universities. Despite the evidence that the efforts of adult educators to open up higher education for older students have borne fruit (adults now constitute the majority of the student population in universities), once they arrive in higher education, students move from being 'adult students' to 'mature students'. Whilst this might be considered a mere shift in nomenclature, we believe that it signifies discontinuity. In order to take account of these new students, we would expect the literature of higher education pedagogy to draw on the decades of work that adult educators have put in to developing appropriate curricula and pedagogies for 'non-traditional' students. The pedagogic focus of large parts of adult education was, after all, on how to adapt and transform traditional teaching practices and the content of courses to include students for whom the standard cultural capital of universities was opaque and alienating. Instead, the new specialism of teaching and learning

This is an edited version of a paper originally prepared for the Global Colloquium on Supporting Lifelong Learning, 2000, Milton Keynes: The Open University.

in higher education has developed without reference to adult education and takes little account of who the students are; instead it concentrates upon the processes and outcomes of the classroom transaction, rather than its content, context or purpose.

We have been involved in a journey, trying to understand why there are so few connections between developments in pedagogy in the education of adults and those in higher education. Our initial project[1] was a literature-based study intended to develop theoretical frameworks for analysing pedagogical writing, and to trace the commonalities and divergences between pedagogic models evident in adult education and other established sectors of education, and those emerging in the relatively new – and relatively undertheorised – field of higher education pedagogy. This, we hoped, would provide the basis for an analysis of the consequences of divergent development for both adult and higher education teaching. The study was UK-based, but utilised sources from throughout the Anglophone world and, to a lesser extent, from European writing originating outside the UK.

We focus somewhat unfashionably on educators, and on the dynamic relationship between educators and learners, understanding the classroom, the lecture theatre, the workplace as communities of practice. We believe that much of the current rhetoric of lifelong learning obscures this essential dynamic, and concentrates on learning in ways that, paradoxically, effectively leave learners without any real identity other than that of 'learners'. In our continuing work, we draw on the work of Lave and Wenger (1991) and more recently Wenger (1998) to try to understand the emerging pedagogic 'communities of practice' – particularly in higher education (Malcolm and Zukas, 2000). These ideas provide sociocultural and pedagogic 'lenses' through which educational practice can be viewed, and help to clarify the reasons for the development of the intercommunal and epistemological splits between fields of pedagogic writing. In essence, they help us to understand why, despite the apparent bridge building of lifelong learning rhetoric, we find only semi-permeable walls.

Building identities

Our research has focused on identifying pedagogic 'identities' implicit in current writing on higher education teaching and on creating a bibliographic map of the literature. Our aim has been not to use these modes as reifications of educational practice, but rather to uncover the identities or 'masks' (Bailey, 1977) attributed to educators within the literature, and to consider their implications. Below, we develop two of these emergent identities to provide a synthesis of our previous work; we believe that this offers a possible framework for considering and evaluating pedagogies in lifelong learning.

We identified at least five pedagogic 'identities' in the literature we surveyed:

- The educator as critical practitioner
- The educator as psycho-diagnostician and facilitator of learning
- The educator as reflective practitioner
- The educator as situated learner within a community of practice
- The educator as assurer of organisational quality and efficiency; deliverer of service to agreed or imposed standards

These identities, or 'versions' of the educator, are neither exhaustive nor mutually exclusive, but represent the range of understandings of pedagogic work apparent in the 'mainstream' higher education literature. In the process of arriving at and analysing these identities, which we describe below, we used a number of conceptual 'dimensions' (some more useful than others) along which we could locate the characteristics and implications of each identity. A more detailed account of both the models and the process of analysis has been given elsewhere (Zukas and Malcolm, 1999).

In this chapter we will compare two common conceptualisations of pedagogic identity in the respective literatures of higher education and adult education: the educator as 'critical practitioner', and the educator as 'psycho-diagnostician and facilitator of learning'. These polarised pedagogic identities are familiar to the adult education community of practice, representing the extreme positions in an ideological tussle that has rumbled through the field for several years. They are chosen precisely because they are illustrative of a major difference between the two bodies of pedagogic literature: the identities are both strongly represented and contested within adult education, whilst in higher education, one identity is dominant, and the other is barely visible. In each case, we explore the prevalence and characteristics of the identity within higher education and adult education writing, analysing the reasons for inclusion or exclusion of particular perspectives. We briefly describe the other three identities, although we do not incorporate them in our analysis.

In order to consider analytically the commonalities and differences between the five 'identities', we developed a number of conceptual dimensions through a process we describe below. In this chapter, we utilise five of the dimensions in order to gauge some of the implications of the critical practitioner and psycho-diagnostician identities for pedagogic practice. They are: learning within a community vs. individualised learning; disciplinary community vs. pedagogic community; moral and social accountability vs. organisational accountability; educator as 'person in the world' vs. anonymous/invisible educator; and student as 'person in the world' vs. anonymous/invisible learner.

The educator as critical practitioner

The political roots of adult education and its strong social purpose tradition, from the activities of the Chartists through to contemporary discussions of 'diversity', have ensured that the 'why' and 'what' of adult education have always been as important as the 'how'; in fact content, purpose and process have been seen as inseparable elements of practice. The current generation of adult education writing has borrowed from a range of political traditions to bring a variety of critical, including feminist, social understandings to bear on pedagogy, and to produce various conceptualisations of critical practice. Postmodernist understandings can be seen as deriving from this same critical tradition. These diverse approaches consider the content of classroom practice as embodying and manifesting the power–knowledge relations that exist beyond the classroom. Of course, this is not to suggest that all adult education writing could possibly be characterised as promoting critical practice; adult education has its share of dull and mechanistic writing on decontextualised classroom techniques. Our point here is that it is a recognisable, familiar and easily accessed 'angle' on the pedagogy of adult education; adult educators are not generally surprised to be asked about the *purpose* of their pedagogic work as well as its processes.

Our reading of the higher education pedagogic literature has revealed a markedly different picture from that evident in adult education. There is a long and respected tradition of critical writing on the purposes of higher education and its various social, historical, epistemological and technological functions. In Britain, Barnett's prolific recent work on higher education and a 'critical being' (1997) is a major contribution to the debate on higher education as a social and political *institution*. In (inter-)disciplinary fields where different positionalities have challenged and transformed the nature of what counts as knowledge, e.g. in women's studies, critical pedagogy has emerged inevitably from the questioning of disciplinary discourses, structures and power relations. ('Critical' here includes feminist approaches – although the debate on their divergences continues (e.g. Gore, 1993).) Thus it is not difficult to find writing on feminist pedagogy, but it tends to be found within the specialist literature of women's studies itself, rather than in the literature of mainstream or 'straight' pedagogy. When we turn to the 'straight' pedagogic literature of higher education, which generally takes 'teaching and learning', rather than knowledge or purpose, as its starting point, versions of critical practice are much harder to find; it is almost like looking at the literature of an entirely different field of study. There are odd exceptions: Webb (1996), Rowland (1999) and Walker (1999) are examples of writers on higher education pedagogy who explicitly consider the 'why' of higher education in conjunction with the 'how'. Walker's references to such familiar guiding lights of critical adult education as Gramsci and Freire are almost unique in the field of higher education pedagogy; her background in South African teacher education may be relevant. Beyond these few independent-minded exceptions, the educator as critical practitioner makes few appearances in the 'straight' higher education pedagogic literature. The instrumental focus on 'teaching and learning', as if it were a subject in its own right, means that higher education pedagogy has become fragmented and artificially dispersed over several distinct bodies of thought and literature.

The educator as psycho-diagnostician and facilitator of learning

Taking the first international exchange between British and North American adult educators (Zukas, 1988) as a point for comparison, a notable difference between British and North American adult education was the absence of psychological models of the learner and the teacher from the British literature. Over the last ten years or more, this difference has been less marked as North American adult education has moved away from psychological models and frameworks as can be seen in examples such as the latest *Handbook of Adult and Continuing Education* (Wilson and Hayes, 2000). In Britain, certain forms of psychology, particularly humanistic versions, have influenced much adult education pedagogy but psychometrics, learning styles and other non-social understandings of the individual have been much less popular. In contrast, psychology has provided the dominant framework for higher education pedagogic writing in Britain. There is a vast literature that begins with a focus on learners and educational transactions. It assumes that educators need to diagnose learners' needs, e.g. by identifying or taking into account learning styles or skills (e.g. Boyatzis and Kolb, 1991), or other individual predispositions, according to a favoured learning theory (Brown, 1993). Once characteristics and approaches to learning are identified, educators facilitate learning by using techniques and tools that meet those needs (e.g. Gibbs, 1992; Grenham *et al.*, 1999). With learning foregrounded to this extent, pedagogy itself is conceptualised as little else than diagnosis and facilitation. This diagnostic approach is favoured by many of the 'founding fathers' of British higher education pedagogic research. In such approaches, psychological theories are used as tools to inform the ways in which practice takes place; in other words, theory determines practice. But, unfortunately, such theories do not emerge from practice; indeed, they are remarkable in that they discount the context and purpose of educational events, and the disciplinary settings in which such events take place.

Of course, not all psychological theory ignores context and settings. Sociocultural psychology has transformed school teacher education and clarified the relational elements of pedagogy; research on situated cognition (Brown *et al.*, 1989) has also emphasised the significance of context for teaching and learning. But such critical psychological approaches have not had a significant impact on higher education pedagogic writing. Why might this be? Tennant (1997: 1) argues that, if the focus is on learning rather than on psychology, 'it appears cumbersome and unnecessary to address the conceptual and methodological problems of psychological theory and research'. This failure to engage critically with the discipline from whence ideas about learning originate has led to arid and somewhat outdated versions of psychology being 'applied' to learning.

A further reason why critical psychological approaches may not have had much of an impact has to do with the divorce of higher education pedagogic research from pedagogic practice, as is often the case in UK institutional structures. Teachers may assume that pedagogic researchers 'know' how it should be done – they are, after all, the experts. As in management education, they may demand to know 'how to'; and psycho-diagnostic and facilitative models offer apparently easy solutions. The contemporary concern with accountability and measurability (Malcolm and Zukas, 1999) encourages the search for such solutions, and the structural separation of higher education teacher training from school, adult and further education teacher training also lessens the impact of research across sectors. Furthermore, the commodification of higher education encourages a conceptualisation of learning as product, rather than process. The psycho-diagnostician is able to diagnose learning needs and facilitate learning through various techniques; learning is then measured to make sure it has happened.

The educator as reflective practitioner

This model of the educator is very common in much of the current literature. It derives in general terms from the work of Schön (Schön, 1987) although it has been subjected to much modification and reinterpretation (e.g. Boud and Walker, 1998; Nicol, Kane and Wainright, 1994). The range of interpretations, and the fact that they are frequently implicit rather than explicated in texts about teaching and learning in higher education, mean that 'reflective practice' has become a rather all-embracing term, which diminishes in significance as its applications increase. It is interesting to note that whilst reflective practice has been much contested as a concept in the literature of childhood education and adult education (such as Bright, 1996; Ecclestone, 1996), its conceptual basis has only rarely been addressed in the higher education literature (Eraut, 1995). In most of its higher education manifestations it is presented as taken-for-granted 'good practice'. The clearest evidence of its conceptual dominance is the way it was incorporated, without explanation, into the language of the ILT accreditation framework (ILT, 1999).

The educator as situated learner within a community of practice

This model is seen most obviously in the work of Lave and Wenger (Lave and Wenger, 1991) who focus on legitimate peripheral participation (through apprenticeship) as a way of learning the 'culture of practice'. It could of course be argued that an informal apprenticeship is in fact the traditional learning route for teachers in higher education. However the current focus on the use of mentoring schemes and similar intergenerational support methods suggests a more structured and conscious approach to the process of professional learning. The attraction of the ideas of cognitive apprenticeship, socialisation and professional evolution, within a community of practitioners, may be that they incorporate the social world into the educator's identity.

The educator as assurer of organisational quality and efficiency; deliverer of service to agreed or imposed standards

There is a strand of writing on teaching and learning in higher education that focuses on the contribution of teaching to the quality of an institution's activities (e.g. Ellis, 1993; Elton, 1987). This is perhaps not a surprising development given the growth in recent years of monitoring regimes intended to test and maintain the accountability of publicly funded services. It does, however, raise important ethical questions about the professional role and priorities of the university teacher, which, in this country at least, have yet to be analysed in sufficient detail. This model frequently coexists with the previous one (the psycho-diagnostician and facilitator), creating a 'scientistic' framework that 'constructs subjects [in this case both learners and teachers] in ways which better enable their regulation and control' (Usher and Edwards, 1994: 33).

We thus have five provisional models to work with. They are not a comprehensive account; for example, we omit the model of the educator as disciplinary thinker, researcher and actor. There is a long tradition of attempts to analyse the epistemological and other characteristics of disciplines, and their impact on people and structures in higher education (Kuhn, 1970; Lodahl and Gordon, 1972; Biglan, 1973; Becher, 1989). Within the general literature of teaching and learning, however, this approach has not really taken root in terms of considering the *pedagogic* implications of the conceptual frameworks of disciplines. Disciplinary questions have moved relatively recently to a new and central position that promises to generate fruitful conceptualisation (e.g. Caddick, 1999). Once again, we need to analyse instances of this approach in more detail before incorporating it into our 'map' of the field.

In addition to omissions, there are some absences – ideas that we might expect to find in the literature, but that seem to occur either exceptionally or not at all. The most noticeable absence is that of the nature of knowledge, and the teacher's role in its production – a question that has exercised the minds and pens of childhood and adult educators for many years, but around which much of the pedagogic writing in higher education seems to tiptoe with excessive caution. This is clearly linked to the previous point about disciplinary frameworks, and also to the vexed question of who is involved in the production and analysis of pedagogic knowledge. The focus on 'learning', and on individuals, often enables writers to sidestep – consciously or otherwise – the question of what exactly is being learned, by whom and why.

Analysing identities

Having tentatively identified certain identities of the educator from the literature, we needed to create tools for analysing them. Our first attempt was to use repertory grid techniques (Fransella and Bannister, 1977) in order to tease out the underlying assumptions of each identity through the generation of constructs. This is useful principally as a 'rough draft' for further analysis, since the constructs identified are inevitably rather crude and approximate.

Briefly, the technique entailed a series of comparisons; each comparison involved three identities, and we considered how, conceptually, two were alike and one was different. We then gave a meaningful name (meaningful to us) for each end of the dimension we had generated. We continued to compare different combinations of identities until we found that we were re-using the same ideas (that is, we had run out of meaningful dimensions). The process helped us identify ten dimensions against which the five usable models could be assessed. In the process of assessment, we rejected one, since it was pertinent to one model only. The final dimensions we identified are shown in Figure 13.1.

We now consider how the two identities most developed in this chapter, the educator as critical practitioner and the educator as psychodiagnostician, differ along five of the most significant dimensions of pedagogic identity and practice.

Learning within a community vs. individualised learning

The 'critical practice' identity is not difficult to situate along this dimension. It focuses on learning within a community; students and teachers are considered to be social and cultural actors with identities emerging from their wider social experiences. The nature of and relations between their communities are likely to be contested, and this will have a bearing on the processes and content of classroom activity. The conscious social orientation of much adult education practice means that 'student-centred' pedagogy

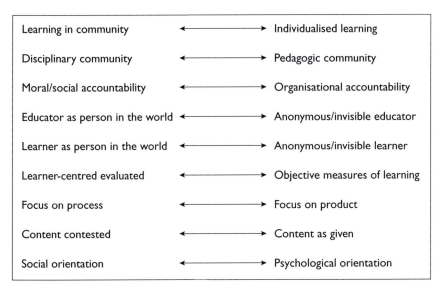

Figure 13.1 Dimensions of pedagogic identity.

has to involve the consideration of community identities. The 'educator as psycho-diagnostician', on the other hand, inevitably focuses on the learner as an individual – specifically, as a manifestation of psychological tendencies, processes and dispositions, which can be understood and utilised for the purpose of learning. Whilst this perspective does not acknowledge relations between individuals, it does not generally extend its scope beyond the classroom transaction to the broader social or cultural context, or the community identities to which this gives rise.

Disciplinary community vs. pedagogic community

Higher education teachers usually conceive of themselves as members of a disciplinary community. The critical practice identity enables teachers to question the content and purpose of their teaching, just as their research questions orthodoxies within the discipline. Within adult education, the knowledge-content of and between disciplines has been interrogated, precisely because the pedagogic role of adult educators could not be divorced from the content of teaching. Critical practice thus allows educators to inhabit 'knowledge-practice' communities, which are simultaneously (inter-) disciplinary *and* pedagogic. The educator as psycho-diagnostician, on the other hand, separates the pedagogic from the disciplinary role, assuming the existence of two separate communities. This assumption enables pedagogy to be analysed simply in terms of 'teaching and learning' rather than as an aspect of knowledge production, and in effect creates a super-fluous community of (decontextualised) pedagogues. Even where pedagogy is discussed within a disciplinary context, for example in geography or chemistry, disciplinary content is assumed to be intact and unquestioned; the pedagogic role is simply to enable students to learn it. Again, the social purpose of higher education is divorced from action in the classroom. This could change with the recent introduction of subject-specific learning and teaching support networks such as Escalate (intended to support staff development related to teaching and learning for academic staff working in education and continuing education; see http://www/escalate.ac.uk), but we wait to see.

Moral and social accountability vs. organisational accountability

Educators are always accountable to their organisation, but this dimension focuses on the primacy of organisational accountability over other forms of accountability. All educators are now under pressure to consider the consequences for their organisations of inadequate performance on quality measures, and to adhere to organisational requirements through ever-increasing scrutiny. Sophisticated methods of checking and measuring have been developed (commonly called quality assurance processes), which ensure that the individual educator works in an organisationally appropriate manner.

The psycho-diagnostician can call on any number of procedures and instruments for describing and measuring pedagogic processes and student learning, which makes it easier for her or him to fulfil these new organisational requirements. The absence of content and purpose from the teaching and learning in higher education approach means that few contradictions should be encountered between 'good' pedagogic practice and organisational requirements; measurable evidence of 'student learning' constitutes fulfilment of both. This may indeed be why so many universities are keen to promote the empiricist quick-fixes of the psycho-diagnostician.

But the advent of subject and academic review, the latest articulation of quality assurance in British higher education, has made it increasingly difficult to prioritise moral and social over organisational accountability. Organisational scrutiny demands approved and codified course objectives and content for quality assurance purposes, reducing the scope for pedagogic responsiveness. Thus, for example, the negotiation of the curriculum with students (a prevalent ideal in adult education pedagogy until recently) is quite incompatible with current organisational demands; where knowledge is a commodity, the customer must be given full, or at least convincing, product information. 'The skills of being an academic are increasingly becoming isolated and fragmented in contexts in which the paramount requirement is to make the work more explicit, so that it can be more easily codified and measured by performance indicators' (Smyth, 1995: 14).

Educator as 'person in the world' vs. anonymous/ invisible educator

The educator as a person in the world – as someone with social identity, and conscious of the 'worldly' baggage present in the classroom – is perhaps such an obvious element of pedagogic identity in adult education that it is taken for granted. We agonise over power relations with students, and conduct vigorous debates about how our gender, class, sexual, or ethnic identity affects what and how we teach. These concerns extend to the content and inclusivity of our disciplines, doubtless informed by the social purpose tradition of adult education and the sociological perspectives that have informed its growing body of theory over time. The 'educator as critical practitioner' is indisputably a person in the world, and this may account for the appeal of, for example, Brookfield's work (1995) to teachers; he addresses them as real people, with real anxieties and frailties. If we turn to the 'educator as psycho-diagnostician', the teacher's reality is generally absent; the teacher has a pedagogic function rather than a social identity. The focus is on the (equally anonymous) learner and the processes occurring within the learner that enable learning to take place. Thus higher education *pedagogy*, where this model is dominant, detaches itself from those issues, such as diversity, that are addressed through social purpose approaches to higher education *policy*.

The learner as 'person in the world' vs. anonymous/ invisible learner

Within the literature of teaching and learning in higher education, despite its frequent focus on 'the learner', there is little recognition of the socio-cultural situatedness of the individual. The learner frequently appears as an anonymous, decontextualised, degendered being whose principal distinguishing characteristics are 'personality' and 'learning style' (Brown, 1993). This approach, typical of psychometrics, can be traced back to the belief in psychology that it is possible, indeed desirable, to be able to predict people's behaviour. In order to do this, it is presumed that we all have characteristics that determine future actions (e.g. learning styles that determine how you learn). But this implies that learners 'have' learning styles, preferences and behaviours located somewhere inside them, which exist free of history, culture or context. Indeed, in order to study the individual, contextual and other factors are deliberately excluded from the scientific equation in order to discover universal truths. Thus, the psycho-diagnostician does not need to consider the possibility that 'learning styles' may be constructed through discursive practices or may arise from the learner's history or sociocultural position, and may not be an 'essential' part of a human being; they are, for the purposes of pedagogic practice, simply there.

The critical practitioner situates the learner very firmly in the social world and in the community of practice. It is impossible to disentangle the learner's situatedness from the educative process. Indeed, in much adult education literature, the age, class, race and gender of learners have been the prime focus of discussion, practice development and policy contestation; an understanding of positionality is integral to an understanding of pedagogy. This has yet to be developed in the literature of higher education pedagogy to any significant degree, despite the vast changes in the student body that have occurred in recent years.

Protective walls

In our exploration of two caricatures of pedagogic identity, we have tried to show the consequences of the split between adult education and higher education pedagogical thinking and writing. We have explored elsewhere some of the reasons why the psycho-diagnostician has gained ascendancy in higher education (Malcolm and Zukas, 2001). Briefly, we have argued that part of the problem lies in the relationship between theory and practice. Theory, rather than representing forms of critical engagement with, and understanding of, practice, appears to take the form of a set of rules for professional behaviour. Teaching, assessment or learning procedures – seating arrangements, student journals, group exercises, action research projects, for example – can be attributed to 'teaching and learning theories', which in turn can be attributed to research on teaching and learning processes. The role of research is to create and refine theories and thus to contribute to the development of rules for practice – in some ways rather like trying out recipes to see if they work.

We are troubled by the epistemological confusion suggested by such a model of research. The psycho-diagnostic higher educator resembles Holmes' 'homunculus with a toolkit' (1999: 89): an anonymous worker, equipped with a portable set of scientistic theories that can be selected as required, and applied systematically to the teaching situation. There is little recognition of theory informing and shaping research, determining the kinds of questions that are asked and the answers that are sought; most crucially there is no hint that the theories that shape research are situated and contestable.

We believe that this naive version of theory has come about in part because of the separation of disciplinary and pedagogic communities in higher education, and the fracture between research-based and pedagogic communities of practice. A new field of practice, staff and education development in higher education, has emerged separate from disciplinary communities. With its foundations in training, the field has promoted a particular set of understandings and language conventions: outcomes, objectives, assessment and reflection, for example. But this separate language encourages the idea that teaching is a separate and essentially different activity from research. It promotes the dislocation of pedagogic thought and practice from disciplinary knowledge and development.

One of our concerns is that such an approach could be seen to support lifelong learning – after all, if one is able systematically to develop teaching as a distinct activity that bears no relation to context, content or purpose, it could be argued that this would then be transferable across sectoral walls. The setting up of a learning and teaching support network generic centre could be seen in this light (http://www.ltsn.ac.uk/about/generic_centre.asp). This could be the basis for a new pedagogy for lifelong learning and teaching. But we believe such an approach omits the most important elements of pedagogy: the relations between educator, student and institution, the social context, purpose and ethical implications of educational work, and the nature and social role of educational knowledge.

For us, the way forward is try to build bridges across the sectoral walls in order to analyse the purposes and consequences of our professional activities. Pedagogy is more than teaching and learning. We assume that it incorporates a critical understanding of the social, policy and institutional context, as well as a critical approach to the content and process of the educational/training transaction. If lifelong learning is the rhetorical vehicle for building such bridges, we should be sure not to undermine its foundations by its narrow linguistic focus on learning.

Note

1   ESRC project no R000222794, *Models of the Educator in Higher Education: A Bibliographic and Conceptual Map. 1998–9.*

References

Bailey, F.G. (1977) *Morality and Expediency: The Folklore of Academic Politics*, Oxford: Basil Blackwell.

Barnett, R. (1997) *Higher Education: A Critical Business*, Buckingham: SRHE/Open University Press.

Becher, T. (1989) *Academic Tribes and Territories*, Buckingham: SRHE/Open University Press.

Biglan, A. (1973) The characteristics of subject matter in different academic areas, *Journal of Applied Psychology* 57(3): 195–203.

Boud, D. and Walker, D. (1998) Promoting reflection in professional courses: the challenge of context, *Studies in Higher Education* 23(2): 191–206.

Boyatzis, R.E. and Kolb, D.A. (1991) Assessing individuality in learning: the Learning Skills Profile, *Educational Psychology* 11(3–4): 279–295.

Bright, B. (1996) Reflecting on reflective practice, *Studies in the Education of Adults* 28(2): 162–184.

Brookfield, S.D. (1995) *Becoming a Critically Reflective Teacher*, San Francisco: Jossey-Bass.

Brown, G. (1993) Effective teaching, in Ellis, R. (ed.) *Quality Assurance for University Teaching*, Buckingham: SRHE/Open University Press.

Brown, J.S., Collins, S. and Duguid, P. (1989) Situated cognition and the culture of learning, *Educational Researcher* 18(1): 32–42.

Caddick, M. (1999) The atelier principle in teaching, paper presented at Research and Practice in Educational Development(s): Exploring the Links, Stoke Rochford, SEDA/SRHE.

Ecclestone, K. (1996) The reflective practitioner: mantra or a model for emancipation, *Studies in the Education of Adults* 28(2): 146–151.

Ellis, R. (1993) *Quality Assurance for University Teaching*, Buckingham: SRHE/Open University Press.

Elton, L. (1987) *Teaching in Higher Education: Appraisal and Training*, London: Kogan Page.

Eraut, M. (1995) 'Schön Shock: a case for reframing reflection-in-action?', *Teachers and Teaching: Theory and Practice* 1(1): 9–22.

Fransella, F. and Bannister, D. (1977) *A Manual for the Repertory Grid Technique*, London: Academic Press.

Gibbs, G. (1992) Improving the quality of student learning through course design, in Barnett, R. (ed.) *Learning to Effect*, Buckingham: SRHE/Open University Press.

Gore, J. (1993) *The Struggle for Pedagogies: Critical and Feminist Discourses as Regimes of Truth*, London: Routledge.

Grenham, G., Wade, P. and Kelly, D. (1999) Active learning at the National College of Ireland, paper presented at Research and Practice in Educational Development(s): Exploring the Links, Stoke Rochford: SEDA/SRHE.

Holmes, L. (1999) Competence and capability: from 'confidence trick' to the construction of the graduate identity, in O'Reilly, D., Cunningham, L. and Lester, S. *Developing the Capable Practitioner: Professional Capability through Higher Education*, London: Kogan Page.

ILT (1999) *The National Framework for Higher Education Teaching*, York: Institute for Learning and Teaching.

Kuhn, J. (1970) *The Structure of Scientific Revolutions*, Chicago: University of Chicago Press.

Lave, J. and Wenger, E. (1991) *Situated Learning: Legitimate Peripheral Participation*, Cambridge: Cambridge University Press.

Lodahl, J.B. and Gordon, G. (1972) The structure of scientific fields and the functioning of university graduate departments, *American Sociological Review* 37(February): 57–72.

Malcolm, J. and Zukas, M. (1999) Models of the educator in HE: problems and perspectives, paper presented to STLHE, Collaborative Learning for the 21st Century, University of Calgary.

Malcolm, J. and Zukas, M. (2000) Becoming an educator: communities of practice in HE, in I. McNay (ed.) *Higher Education and its Communities*, Buckingham: SRHE/Open University Press.

Malcolm, J. and Zukas, M. (2001) Bridging pedagogic gaps: conceptual discontinuities in higher education, *Teaching in Higher Education* 6(1): 33–42.

Nicol, D., Kane, K.A. and Wainwright, C.L. (1994) Improving laboratory learning through group working and structured reflection and discussion, *Educational and Training Technology International* 31(4): 302–310.

Rowland, S. (1999) Surface learning about teaching in higher education, paper presented at BERA Annual Conference, University of Sussex.

Schön, D.A. (1987) *Educating the Reflective Practitioner*, San Francisco: Jossey-Bass.

Smyth, J. (1995) *Academic Work: The Changing Labour Process in Higher Education*, Buckingham: Open University Press.

Tennant, M. (1997) *Psychology and Adult Learning* (2nd edn), London: Routledge.

Usher, R. and Edwards, R. (1994) *Postmodernism and Education*, London: Routledge.

Walker, M. (1999) Doing criticality: mapping a HE project, paper presented at BERA Annual Conference, University of Sussex.

Webb, G. (1996) *Understanding Staff Development*, Buckingham: SRHE/Open University Press.

Wenger, E. (1998) *Communities of Practice: Learning, Meaning and Identity*, Cambridge: Cambridge University Press.

Wilson, A.L. and Hayes, E.R. (2000) *Handbook of Adult and Continuing Education*, San Francisco: Jossey-Bass.

Zukas, M. (ed.) (1988) *Transatlantic Dialogue: A Research Exchange*. Proceedings of the Joint SCUTREA/AERC/CASAE Conference. Leeds: University of Leeds.

Zukas, M. and Malcolm, J. (1999) Models of the educator in HE, paper presented at BERA Annual Conference, University of Sussex. Available at http://www.leeds.ac.uk/educol.

Index